ETHICS
FOR
POLICYMAKING

Recent Titles in
Contributions in Political Science

Ethics for Policymaking

A METHODOLOGICAL ANALYSIS

Eugene J. Meehan

Contributions in Political Science, Number 257
Bernard K. Johnpoll, *Series Editor*

GREENWOOD PRESS
New York • Westport, Connecticut • London

Library of Congress Cataloging-in-Publication Data

Meehan, Eugene J.
   Ethics for policymaking : a methodological analysis / Eugene J.
Meehan.
      p. cm. — (Contributions in political science, ISSN 0147–1066 ;
no. 257)
   Includes bibliographical references.
   ISBN 0–313–27342–1 (lib. bdg. : alk. paper)
   1. Policy sciences—Moral and ethical aspects.   I. Title.
II. Series.
H97.M44   1990
320'.6—dc20   89–25763

British Library Cataloguing in Publication Data is available.

Library of Congress Catalog Card Number: 89–25763
ISBN: 0–313–27342–1
ISSN: 0147–1066

First published in 1990

Greenwood Press, 88 Post Road West, Westport, CT   06881
An imprint of Greenwood Publishing Group, Inc.

Printed in the United States of America

The paper used in this book complies with the
Permanent Paper Standard issued by the National
Information Standards Organization (Z39.48–1984).

10 9 8 7 6 5 4 3 2 1

Contents

Acknowledgments

Writing a preface to a book is a bittersweet experience: although it signals the end of drudgery, the respite is only temporary; and if it provides a welcome opportunity to acknowledge one's debts, they are always too numerous to allow this to be done properly. In the present case, my major individual creditors include: first, the various friends who read and commented on the manuscript (notably Ronald D. Brunner, Marcelo Dascal, James Doyle, Pauline Rosenau, Paul Roth, Larry Spence, William Zanardi, and my former colleague Hans Michelmann and his cohorts at the University of Saskatchewan—Joseph Garcia, Allan McCloud, Jene Porter, Duff Stafford, Jeffrey Steves, and Gudrun Klee); second, my wife Alice, who suffers through each of my writing efforts more-or-less tolerantly; and, third, my past students, who contributed far more than they realize—or care. Each of these persons has been sacrificed to some extent on the holy alter of book production; some have been exploited quite ruthlessly. None bears any responsibility for what follows.

My intellectual debts, in the broader sense in which we all borrow from other thinkers, are literally beyond identification. It is quite impossible to tell, at this stage of life, where others leave off and I begin—nor in all honesty does it matter very much. The normal channels for acknowledging the sources of such influences (footnotes and bibliographic references) are for the most part closed. Happily, that is less of a problem in the present volume than might otherwise be the case. To borrow a felicitous phrase from Larry Spence, this is not a "book about books," but a sustained argument in favor of a particular perspective on the relationship between normative judgments or arguments and policymaking, advocating a somewhat different approach to providing a justification for acting in a particular way, whether individually or collectively. No "imprimatur" can be produced for such efforts. Indeed, footnotes and references are a potential distraction rather than an asset, for they tend to raise irrelevant questions about sources and antecedents, and thus shift attention from the central thrust of the argument. I have therefore minimized the number of footnotes, and provided only enough bibliography to suggest the overall conception of "philosophic ethics" from which the discussion begins. Those seeking a "guide to the literature" will have to look elsewhere; the objective here is to produce as clear and coherent an argument as possible for an approach to normative affairs that can provide the needed foundation for individual and collective decisions.

1

Introduction

Objectives and Constraints

This volume continues and extends a study of the intellectual foundations of individual and collective action that has now been in progress for a number of years. (The bibliographic note at the end of the chapter summarizes the results that have been published to date.) The overall objective of the study is to establish the knowledge requirements, empirical and normative, for defensible or corrigible policymaking. However, the meaning of "knowledge" and "policy," as well as such related concepts as "epistemology," varies so widely in both everyday and technical usage that the precise content and significance of the objective, and the extent to which the effort to achieve it has been properly directed—not to say successful—cannot be assessed until the meaning of basic terms has been stabilized. The problem is not unique to the present inquiry; differences in the way in which those, and other similar terms, are defined and applied is a major source of misunderstanding and disagreement among those concerned with furthering the quest for knowledge in almost every field, particularly those outside the physical sciences.

In the circumstances, it might seem the course of wisdom to avoid conventional terminology altogether and rely instead on descriptive statements, or invent new labels to replace those in use. However, there are good reasons to insist on the legitimacy of using "knowledge," "policy," and other related terms in ways that further a systematic effort to provide the intellectual foundations for human actions. Most importantly, the assistance that might be obtained from closely related fields of systematic inquiry would have to be foregone if that strategy were adopted. The traditional labels are therefore retained, but the meaning attached to them has been restricted in ways that allow productive borrowing from other disciplines, and suggest the kinds of inquiries needed there or elsewhere to further the overall enterprise. Briefly, a set of fairly precise meanings is developed within the theoretical apparatus used to determine the intellectual requirements for directing human actions. Since meanings created in this way are likely to differ from at least some of those in current use, that places an additional burden on both author and reader; the text must be written using the meanings found in the limiting or precising definitions, and read in the same terms. Disagreements about the validity of applying a given label to a particular meaning should be reduced by the use of such definitions, although they are unlikely to be avoided altogether. In any event, only those inquiries and arguments that employ the same set of meanings will be relevant to, and potentially useful for, fulfilling the purposes of the present inquiry. It should be emphasized, however, that the acceptability of the proposed conception of "knowledge" is far less important for the argument that follows than either the validity of the analysis used to identify the intellectual requirements for directing actions or the usefulness of the findings for improving intellectual performance, particularly as it relates to the conduct of real-world affairs.

Given the overall purpose of the inquiry, the two tasks to be completed first were: (a) to identify or determine the intellectual requirements, both empirical and normative, for directing human actions, and (b) to develop a theoretical apparatus, a set of fundamental assumptions, able to show how those requirements could be fulfilled within the limits of human capacity as presently understood and subject to all of the relevant environmental restrictions. The two tasks were reciprocally contingent; the limits or constraints encountered in one area directly influenced the possibilities available in the other.

Analytically, the crucial factor was the theoretical structure, for it provided the integrating mechanism that linked the various elements required to fulfill the overall purpose. The intellectual requirements were identified within that context; the meaning of key terms was defined there. Once the basic theoretical apparatus was reasonably complete, its validity and usefulness could be explored through the connection to directing human actions. Systematic testing was carried out in three major areas: first, the direction of collective actions or public policymaking; second, the conduct of inquiries meant to produce knowledge that could be used for making defensible policies; and third, the education of individuals in ways expected to improve intellectual performance in areas that impinge on individual or collective policymaking.

The usefulness of the analytic apparatus for assessing governmental performance and suggesting improvements (for evaluating policymaking by public authority) was explored in extended studies of two federal activities: first, the public housing program, which was traced in some detail from its origins in the New Deal through the beginning of the 1980s[1]; second, the Inter-American Foundation, a small agency created by the Congress in the early 1970s to learn how to manage overseas development assistance.[2] The usefulness of the theoretical structure for criticizing academic inquiries meant to provide knowledge that could be used for making or improving policies was checked against a sample of recent work in economic theory, selected because economics is usually regarded as the most powerful of the social sciences.[3]

An effort to create an education program able to improve intellectual performance of the kind required for defensible policymaking, has served as the primary channel for developing and testing the overall theoretical structure.[4] A course of study or training program derived from that apparatus provides an exceptional opportunity to test its validity and usefulness for directing actions. The principal objectives of such training, which can be summarized very succinctly as the "Three As" of education, are open to reasonably adequate measurement and thus provide a good indication of the extent to which the theory can fulfill its proposed functions. That is, an individual's capacity to *acquire* knowledge self-consciously and critically, to *augment* or add to the existing supply of knowledge, and to *apply* such knowledge efficiently and effectively in public or private affairs can be measured at least well enough to assess the effects of training and provide the information needed for improving the underlying theoretical apparatus.

The results obtained from these, and other, tests and applications have been uniformly positive and in some cases, exceptional. That is not to claim that the theoretical apparatus has been "proved," for such terms are inappropriate. But it is demonstrably useful for criticizing intellectual activity and suggesting ways of improving it, particularly where the activity relates to the formulation of public policies. And what is more important, training programs using materials derived from the theory have consistently produced improved critical performance by both academic and nonacademic persons, in the United States and in Latin America.

Until now, most of the development and testing has been targeted at the empirical or "scientific" part of the intellectual apparatus required for directing human actions. The normative or ethical requirements were elaborated only to the point where they could be identified in broad terms and integrated into the overall structure. That emphasis is here reversed. The primary goals of the present volume are a detailed statement of the *normative* requirements for directing actions and an elaboration of the theoretical structure sufficient to show how those specific requirements can be fulfilled. Only so much of the empirical apparatus has been included as is needed to follow the course of the argument.

The approach to inquiry maintained throughout the study has been methodological rather than substantive, in the broad sense of "methodological" that extends beyond mere technique or procedure (and would be labeled "epistemological" if philosophic usage were different). That focus is retained here. The aim is to produce a clear statement of the analytic characteristics of a normative structure adequate for directing human actions in ways that can be defended within the limits of human capacity and not to establish its substantive content, to clarify the kinds of evidence and argument that are needed for adequate criticism or justification of normative judgments and not to justify, criticize, or defend any particular normative position. Some substantive assumptions must be made before an adequate theoretical framework can be created, but their function is to identify, and bound, the kinds of evidence allowed in justification or criticism.

The purposes that direct the present inquiry differ considerably from the purposes more commonly pursued within the mainstream of contemporary social science (and within ethics or moral philosophy as well). Because the implications of those differences are extensive, for both the kinds of questions that are raised and for the criteria of adequacy that are applied to proposed responses, some underscoring is essential. The effect of differences in emphasis is magnified by the need to ground justification or criticism of human actions, whether physical or intellectual, in the relation between actions taken and purposes sought; purposeless actions cannot be criticized or improved. The problem of criticism is complicated further by the need to deal with purposes that are stated using analytic rather than practical or everyday concepts, and at several different levels of generality. In global terms, the purpose of these studies is to articulate as fully as possible the kind of intellectual structures (knowledge) that is required for *directing* individual or collective actions in ways that can be justified or defended out of human experience within the limits of human capacity. Those who seek to fulfill other purposes, identified at the same analytic level but within a different framework—an "explanation" of events as that term is used in the philosophy of science, predictive capacity with respect to the future, the capacity to control future events knowingly and systematically, or a "model" of some portion or aspect of the world as experienced, among others—may not necessarily, or even usually, accept and apply the same set of basic assumptions. But argument and criticism carried on across the boundaries of two or more different sets of fundamental assumptions may not intersect sufficiently for discourse to be productive, or even meaningful. Systematic improvement of intellectual performance, justification and criticism of knowledge claims, must proceed from a foundation of known, though not necessarily shared, basic assumptions. Conclusions are inseparable from the assumptions and reasoning on which they depend.

Further, even if agreement is reached with respect to the overarching purpose of inquiry, disagreement about the more limited purposes assumed to be necessary prerequisites to the achievement of that overall purpose remains possible or even likely. In the present volume, for example, the *normative* purpose of inquiry, the purpose to be achieved or fulfilled by directing human actions, is taken to be the maintenance and improvement of the conditions of life of some human population. Those who agree on that overall purpose may nevertheless dispute its various corollaries, in which case the other assumptions required for achieving the overall purpose are also likely to differ. That is, if different ancillary or contributory purposes are accepted, then different assumptions will be required to fulfill them and that will both alter the content of the justification provided for particular decisions and affect the validity of criticism targeted at propositions generated from alternative sets of assumptions.

To state the point somewhat more broadly, every assertion depends for its validity on a set of underlying assumptions: that is the primary sense in which it is legitimate to claim that *every* proposition is "theory-laden." Some of those assumptions, or perhaps all of them, may remain unstated or even unrecognized. Indeed, given the complexity of the intellectual apparatus, it is impossible to be certain that *all* of the assumptions used for directing real world actions have been brought to consciousness and articulated fully. Criticism and improvement of knowledge are possible, but only by focusing on the products of judgment, the conclusions or knowledge claims, rather than the process. Once some knowledge claims have been established, and in an ongoing world that is usually the case, other claims to know can be tested against them. And the whole apparatus can be tested at least partially against alternative competing knowledge systems. In effect, unless *some* set of assumptions is taken as given, knowledge claims cannot be tested. Such limits are somewhat obscured by the ongoing character of the intellectual enterprise; since every argument begins *in media res*, the initial assumptions on which arguments depend are easily overlooked.

In these terms, to be amplified considerably in due course, the limitations inherent in the canons and conventions of argument and criticism currently accepted in policymaking cannot be eliminated, and performance cannot be improved demonstrably in any deliberate way (and their patent inadequacy provided the initial impetus for these inquiries) until a common set of assumptions is accepted and applied by those involved with direction, justification, and criticism of actions. A prerequisite to success in that effort is a clear statement of the conditions that must be met before the policymaking enterprise can succeed. Development of a valid critical apparatus would not be guaranteed thereby, of course, but until those limiting conditions have been established, the criteria used to decide the acceptability of particular proposals or to settle conflicting claims to know cannot be determined. One major purpose of these inquiries has been to articulate those fundamental requirements, however tentatively, and suggest a set of assumptions that makes it possible to fulfill them.

Obviously, what is proposed here is only one way of dealing with the problem; others are always possible. No set of analytic requirements is or can be definitive or absolute. Nor can there be a warrant for claiming an irrefragable system of assumptions, a critical apparatus that is somehow immune to criticism. To the contrary, open competition among alternative assumptions is an essential element in any ongoing effort to create and improve knowledge intended for directing real-world actions. Accepting an overall purpose for inquiry makes possible a level of testability that is adequate if imperfect. But that overall purpose is also open to dispute and subject to change based on experience. It may seem unlikely that the need to produce knowledge adequate for directing human actions will be disputed, or that the search for such knowledge will be abandoned, but the principle must be honored if the integrity of the theoretical apparatus is to be maintained.

The need for some set of basic assumptions to serve as a foundation on which knowledge adequate for directing human actions on defensible grounds can be created serves to emphasize the importance of the role played by normative judgment in the overall apparatus. Analytically, the normative purpose to be sought through action must be specified before the evidence needed to judge among alternative competing sets of fundamental assumptions can be generated. The claim that the knowledge created on the basis of a given set of assumptions "works," or that it corresponds reasonably well with past human experience, even if fully conceded, does not provide a sufficient base for controlling quality. Given a commitment to directing actions, the necessary precondition to accepting any specific assumption in the knowledge system is to demonstrate that it is needed for achieving the overall normative purpose for which the knowledge is to be used. With respect to any claim to knowledge, the assumptions on which the claim depends must at a minimum be adequate to meet experiental and methodological criteria established for the field of inquiry. The analytic framework employed here underscores the need to go further and ask whether the purpose itself is worthy of pursuit—a matter of substantive and normative concern and not a methodological issue. In effect, criticism and justification of claims to know must extend beyond their empirical and methodological or analytic dimensions to include the normative purposes that knowledge is expected to serve. "Informed opinion," which is the ultimate testing ground for all knowledge claims, must therefore be informed and competent in all three areas for any situation where recommendations for action are put forward or required. The argument that follows seeks to establish a set of criteria that can be used to assess such overall competence, and to elaborate a critical apparatus that can, at a minimum, provide a point of departure for future improvements.

The Action Focus

The justification for an action focus, for seeking to determine the intellectual requirements for directing human actions rather than trying to establish knowledge requirements in general terms, is found at two mutually supporting levels of analysis. In everyday affairs, action is a constant and irreducible feature of every human life and at least some human actions have consequences of considerable human significance. Put another way, human preeminence on earth, and the conditions of life of the human population, are largely a function of intellectual capacity, of the knowledge that the species has been able to create and apply. Human actions, individual and collective, provide the essential mechanism through which knowledge functions to modify or improve the human condition. That is already sufficient to justify efforts to bring human actions under intellectual control. A search for knowledge that "works," in the sense of satisfying normative/pragmatic criteria of acceptability, is readily produced in that context. The meaning of "work" can be determined at a level of precision that suffices for criticism and improvement once a set of fundamental normative assumptions has been accepted.

The methodological reasons for accepting an action focus in the search for knowledge are still more compelling. The central problem in any effort to generate valid knowledge is to identify or create the set of assumptions that is needed for criticism or improvement of knowledge claims. But a justification for accepting some claims and rejecting others is beyond reach until the set of purposes for which the knowledge will be used has been specified. Those purposes in turn depend on an initial normative commitment; it generates the set of assumptions that are used to determine importance or significance. An action focus is therefore a basic requirement, for purposes cannot be achieved without actions. Any number of theroretical structures can be used to generate knowledge, but the normative assumptions accepted by the inquirer actually determine which of the proposed structures is actually employed. Normative purposes in turn require an assessment of the limits and possibilities available to the species within the boundaries of existing capacity, so far as it can be determined. The chain of reasoning leads inexorably to the need to inquire into the intellectual prerequisites for directing human actions on defensible grounds.

The basic normative commitment proposed here is to a systematic effort to maintain and/or improve the conditions of life of some human population. The assumption, simply stated, is that if anything has significance for living humans it is the individual human life. That commitment, sometimes called "radical individualism" (in ethics), seems unavoidable. The assumption is justified by a relatively simple *reductio*, for denying the significance of human life to living humans seeking to assess significance would serve to make the knowledge-seeking enterprise absurd or pointless. *Homo mensura*, then, will appear as one assumption in any knowledge system meant for achieving human purposes. There is no need to deny that knowledge can be created from other assumptions, or even to claim that knowledge which is not useful for directing human actions is unworthy of credence, though such extreme positions might be defensible. But for the species as a whole, two of the more fundamental assumptions that can be defended for use as guides in the quest for corrigible knowledge are: first, that some body of knowledge, some set of assumptions must be created and justified that can serve to direct human actions on defensible grounds; second, that such knowledge must be assessed or evaluated by reference to pragmatic criteria in which the individual human life appears as the primary unit of significance.

Analytically, the case for using human life as the fundamental base for normative judgments, and therefore for accepting an action focus, can be made in much stronger terms. For once it is agreed that knowledge must be tested or validated as fully as human capacity allows, that the accuracy and reliability of knowledge claims must be determined as clearly as possible, a commitment to an action focus is forced. Of course, the need for testing is sometimes denied and the possibility of testing in a meaningful way can be repudiated, but such denials are self-defeating. It is a commonplace that the reliability and accuracy of knowledge claims vary dramatically from field to field and within fields. Therefore, if knowledge is to be employed for humanly significant purposes, it is clearly necessary to assess its quality, if only to allow the needed weighing of the effects of risk on choice. That forces reliance on some kind of pragmatic criteria. Efforts to assess knowledge claims by reference to the attributes of the person who makes the claim have long since been abandoned, and rightly so. The procedures used to produce knowledge cannot guarantee its quality, claims made on behalf of alleged "scientific" methods not to the contrary. Procedure can guarantee product quality only within fully closed and calculable systems of interactions, that is, within logic or mathematics. And the sensory dependence of the species, which seems established beyond serious dispute, effectively precludes assessments of quality based on a direct comparison of the content of reality and the content of a knowledge claim, even if the special requirements that apply to the normative domain are left aside. Reality is not directly accessible through the senses.

Finally, in an era when the capacity of electronic computers is very consistently overestimated, it may be worth emphasizing the inability of any formal or logical apparatus to resolve the kinds of problems involved in the creation and application of knowledge. If sensory dependence is accepted as one prime limit on human capacity, knowledge systems must be grounded in human sensory experience. Yet even the simplest claim to know, stated in descriptive terms (A dog is in the yard), involves an irreducible element of creativity, a judgment—a process that cannot be reduced to simple rule applications. The procedures needed to link raw perceptions or observations to membership in a class of things, which must be employed in order to determine that there is a member of the class "dogs" that is related in observation to a member of the class "yards" in a particular way, are translogical though they may involve a calculation. In the last analysis, such judgments are tested against the judgments of other observers; there is no non-human, disinterested, or neutral authority to which an appeal can be made. The *only* way to test a human judgment of this kind is against another human judgment. Judgments differ demonstrably in quality, and good reasons can be offered for preferring one judgment to another in a wide range of cases. All such preferences are based ultimately on a consensus of informed opinion, on a set of conventions developed within a field of inquiry or action. Disagreements among informed and competent judges cannot be settled unless a significant and resolvable difference in assumptions or information is located or discovered.

Some means of evading the limit imposed by the need to rely on judgments is essential; otherwise formal logic is of little use for creating and applying knowledge, and logic provides the essential dynamic force in any knowledge system. The "solution," which is a commonplace in the philosophy of inquiry, is to ignore the processes used to make judgments and concentrate on logical replication of the conclusions, of the products of judgment; it makes use of a standard technique for dealing with "black boxes" in electronic engineering. The task of producing knowledge, within that perspective, is precisely analogous to trying to create a logical apparatus that reproduces the external characteristics of "black box" performance. The assumptions built into the logic must not conflict with assumptions accepted by the person who produces the judgment, but there is no way to justify assuming that the axioms incorporated into the logic replicate the internal operation of the black box, nor is there any need for such an assumption. So long as the logical apparatus is created with a specific analytic function in mind, and linked firmly to the conduct of human affairs and human experience, successive applications can lead to corrections that eliminate discrepancies, producing in time intellectual tools of immense power and accuracy.

To conclude, in a sensory-based knowledge system, the results obtained by testing knowledge in action against purpose emerge as the only viable basis available for asserting, justifying, or criticizing, claims to knowledge. Despite the hazards associated with the use of such pragmatic criteria, no acceptable alternative has been found. For the purposes that engage us here, experience suggests that those criteria will suffice. The intellectual foundations of action, systematically pursued, turn out to be grounded in some set of normative judgments; they depend on an agreement to use informed and competent human judgment as the ultimate guarantor of knowledge quality. Testing in action is not possible without an initial normative commitment, acceptance of an overall normative purpose to be sought through action, in the same way that the overall purpose of a given sport or game determines the criteria used to test and improve actions taken within the framework of its rules. Detached from the overall purposes of a game, which are essentially "normative" in the sense used here, actions lie beyond justification or test.

Implications of an Action Focus for Inquiry

The detailed argument needed to support this rather summary statement of the position taken here is left to the main body of the text. But a few basic points relating to the characteristics of action, and their implications for the present type of inquiry, may clarify the rationale and help to shape the context for the following discussion. Bear in mind that the focus of criticism, for reasons already considered, is the *action* and not the actor, and the "purpose" sought is always stated in analytic rather than everyday terms. Further, the critical base is valid only for voluntary actions, those open to choice by the actor. Involuntary actions cannot be criticized or improved; they are simply part of nature, like a falling leaf or a rainstorm. Not every human action is purposeful, and if the purposes of the actor cannot be determined and translated into analytic terms, the action cannot be criticized or improved (unless a purpose is first attributed to the actor, and that is at best a risky business).

The first type of problem encountered in efforts to produce and justify the knowledge required for directing actions is a function of the analytic complexity of the basic concept. Every voluntary action has three major analytic dimensions, can be examined critically from three different perspectives—empirical or experiential, normative, and methodological. Justifications for actions must satisfy criteria of adequacy appropriate to each of these three perspectives. Viewed empirically, an action appears as an effort to produce a specified future outcome by introducing a present change into the environment. Criticism and justification focus on the question: "Does the evidence suggest that the change to be introduced into the situation is likely to produce the desired outcome?" Viewed normatively, a voluntary action serves to reify a preference for one future state of the world rather than for any of a specified set of alternatives, each attainable with some degree of risk or uncertainty—voluntary actions are analytically indentical to choices. Criticism is concerned in this case with the question "Can reasons be found in human experience for maintaining that preference or priority?" Finally, the acceptability of the justifications or criticisms produced in response to each of these queries will depend on the methodological assumptions used to produce them or on their theoretical relation to the purpose at hand and the content of past experience.

Closer examination of the conditions to be satisfied before an "improvement" can be made in human actions raises other slightly different, but no less important problems for the inquirer. Strictly speaking, actions cannot be improved, despite the implication to that effect in everyday usage. Actions are what they are. Only performance can be improved. And when an "improvement" in reasoned performance appears, it is due to changes that occur within the set of assumptions used to direct actions; different assumptions force a different action in pursuit of a specified purpose. The action has not improved; another action has been substituted for the first. In effect, improvements in the quality of human performance require a change of actions rather than their improvement. And if improved performance is due to changes in assumptions, then it cannot occur unless actions are *forced* (logically) by a set of known assumptions. The results of action serve as a test of the assumptions that directed the action and not of the action per se, and that relation must be reflected in procedures used for correcting performances that employ those assumptions—again, a very important matter for policymakers to take into account where policymaking is construed as the direction of human actions.

To make the point somewhat differently, improvements in human performance are contingent upon learning, upon improvements in the knowledge used to direct actions. It follows that the minimum conditions for learning, which can be stated fairly precisely, are also the minimum conditions for improvements in policymaking. Those limits are quite severe: if the goal is to produce a foreseeable outcome, a set of assumptions must be accepted that suffice to force a particular action under specified limiting conditions. Before human actions can result in learning, in improvements in the knowledge used to guide action, the purpose of the action (the outcome sought through action) must be stated with sufficient precision to allow a clear judgment whether that purpose has been achieved. The set of assumptions on which the action depends must also be articulated in enough detail to show logically or formally that a particular outcome can be expected to follow from the action. Under those conditions, the results that actually appear can be compared to the results anticipated, providing both a test of the assumptions that forced the action and the evidence needed to correct them, or more accurately, to modify the probability of success attached to their use.

It is worth noting parenthetically that what is tested by action is the full set of assumptions that is used to direct the action, *taken as a whole*. As noted earlier, when judgments are involved, that full set of assumptions cannot be known; criticism is based on a reconstruction of the grounds for judgment. In effect, a partial selection is assumed to be complete and that allows calculation of implications; the procedure is made feasible by adding a *ceteris paribus* clause. But if expectations and outcomes differ, the faulty assumption in the structure may be extremely difficult to locate, particularly in cases where the error is due to a missing assumption (included in the *ceteris paribus*) and not to an inadequacy in one of the articulated assumptions or an error in calculation. Even if the outcomes correspond perfectly with expectations, some measure of uncertainty will always remain attached to the knowledge employed, because of the unknowns linked to it through the *ceteris paribus*.

Voluntary actions provide a mechanism through which empirical and normative knowledge can be combined to fulfill normative purposes in the real world. Efforts to impose quality control on the empirical and normative knowledge used to direct actions are complicated by the need to function in an ongoing intellectual system in which a variety of purposes is already being pursued, and a range of conventions, techniques, and performance standards has been created for assessing efforts to fulfill them. The precise nature of the problem is perhaps best illustrated by reference to the physical sciences. For the most part, those disciplines have concentrated on fulfilling two primary purposes: predicting future events and controlling (preventing or producing) future events by present actions. Within the sciences, each of these purposes serves as a criterion for assessing knowledge produced. Obviously, if the purpose of inquiry is to predict future events, then successful prediction is a good indicator of success. But for directing human actions, knowledge that is adequate for predicting future events is not sufficient;

future events must be *controlled* by present actions, and the knowledge required for that purpose must satisfy more stringent evidentiary requirements. Therefore, if empirical or scientific inquiries are to create knowledge that is useful for directing human actions, the purposes of such inquiries cannot be limited to prediction. Further, even the capacity to control future events, taken alone, may not be a good indicator of successful inquiry, for the future events that can be controlled using the knowledge that has been created may not be normatively significant. Moreover, the technological capacity needed to apply the knowledge produced must actually be available if the knowledge is to serve as a basis for action, yet that requirement need not be either necessary or desirable within a particular scientific field. It is possible, in other words, to fulfill critical standards that are perfectly adequate given one (legitimate) purpose yet fail with respect to other standards even though analytically the purpose (controlling events) is "the same" in both cases. Similarly, if the conceptual apparatus used to produce a particular theoretical structure cannot be linked to an adequate set of normative concepts, then it cannot be used in the direction of actions, however powerful the body of supporting evidence may be.

Construing voluntary action as a mechanism for combining empirical and normative knowledge to achieve some human purpose serves to emphasize further the primary role of normative assumptions in the development of an intellectual apparatus able to direct actions. Empirical purposes are always contingent upon normative purposes; they are pursued because they are necessary prerequisites to the fulfillment of a normative purpose. There would be no reason to seek ways of achieving a particular outcome unless it had already been established that the outcome was normatively desirable. "Curiosity" might lead someone to undertake such an inquiry, of course, but in a knowledge system meant to fulfill the requirements for directing actions, the principal justification for any empirical inquiry is that the knowledge sought or produced is needed to fulfill an established normative purpose. Theoretical pressure to round out the available knowledge supply in a given field might seem persuasive, but that would only be the case if the field as a whole was deemed sufficiently important to warrant the effort, and that is a normative matter. The doctrine of "knowledge for its own sake" is merely grotesque in a world of serious resource scarcities.

If testability is to be an essential characteristic of knowledge claims, the set of priorities used to direct actions must be ordered transitively. That in turn forces selection of an overriding purpose for action; otherwise, it would be impossible to choose among alternative, competing subordinate purposes. The "ultimate" purpose, which may be stated in quite general terms, provides the limits that determine the acceptability of the various side effects generated out of efforts to achieve contributory purposes, as the football coach in a secondary school is not permitted to risk the future health of the players in an effort to fulfill the short-run objective of winning a particular game.

Although selection of such an ultimate purpose sounds a formidable, or even impossible, undertaking, it turns out in practice to be a relatively simple matter. Given the overwhelming importance of human life in the panoply of human concerns, the ultimate normative purpose of human inquiry can in all cases be taken as the maintenance and improvement of the conditions of life of *some* human population. That leaves open such questions as which human population should serve as the focus of judgment, or how the various populations affected by action should be treated when preferences are being justified, while supplying an adequate point of departure for creating a defensible preference system. It may be necessary to supplement or elaborate that ultimate purpose in various ways, but outright elimination, or even direct substitution, would lead unavoidably to absurdity.

Once a purpose for human actions has been established, whether ultimate or proximate, it remains to create a theoretical or analytic structure able to direct efforts to achieve it, or to criticize proposals for doing so. The structure will consist of sets of assumptions whose content is determined by the purpose to be fulfilled: their form is a function of the way in which assumptions are combined to fulfill the purpose; their substance depends on the actual content of past human experience. The overall apparatus will contain both limited and specific structures, sets of narrow assumptions used for dealing with highly specific purposes in carefully defined situations and broader, more generalized structures, created inductively from such specifics. At the base of the overall system lies a set of primary assumptions that is incorporated into *every* knowledge claim generated within the apparatus. Those basics will refer, among other things, to the intellectual capacity of human actors, to the limiting conditions imposed by natural processes, and to the availability of resources, including relevant knowledge. They will also include the conventions that determine the kind of evidence that should be accepted for particular kinds of generalized propositions about empirical or normative relations. A theoretical apparatus of this order will be testable by reference to (1) its capacity to account for the success or failure of past efforts to achieve the purposes for which it was created and (2) its capacity to direct the creation of knowledge useful for controlling human actions in accurate, reliable, and normatively acceptable ways.

An Illustration of the Process: Athletic Coaching. Perhaps the best illustration of the analytic considerations involved in creating knowledge of the kind under discussion is found in athletic coaching. Beginning with the overall purpose of a game such as football or golf, athletic coaches work backward, analytically if not historically, seeking to create a structured set of second-order purposes whose fulfillment is necessary and/or sufficient for achieving that overall purpose. The search will, if successful, force articulation of further levels of purposes ancillary to those already identified, and development of ways of achieving them. The process is bounded on the one hand by the ultimate purpose of the game, for that must be accepted before criteria of relevance and significance can be created, and on the other hand by the rules of the game and the limits of human capacity. Such limits perform exactly the same function in coaching that the rules governing the operation of the natural universe play in physics. The process of elaboration and development continues until success is achieved reliably and efficiently enough to satisfy normative requirements, or until practical/analytic limitations intervene to end the analysis.

Taken as a whole, the set of ancillary purposes developed by those who play and coach football, and the means devised for achieving them, amount to a "theory of play" for the sport. That theory is stated in a "coaching language," developed concurrently with the theory of play and meant to further improvements in the theory. A theory of play of this kind provides grounds for directing the actions of individual players in stipulated circumstances, for developing exercises for those seeking to improve their performance, and for criticizing their performance constructively. Over the long run, a well-developed theory of play can increase the probability that the purpose of the activity will be achieved as fully as resources allow. A sound theory cannot guarantee success, but it can lead to changes that are recognized as improvements by the community of "informed and competent" observers. Performance in real games provides the data that are needed to substantiate the judgment of "informed opinion" at the same time that it produces the evidence used to test and improve the theory of play itself.

Some of the major possibilities and limitations inherent in the kind of analysis undertaken here are nicely illustrated by the functioning of theories of play in athletics. Such theories are quite useless, for example, as a basis for developing motivation among the players; that require a theory of motivation rather than a theory of play. Further, if a theory of play can suggest ways of improving individual performance, such improvements are necessarily a function of the players' individual efforts. More important still, good coaching usually seeks to generate some measure of self-coaching among players, to develop players able to learn from experience and use the learning to improve performance without external assistance. In effect, individual players are encouraged to deal with their own actions using the theory of play developed by the coach (and perhaps modified or enriched by personal experience).

Two other characteristics of the development of the intellectual foundation on which athletic coaching depends bear special emphasis here. First, theories of play cannot be created or improved outside the context provided by real contests; the structure must be generated inductively, meaning that it begins with, and is constrained by, real world experience rather than proceeding formally from *a priori* assumptions. Second, a theory of play is always stated in generalized terms and must be applied; application requires acts of judgment on the part of the user, whether coach, player, or spectator-critic. Each application of the theory serves both to test the theory and to provide the evidence needed to extend and elaborate it.

A theory of play in sports is an "open" structure and not a closed system, or logic. For both practical and methodological reasons, the essence of the theory must be captured in a logic or calculus, however tentatively and uncertainly. Yet no theory of play can produce the kind of complete specification of the actions needed to achieve a given purpose that being "captured in a logic" implies, for the same reasons that the procedures learned in medical school must be augmented in the performance of any specific operation. In effect, those who apply theories to real world affairs actually complete the theory at the time of application, adapting a generalized structure to the particular requirements of the situation at hand. This creative aspect or dimension of theory (or policy) application has some very important implications for the way in which theories or policies should be formulated and administered, particularly in the conduct of collective affairs, and for the kinds of organizational or institutional arrangements that should be created for applying policies if they are to be improved over time out of experience.

Analytically, development of a theory of play, whether for thinking or for athletics, proceeds in a relatively straightforward manner, beginning with an overall purpose and working backward. Historically, however, the situation encountered in real cases is likely to be quite different, for theoretical development necessarily occurs in an ongoing environment where purposes have already been accepted and means for seeking to fulfill them are already in place. The policy analyst in particular is usually placed in a situation akin to that of the football coach whose players have "played the game" before but without systematic instruction, or worse, the violin teacher whose students have already acquired habits or ways of performing that must be unlearned before further progress is possible. Strictly speaking, the psychological problems encountered in efforts to adapt current practice to analytic requirements are not a matter for concern here. Analytic requirements are fixed by the purposes sought and the resources/capacities available for achieving them. If the analysis is valid, the requirements *must* be met, else success is only accidental. However, it is worth pointing out that efforts to improve real world performance by living persons must begin with those persons as they are presently, otherwise the theory of play will not function properly. The athletic coach who complained because the players could not fulfill the requirements of the theory of play would be advised, rightly, to change the theory of play. The same limitations hold for intellectual structures meant to assist real people with the conduct of real world affairs. In the last analysis, the capacities, limitations, and needs of human "players" and not the requirements of logic, control acceptability.

Bibliographic Note

The theory of knowledge on which the present argument depends originated in the 1950s on a foundation supplied by then-current philosophy of science.[5] Although it contributed greatly to the clarification of the methodological foundations of social science, the inadequacy of the "deductive paradigm" of scientific explanation that dominated the field at that time was readily apparent even from informal efforts to apply it to real-world affairs. There were two basic problems with the paradigm: first, if the formal requirements for scientific "explanations" were enforced rigorously, they could rarely if ever be met within social science and performance was unlikely to improve in the near future; second, and much more important, even if those requirements could be satisfied, the resulting knowledge did not always provide an adequate base for action and testing/corrigibility remained a serious problem. The basic modifications introduced into the deductive paradigm flowed from a recognition of the role of purposes in testing and improvement of human performance—of the importance of employing a pragmatic criterion for the criticism and improvement of knowledge. The critical focus was therefore transferred from the logical characteristics of the knowledge claim to the sets of purposes for which knowledge was required and the conditions of their fulfillment.[6] The empirical portion of the modified theory of knowledge was published in 1968[7]; a summary version of the normative or ethical part of the theory appeared in the following year.[8] An integrated statement of the complete position, focused on the intellectual requirements for directing human actions on defensible grounds and concentrating most heavily on the empirical or scientific dimensions of knowledge, was published in 1971.[9]

In the following decade, the epistemological/methodological structure was tested as fully as resources and circumstances allowed. In particular, the value of the apparatus as a pedagogical tool, as a base for instruction that could improve the cognitive or critical performance of students, was examined at various educational levels from elementary school through graduate training in both the United States and Latin America. The results, although very tentative and based on a relatively small body of data, were uniformly encouraging.[10] Concurrently, the analytic structure's value as a critical tool for assessing the quality of public policymaking was tested fairly extensively, focusing on the American federal government's activities in the field of public housing.[11] The results were again quite positive. (Such terms as "encouraging," or "positive" are based on the informal judgments of those involved with the experimental programs, supplemented by "paper and pencil" testing.) And finally, the value of the theory as an aid to those actively engaged in making public policy was studied with the cooperation of the Inter-American Foundation in Rosslyn, Virginia, a federal agency created by the Congress in 1970 and charged with learning how best to carry out overseas development assistance humanely and effectively. Once again, the results were most encouraging.[12] The basic theory was therefore revised to incorporate the modifications and refinements suggested by a decade of teaching, application, and evaluation, and published in 1981.[13] A text version of the theory, targeted at the beginning undergraduate or the upper-level secondary school student, appeared seven years later.[14]

Among the findings to emerge from the application of the theoretical apparatus to federal policymaking, two points stand out as particularly significant: first, the knowledge required for directing actions on defensible grounds was not usually available; second, where such knowledge *was* available, it was usually ignored by those responsible for making policy. Both those who directed the rule-making apparatus and those who criticized the performance depended heavily on assumptions that were usually untested, often untestable, and sometimes known to be grossly erroneous. Discussions that took place during the policymaking process tended to focus on procedural rather than substantive issues; there were few signs of significant learning and fewer still of the use of such learning to improve performance. Indeed, it could be argued with some force from the evidence produced by a detailed study of the public housing program in the United States that human populations living in late twentieth-century industrial society might do well to avoid the ministrations of public policymakers as their eighteenth-century ancestors had profited by avoiding doctors and hospitals, and for many of the same reasons. Because that rather pessimistic conclusion ran contrary to the received wisdom of the times, a suitable demonstration seemed advisable.

A study of the adequacy of the empirical or scientific knowledge available in the social sciences for use by the policymaker was undertaken first, targeted at economics since that is generally considered to be the most powerful and sophisticated of the social sciences. A parallel study of the normative knowledge currently used for directing human affairs, based on the detailed critical apparatus developed in the present volume, is in progress. A survey of major academic publications in American economics, including econometrics, and covering the decade from 1970 to 1980, was completed in 1981. The findings to date have been quite uniform: if such specialized subfields as agricultural economics (where the approach to inquiry is controlled mainly by criteria obtained from the adjunct field rather than by those employed in economics) are excluded, economic "theorists" rarely if ever produce the kind of knowledge required for policymaking. At best, economic "theories" are useful for predicting future events, although accuracy and reliability decline dramatically over very short time spans—weeks at most. Economics emerged from the study as a field of inquiry more closely resembling meteorology than one of the experimental or engineering sciences, and rarely if ever able to approach the level of accuracy and generality commonly achieved in meteorology. Further, and more ominously, the usefulness of economic theory in policymaking is unlikely to improve over the long run barring major, and highly improbable, changes in the approach to knowledge development taken by the field.

2

Action: The Intellectual Foundations

Meaning and Derivations

If the intellectual requirements for directing human actions are to be stated persuasively, the class of events labeled "actions" must be provided with an adequate meaning or definition. A precisely equivalent problem appears in the field of medicine if a definition or meaning is sought for such concepts as "mumps" or "cancer." The requirement cannot be satisfied by consulting an ordinary dictionary, which merely provides an uncritical summary of current practice; the equivalent of the kind of meaning provided by a medical dictionary is needed. Concepts intended for use in the conduct of human affairs must have meanings that are linked to the requirements for conducting such affairs in an acceptable manner. As in medicine, definitions cannot be either arbitrary or capricious; they must correspond well to human experience with the "thing" that has been defined. However, given the scope and diversity of human actions, efforts to define the class in the same way that medicine has defined such concepts as mumps or cancer, by generalizing observed characteristics of particular cases of each disease, are unlikely to succeed. Definitions created by that procedure would be subject to endless exceptions and qualifications; members of the class would be quite heterogeneous in their other attributes. With respect to concepts such as "action," a somewhat different approach to meaning and definition is needed.

The problem is resolved fairly readily by creating an analytic definition or meaning for the concept. That is, the meaning of "action" can be stated in terms of the human capacity to produce change in the environment—defined by specifying the necessary and sufficient conditions for an action to occur in terms of environmental change. Thus, an *action* occurs whenever the capacity to produce a change in the environment is present, whether that capacity is vested in an individual or a collectivity. Since capacity *must* be exercised, either by positive action or "negatively," by failing to act, the presence of capacity is an adequate indicator for action. Whether or not the capacity is used, the forced effect of the action that follows is a world that is in some respect different than it would otherwise be had the capacity been used in a different way. If capacity is used positively, in the ordinary meaning of "act," it will either produce a change that would not otherwise take place, or prevent a change from occurring that would otherwise be expected to happen. If capacity is not exercised, either changes that could have been produced will not take place or changes that could have been prevented will follow. In either case, the world will be different in some way than it could have been had the capacity been otherwise employed, and an "action," as defined, will have occurred. The world actually produced, or expected to be produced, can be compared to the world that could have been produced had capacity been exercised differently, thereby providing a base for criticism and improvement of the exercise of capacity—of action. Not every change that is observed can be attributed to human action, of course, and not every action is significant; the critical apparatus must therefore include both the grounds needed for attributing causality to some prior event or action and some means for separating what is significant from what is trivial.

Defined as the exercise of real human capacity to produce change, actions may be either voluntary or involuntary. Only voluntary actions, those that can be performed or avoided at will, are amenable to criticism. Involuntary actions, those performed willy-nilly by the person, will also produce change but they are not open to criticism for they cannot be altered. "Actions" that lie wholly beyond present human capacity can also be disregarded, although they may be both conceivable in the present and possible in the future. Finally, the dogmatic determinist's insistence that *all* human actions are somehow determined and therefore no action is "really" voluntary can also be ignored. If the determining factors cannot be specified, that extreme position has no practical implications. For the remainder of the discussion, then, the term "action" is reserved strictly to the voluntary exercise of human capacity to produce change.

When action is defined in this way, voluntary actions are precisely equivalent to choices. The exercise of capacity (action) always creates a world that is different than it would otherwise be. If the action is voluntary, the capacity to produce change need not be used; if capacity is not used, the world of the future will take the shape dictated by the drift course of events, and it will differ in at least some respect from the world that would have appeared if capacity had been exercised positively. It follows that whenever there is a genuine capacity to produce change that can be controlled voluntarily, the person who controls the use of capacity will, unavoidably, produce one of two or more different alternative future states of the world, and will therefore make a choice. The substance of the choice, the "thing" that is chosen, is the content of one member of the set of alternative future states available to the actor. The content of the full set is determined by the actor's capacity to produce change at a given time and place, *plus* the future outcome projected by allowing the drift course of events to flow unhindered. In effect, any actor with the capacity to produce change is *forced* to choose from among two or more alternative, different film clips of the future. One clip will contain the future to be expected if events are allowed to run their course; the others will contain the future states expected to follow from each of the actions available within the actor's capacity. Since either action or inaction will reify one member of the set of film clips, capacity alone is sufficient to force action or choice.

Defining action in terms of an actor's capacity to produce change, which serves to equate action with choice, benefits policy-related inquiry in several important ways. First, it allows an accurate determination of the intellectual requirements for directing actions and therefore provides the needed leverage point for criticizing and improving performance. Second, because that meaning corresponds reasonably well with the preferred meaning in current usage, the risk of confusion inherent in the use of limiting or precising definitions is much reduced. Third, the definition serves to emphasize the crucial role played by normative judgment or preference both in the direction of actions and in the criticism and improvement of performance. Fourth, focusing criticism, or justification, on the action rather than the actor, tends to reduce the risk of *ad hominem* arguments. The actor's identity is used only to determine capacity; once that has been established, identity can be ignored. There is no need to examine the actor's awareness, intentions, willingness to act, or other subjective attributes; such data are useful for criticizing the actor but irrelevant to criticism directed at actions. Of course, the allocation of rewards and assignment of blame to persons will be based at least in part on such considerations, but judgments of actions cannot be transferred automatically to the actor who performs them. The critical apparatus being developed here is meant *solely* for dealing with actions. Finally, focusing on the actor's capacity to produce change greatly simplifies the treatment of "nonactions"; inaction is one of the actions that can be chosen, and the results of inaction, the failure to exercise available capacity, are included automatically among the set of outcomes from which a choice must be made.

The direction, justification, or criticism, of voluntary actions will be based on a comparison of the consequences projected to follow from each of the actions available within the actor's capacity. In principle, criticism and justification could focus on the actor, the action taken, the consequences of action, or some combination of all three factors. But the normative assumption made earlier that maintenance and improvement of the conditions of life of some human population is the ultimate or overriding purpose of all human actions, which seems unavoidable, serves to force attention to the consequences of action.[1] If justification and criticism are concerned with the effects of action on individual life, they must be based on the consequences of action, for that is where the effects of action are found. Equally important, neither of the other two potential focii for justification and criticism is viable. Criticism based on the identity or attributes of the actor has long since been condemned; the inadequacies of *ad hominem* argument are well known. Efforts to base justification of criticism on the intrinsic characteristics of an action lead invariably to anomalies and inconsistencies so long as the consequences of action cannot be ignored, for the same action may produce quite different outcomes in different situations. At a minimum, the critical apparatus would have to take into account both actions and their consequences. However, it is not necessary to deal with both factors; all of the normatively significant dimensions of action are incorporated into the outcome or consequences, and nothing is gained by adding a detailed examination of the intrinsic characteristics of the action.

Systematic comparison of outcomes does make possible an adequate, if imperfect, justification for actions or choices (preferences). Indeed, that basis for action is recognized implicitly in much of everyday behavior. Faced with a criticism of an action (What you did was wrong! for example) the most common response, "What else could I have done?" implies the need to consider alternatives. What is usually missing is an adequate grasp of the intellectual requirements for answering such questions in a competent way. Justifications based on comparisons of outcomes will be uncertain, and may not be very powerful; serious disagreements may remain after every effort to reconcile them has been exhausted. Uncertainty is unavoidable: the capacity to provide a justification for the kinds of preferences expressed by the fabled Roman Emperor who, after hearing the first finalist in a singing contest, promptly awarded the prize to the second, simply is not available to ordinary humans.

A comparative approach to justification of actions is well suited to normative inquiry that seeks to improve real world performance once the established limitations on human capacity are taken into account. First, it allows the user to avoid much of the traditional terminology

of ethics, which greatly simplifies conceptual and argumentative requirements. Such terms as "good" and "bad," "right" and "wrong," or
"just and unjust" are unnecessary, and inappropriate, in comparative
criticism. Instead, the concepts employed must identify the significant
dimensions of individual life to be used in comparisons—there is no
need to assess particular life states. Even if an outcome could be judged
good or bad, for example (and it has thus far proved almost impossible
to supply guidelines for making such judgments), the problem of justifying actions or choices would remain unresolved. The alternatives
would still have to be compared in ways that would support a judgment
to the effect that one was "better" or "more just" than the other—and
in fact the proposed approach to justification allows that mode of conceptualization if the user can meet established standards for defending
preferences. Absolute criteria are unnecessary; even if the best and the
worst outcome could be identified, that would suffice only for those
situations where one of the two extreme cases actually appeared as part
of a two-outcome set. In a preference system focused on consequences,
an adequate justification need only provide reasons for preferring one
outcome within a given set of options. The preferred outcome need not
be "good" or "just," and an outcome judged "good" or "just" need not
be preferred. The procedures by which such preferences can be established and justified, the requirements and limitations associated with
them, will be considered in detail in chapter 6.

Actions or choices that are based on a deliberate or systematic comparing of outcomes will be labeled *reasoned*, (not "rational") to distinguish them from actions that are either justified on other grounds or
wholly lacking in justification. The definition is weak, and the quality
of the reasoning can vary greatly. No more is needed, however, than
some reason(s) for preference, based on known comparisons, to provide
a normative starting point that can be improved over time. If comparison
supplies reasons for preferring one outcome to the other available alternatives, that preference can be generalized to produce one of the
instruments needed for directing actions (here labeled a *priority* or
preference-ordering). The reasons offered for the preference are tested
against prior experience, including the overall human reaction to the
experience; use of the priority can produce further evidence to support
or refute the initial judgment. If comparison fails to produce grounds
for preference, the choice is a matter of indifference given the estab-
lished/accepted normative system.

The further question whether the established set of priorities is adequate can be answered by reexamining the available outcomes in a
real, particular choice in the light of past experience and an overall
construction of human potential derived from that experience. Nor-

mative justification or criticism, like the testing of any theoretical structure, can take place at two different analytic levels. In the first case, a preference is justified by showing that it is required by an established priority; in the second, the results obtained by applying an established priority are compared to the results that would be obtained if other, different priorities were adopted, seeking reasons in experience for accepting one outcome rather than another. In effect, arguments about preferences or priorities always focus on the same basic elements: the content of the particular choices from which the priority was created, the relevant body of past experience, and the set of generalized assumptions that have been derived from that past experience and are currently accepted and used.

THE INTELLECTUAL REQUIREMENTS FOR DIRECTING ACTIONS

The intellectual apparatus required for directing actions or choices is formidable and complex; the analytic framework needed to identify those requirements, and to criticize efforts to fulfill and apply them, is both elaborate and difficult to apply. At a minimum, reasoned direction of human actions depends on the fulfillment of six major intellectual requirements, each a formidable challenge to current research capacity in the social sciences. (1) If actions are defined by reference to an actor's capacity to produce change, and the justification for action is to be found in a systematic comparison of the available outcomes, carried out in the light of past experience, the actor's capacity to produce change must be specified—the range of actions available to the actor at a given time and place must be identified. (2) The extended set of consequences expected to follow from each of the actions lying within the actor's capacity, together with the outcome to be expected if the drift course of events is allowed to continue unhindered, must be projected on the future—a procedure limited by the available supply of knowledge, resources, and technology. (3) A set of concepts is required that can capture the normatively significant dimensions of each projected outcome; the projections may be made using such concepts or they must be translated into suitable concepts afterward. (4) The preferred outcome within the available set must be identified, and the selection justified; the result can then be generalized into an instrument (priority) able to identify the preferred outcome when applied to appropriate situations. (5) If actions are to be "directed" in the narrower and more specific sense of the term, an action program is required that will produce the preferred outcome when applied under stipulated conditions. (6) Finally, because it is unlikely that an action program will produce the preferred outcome accurately and reliably in all cases, particularly in the early stages of development of a field, and because testing in use is in any case good strategy, a monitoring system is needed that can be used to adjust both the empirical and the normative elements in the intellectual apparatus used to direct actions by reference to the outcomes actually produced.

In addition to these basic intellectual requirements, reasoned actions depend on the availability of a supporting apparatus adequate for generating, applying, and testing knowledge claims. That apparatus includes descriptive data, conceptual frameworks, measurement standards, and so on, plus an adequate language and enough calculating capacity to explore fully and accurately the content or implications of generalized propositions. Both language and logic must be taken as given here, but in real cases each is an important potential source of error and disagreement.

Every effort to provide a justification for a human action, or to criticize an action systematically, will in due course be forced to satisfy all of these intellectual requirements, regardless of the point at which inquiry or criticism begins. A brief examination of each of the major elements in the structure will serve to fix the precise meaning of key terms, indicate the kinds of purposes to be fulfilled, identify some of the problems encountered in efforts to fulfill them, and suggest some of the questions to be answered by policy-related inquiries. A summary sketch of the major requirements that an adequate theoretical apparatus must satisfy, stated in analytic terms, occupies the remainder of the chapter; no particular sequence of historical development is implied by the order of presentation.

The Actor's Capacity

Systematic criticism is directed at actions rather than actors; an adequate justification for action is based on a comparison of all of the outcomes actually available to a specific actor (who may be either an individual or a collectivity) at a given time or place. Their content depends on (1) the identity and attributes of the actor and (2) the situation in which the action occurs. The first step in justification or criticism is to establish the set of actions lying within the capacity of a real world actor in a specific situation. Capacity cannot be inferred from formal authority alone; the set of outcomes included in a choice must be genuinely attainable and real capacity may differ greatly from formal authority. Technically, capacity is an attribute of the actor that is independent of either the actor's awareness of it or his or her willingness to carry out a particular action. It includes everything that is possible for the actor at a given time and place. To illustrate, a dog that has been trained to remain within a given area by systematic conditioning has the capacity to leave the area but cannot exercise it. On the other hand, the dog may be willing to climb a tree in pursuit of a squirrel, and may even try to do so, but normally lacks the needed capacity.

What is actually possible for a given actor, the full scope of the actor's capacity, whether individual or collectivity, at a given point of time in a specified situation under existing institutional arrangements and with current personnel may be difficult or even impossible to determine with any degree of accuracy. In fact, one of the hallmarks of political skill is the ability to estimate in advance the amount of support that can be organized behind a stated measure at identifiable cost within a specific legislative body at a given point in time. Nevertheless, the suggested meaning for "capacity" must be maintained, for if capacity is restricted to what is *psychologically* possible, the established norms in the society then become a self-fulfilling ordinance.

Further, the definition accepted must allow the user to distinguish between real capacity and formal capacity, particularly in the actions of collective bodies. If real capacity is much less than formal capacity, to take one example, then it is merely foolish to judge performance by reference to the latter. And conversely, the failure to exercise real capacity needs to be treated as part of foregone potential. Self-governing or "democratic" communities tend to regard underutilization of authority as highly desirable, justifying that position, most commonly, on assumed high and unchangeable levels of both incompetence and venality among those who govern. That has the unfortunate consequence of blurring the importance of major disjunctions between real and formal authority (usually a primary indication of institutional inadequacy). The systematic underutilization of social potential suggests that those who live in the society, if they do escape some of the more serious disabilities associated with governmental incompetence and malpractice (a point that remains to be demonstrated), do not enjoy the full potential benefits of membership in an organized collectivity. In an era when it is increasingly apparent that the major factor determining the kinds of lives that most individuals lead is the sovereign government that controls the territory of residence or citizenship, that is a very serious weakness.

In principle, the justification of actions requires a full exploration of the actor's capacity, a careful comparison or weighing of *all* of the outcomes available for choice. In practice, that goal is almost never achieved even in very simple situations. Indeed, in any real case the actor's capacity might change in the time required to complete a detailed exploration of potential. Most of the time, only a small portion of the total number of options actually available is explored, and most of them are discarded rather summarily. Experience, habit, and training combine to focus attention on particular actions and their related outcomes. Thus individuals rarely include the effects of hurling themselves in front of passing vehicles when considering how to exercise their capacity, though most persons who live in urban areas face that "choice" many times each day. Nor does a person engaged in purchasing a luxury item for a member of the family usually stop to weigh the consequences of making the purchase against the consequences of spending the same resources to provide food and clothing for the starving. Selectivity is commonplace, and necessary. Otherwise, even simple everyday concerns would be virtually impossible to manage without risking nervous collapse.

However, it should be noted that selectivity is often and perhaps usually exercised unconsciously and uncritically, and its effects are therefore readily overlooked. Two types of protective measures seem called for in the circumstances, particularly within self-governing societies: at a minimum, the members of the society, and more particularly those responsible for directing collective actions, should be sensitized to the influence of selectivity on current practice; and in most cases, systematic monitoring of the consequences flowing from current practice, particularly for areas deemed significant in the hierarchy of collective priorities, is highly desirable. Such considerations are not new, of course, but their importance is well demonstrated by recent studies of such topics as the depth and pervasiveness of both racial prejudice and anti-feminine bias in American institutions and practices, among others.

Projecting the Outcomes

The justification for an action or choice is found in a comparison of the outcomes available to a specific actor at a given time and place. The ability to project the content of those (future) outcomes with some measure of reliability is therefore a necessary precondition to justification. In every case, one outcome must contain the future state of the world anticipated if the actor's capacity is not exercised, if the drift course of events is allowed to continue. Each of the other outcomes contains the projected results of specific actions, of the positive exercise of capacity. Both types of projections are uncertain or risky, and the amount of risk, as well as the substantive content of what is risked, needs to be taken into account when projected outcomes are being examined for preference.

The instrumental requirements for projecting the outcome expected if natural events are allowed to run their course are quite different from those needed to project the effects of human actions. The distinction is readily illustrated. If one species of flowers found in nature is regularly observed to bloom some two weeks after another, that information can be generalized into a simple pattern: Species A will bloom about two weeks after Species B. Combining that pattern with an observation (noting that Species B has bloomed today) leads logically to the prediction that Species A will bloom in about two weeks. The added assumption "Other things equal," or "If nature is allowed to run its course unhindered," is commonly suppressed. Once established, an apparatus of that kind can be used to project the drift course of events onto the future.

Such structures do not provide an adequate intellectual base for predicting the effects of action, hence they cannot be used to project the other outcomes from which choices are made. To illustrate, efforts to speed the blooming of Species A by hastening the blooming of Species B (say by supplying artificial sunlight) will succeed only if the relation between the two bloomings is "causal." Otherwise, the effect of acting on the generalized pattern is to destroy its predictive capacity. For predicting the effects of action, a causal relation *must* be assumed between the action and its consequences; that assumption is not necessary if the purpose is only to predict the outcome of the natural flow of events. The term "causal relation" implies something more than a constant conjunction of events: the supporting evidence must include situations in which the antecedent event presumed to be the "cause" of the outcome was a human action, an event produced deliberately in an effort to secure the projected outcome. A causal relation may state either the necessary and/or the sufficient conditions for a particular event to occur, but that is not enough to distinguish it from any constant conjunction of events. A causal connection assumes further that the relation between two specific events will hold regardless of the way in which the first event or change is produced.

For convenience, instruments with only predictive capacity, that do not assume a causal relation between events, will be labeled *forecasts*; instruments that do incorporate a causal assumption will be labeled *theories*. Forecasts function by transposing a set of correlations from past experience onto the future; since they do not contain a causal assumption they cannot be tested experimentally and cannot provide a basis for action. (Unless a causal relation is assumed, there could be no justification for acting on the relation.) Of course, an instrument that is developed as a forecast may actually incorporate a causal relation, but the supporting evidence need only justify it *qua* forecast. A theory also transposes a set of past correlations onto the future, but one of the elements in the correlated events must be a human action (the connection may be established either directly or indirectly). The causal assumption makes it possible for a theory to serve as a basis for action, and thus provides the necessary logical foundation for experimental testing; if it is assumed that A somehow "causes" B, it follows that performing action A can be expected to produce result B. Although those meanings correspond fairly well with usage in the experimental sciences, and are strongly recommended for adoption within social science, particularly by those concerned with policymaking, current usage varies widely and few of the structures labeled "theories" within social science are supported by evidence that is adequate to establish a causal relation among the elements or events it contains. What is important in the present context, is to link the evidentiary requirements for the instrument to the function it is expected to perform. Excepting those cases where the status of the instrument is already well established, the function to be performed determines the evidence needed to justify accepting and using the instrument for that particular purpose.

The Normative Concepts

Justification of actions requires a comparison of outcomes; comparisons necessarily involve observations of two or more things using a common set of continua, a defensible selection of concepts or variables. In principle, the outcome of any human action can be stated in an infinite number of different ways, each equally accurate. But for purposes of action or choice, the statement of outcomes must capture their normatively significant dimensions; hence, the set of concepts employed must be adequate for that purpose. Given the commitment already made here to maintaining and improving the conditions of life of some human population as the overall or ultimate purpose of action, the normative concepts will refer to the attributes of individual human lives. There is no implication that all human lives will be taken into account in every system of preferences, or that the effects of action on different individual lives will count equally in all cases. But the concepts employed in any statement of the consequences of action must refer to the conditions of life of some selection of persons, otherwise the action cannot be justified or criticized adequately out of human experience.

Detailed discussion of the characteristics of an adequate set of normative concepts, and the problems encountered in efforts to create and apply them, is reserved for chapter 5. In general, however, two basic kinds of requirements will have to be fulfilled by an adequate conceptual apparatus. First, the dimensions of individual life that are considered significant must be isolated and the selection justified; second, indicators that will allow an observer to measure changes in the values of these variables can then be created. Of course, the relative significance of any given attribute or characteristic of a human life varies with the situation, but that is not a matter for serious concern; differences are eliminated automatically by systematic comparison of the outcomes. Put another way, any concept may be "normative" or normatively significant depending on the situation; other aspects of the situation determine the amount of significance that should be attached to the particular values that it takes. The danger to be avoided is the omission of significant dimensions of individual life from the conceptual apparatus. What is omitted can play no part in either judgment or justification; otiose concepts are eliminated during the comparison process on which justification depends.

It should be noted that the concepts employed in the structuring of outcomes can be very complex constructs, comprising a number of other concepts that may also, under some circumstances, be considered "normative." Thus the overall concept of "the quality of individual human life" will upon analysis be shown to comprise other complex concepts such as "the state of health of the individual," which in turn can be analyzed into still other concepts such as "condition of eyesight," and so on. Concepts that are regarded as normative in one context may appear as indicators for other normative concepts in a different context—"condition of eyesight" may be used to measure "the quality of individual life," for example. A full statement of the apparatus required for identifying the normative concepts employed in reasoned choice and of the problems that arise in efforts to measure their values is set forth in chapter 5.

Once a selection of normative concepts has been agreed, they must be linked through a network of theories to the set of concepts used to project the available outcomes, to the concepts found in the theories and forecasts used to make the projections. If the historical development of the available intellectual apparatus had been guided by analytic requirements, such relations would already be well established. Inquiry would commence with a normative commitment; therefore, the goals of inquiry would already be stated in normative terms, and theories would make use of concepts whose relations to normative requirements were already established. But historically, empirical and normative concepts have developed independently, and the concepts commonly used in theories and/or forecasts do not usually refer to the normatively significant dimensions of individual human life. Indeed, they can only rarely be linked to human lives in an effective and defensible way. The conceptual and theoretical disjunction between them is a formidable barrier to improving the quality of policymaking, particularly in collective affairs, the more so because those engaged in the development of theories and forecasts tend to regard their work as somehow "scientific" and therefore fundamentally unrelated to normative matters— in effect, mistaking a normative commitment for an "unscientific" or even "antiscientific" bias. For purposes of action or choice, any theory that cannot be linked to a set of normative concepts is useless, but that assessment is unlikely to be shared by those who produce such theories and validate them by reference to the established conventions of the field in which they are produced.

The nature of the problem is most readily visible in such fields as economics, where the concepts commonly used in forecasts and theories rarely if ever relate to the lives of particular individuals.[2] Within economics, a set of "evaluative" terms has been created, but they refer invariably to features of collectivities or systems (inflation and growth rates, employment levels, price stability, efficiency, and so on); in many cases, they are very difficult to operationalize, not to say relate to the conditions of life of particular persons. Thus, increases in aggregate income or wealth, which are commonly taken as an indication of improved economic performance, may in fact coincide with significant increases in the misery and deprivation of ever larger populations: that aberration was noted long ago by Charles Dickens, was duly enshrined by Marx, and can be documented repeatedly with respect to Third World development. In general, concepts that deal with population aggregates, even in those rare cases where they refer to such normatively-significant aspects of life as infant mortality rates or the incidence of particular diseases, are useful mainly for locating social problems; they are not very helpful in efforts to resolve them, in policymaking.

Preferences/Priorities

Given a set of two or more outcomes, available within the capacity of a known actor, projected with reasonable accuracy and reliability by using instruments that incorporate a causal linkage (theories), and stated using concepts that capture the normatively significant dimensions of each outcome, direction of action requires a device for selecting the preferred outcome in the set. The apparatus must be justifiable prior to use. An instrument able to perform that function, to select or locate the preferred outcome in a given set, will be labeled a *priority* or preference-ordering. Creating and justifying such instruments is, of course, the central task in an action-oriented normative inquiry and the principal concern in the present discussion.

Detailed consideration of the development, structural characteristics, and justification of priorities is reserved for chapter 7, but a few basic points may serve to clarify the nature of the instrument. First, each element in a priority or preference-ordering is a complete outcome, projected as fully as current theoretical capacity allows. When an action is introduced into the environment, it sets in motion a chain of events that will run its full course unless further action is taken, or external events intercede. In effect, choices are made among film clips of the future, each containing the set of consequences projected to follow from one of the available actions. To the extent that it can be anticipated, the full chain of events, the full content of each clip, must be taken into account when choices are justified. In practice, every projection of future events remains incomplete and uncertain; repercussions of actions may go on forever, but the human capacity to trace them is limited, often quite drastically. If that is a source of concern it may also be cause for rejoicing, for the limits on human capacity provide a welcome escape from both infinite regression and endless repercussions. A priority, then, will consist of a generalized set of outcomes, each of which may be quite extensive and complex, ordered to show the preferred outcome. The general form of the structure is comparative and limited: Prefer outcome A to outcomes B, C, D,...N, for example. A priority is generalized in form and is expected to apply to any situation in which the same selection of outcomes is available for choice.

Priorities are created inductively, are generalized out of past experience, and are limited by that experience, in much the same way as empirical knowledge. Insisting that normative knowledge be grounded in and limited by experience very profoundly influences the character of normative inquiry, and the kind of apparatus that can be produced. First, inductively based knowledge is always contingent upon prior experience with specific cases whether the goal is to establish a causal relation or a preference. Regarded analytically, priorities are generalized from prior solutions to particular cases. Second, the search for reasons for preferring one outcome to another, like the search for the cause of a particular event, always begins and ends with a particular case; the availability of a number of cases only facilitates the search. Third, priorities, like causal patterns or theories, can be used only for dealing with recurring situations. Finally, because priorities are inductively grounded, each priority has an independent justification and since only those cases that actually appear in real world situations need be solved, the overall apparatus, the full set of priorities accepted and used by an individual or collectivity, need not be integrated. The elements of the set, the individual priorities, cannot be inconsistent, for that would preclude testing. A transitive ordering of priorities is therefore essential, but transitivity is testable only at the points where priorities intersect. In an inductively based set of priorities, all of the elements may not intersect, and that opens the way to a level of internal inconsistency that is unlikely to appear in a normative apparatus generated deductively out of first principles. Such inconsistency causes no special problems so long as user and critic are sensitized to the hazards associated with inductive inquiries.

Action Programs for Achieving Preferred
Outcomes (Policies)

Once the preferred outcome in a set of options has been established for a particular case, or identified by applying an already-accepted priority, it remains to actually produce that outcome and thus complete the action. An action program, a set of rule-directed actions expected to produce the preferred outcome, is an essential part of the overall intellectual apparatus. A set of rules that is able to perform that function, which corresponds precisely to a cookbook recipe or the prescribed mode of medical treatment for a particular illness, will be labeled a *policy*. That meaning corresponds well with common practice in such areas as Department of State policy papers, but in everyday affairs, and in academia, usage varies enormously and not everything that is labeled a "policy" will have the capacity to direct human actions to a normatively preferred outcome.

A policy may consist of a single rule, such as "All merchandise may be returned without penalty within forty-eight hours of purchase so long as it has not been damaged." More commonly, particularly in collective affairs, policies take the form of a collection of rules, often quite extensive, and are labeled *programs*. The sets of rules that make up the substance of a policy are extrapolated from the causally linked theories used to project the available outcomes. Since each outcome must be genuinely producible, the technological capacity needed to implement the theories used to make such projections must already be in place. Indeed, the consequences, desirable and undesirable, associated with any given action include the effects of using specific equipment or technology—they are incorporated directly into the projections.

Policies serve to apply or reify priorities. They must, therefore, entail a set of actions that is expected to produce the preferred outcome in a given situation with some estimated degree of reliability. The justification for a policy is found in its ability to produce the outcome indicated by a priority; the justification for a priority is its ability to indicate the outcome that is preferred in particular cases. The justification for a particular preference, on the other hand, and the ultimate justification for every policy, is found in past human experience with the various alternatives, including both affective reactions and cognitive considerations.

Actions function as the point of integration for priorities, preferences, and policies, and therefore as the testing ground for each of those elements. Rigorous analytic separation is essential, for collapsing priority and preference eliminates justification, and collapsing priority and policy converts a normative structure based on systematic comparison of consequences into a rule ethic (which is in principle untenable). Empirically or experientially, however, the separation is often difficult to establish and maintain. For all practical purposes, priorities and policies are tested in combination and the implications of the test may be indeterminate for either or both elements if the test design is inadequate. Three major possibilities must be taken into account: first, the outcome produced by applying a policy may conflict with an established priority, and if no reason is found to change the priority, the policy will have to be altered; second, if the outcome is different than expected, but reasons are found for considering it preferable to the projected outcome, it may be necessary to retain the policy and change the priority; third, if the policy produces the preferred outcome but experience gained by living with that outcome suggests that one of the others is actually preferable, both priority and policy may be modified.

So long as testability is considered essential, such complications seriously handicap the policymaker. To meet testability requirements, policies must be stated with sufficient richness and precision to *force* a particular set of actions under stipulated limiting conditions. Unless the actions are required logically by the set of assumptions incorporated into the policy, there is no test. Yet there is a limit to the completeness with which actions can be specified when the objective is to alter the human condition in particular ways. The most powerful policy that can be created provides a complete statement of the actions needed to produce a particular outcome, states the sufficient conditions for an outcome to occur. In such cases, no interpretation is required, or desired, and the policy can be implemented by an automaton, for it amounts to a debugged and noise-free computer program. It may be possible to develop policies of that order for some industrial uses, but even routine administration of relatively trivial human affairs will usually raise problems that cannot be resolved in an acceptable manner using a fully computerized policy.

That raises the major problem encountered in efforts to test and improve policies, particularly in collective affairs. For all practical purposes, every policy must be formulated in terms that allow implementation by a human individual exercising some element of judgment, interpretive capacity, or discretion. The application of a policy is a creative process; the element of creativity in application can be reduced but not eliminated. The nature of the process is readily illustrated from such fields as medicine, where individuals can be "taught," or can learn, how to perform very complex operations such as the removal of an appendix. In that sense, a "policy" or standard operating procedure is developed for controlling the process. But such operations cannot be automated because of the amount of variance encountered in real world cases; appendixes, like the bodies in which they are housed, can vary greatly in size, shape, functioning, and so on. Even a "super automaton" able to take into account all of the complexities previously encountered in such operations would be unable to deal with a situation in which a difference appeared for the first time. Some measure of interpretation and adaptation is unavoidable in virtually all cases. Strictly speaking, a policy that must be interpreted before it can be applied is "untestable." What is actually tested in such cases is the adaptation of the policy, the set of more detailed rules (if any) used to apply it. However, the overall structure is also tested for its ability to generate acceptable modifications in use, and that is its most important function, particularly in the management of collective affairs.

If the application of policies is rarely if ever equivalent to pushing a button or following a strict routine, the implications for those who create policies are both extensive and serious. Under such conditions, policymaking is more concerned with bounding or limiting classes of actions than with precise specification of actions. The crucial question becomes, What amount of freedom of interpretation can be left to the various levels of administration that are involved with application (that lie between the policymaker and the population affected by the policy) without losing control over the outcome? Further, identification of the kind of information that is needed to test and improve the various elements of a complex policy that is administered by a hierarchically ordered administrative system is then essential. Yet even with substantial investments of time and resources, that task may prove impossible, particularly in the short run, unless present knowledge of such processes and of methods for controlling them is augmented very substantially.

Monitoring

The last of the intellectual requirements for directing actions is a monitoring or reporting system that will provide the information needed to test and improve the intellectual apparatus over time. The requirement is indirect, due in part to the uncertainties involved in assessing actor capacity and projecting outcomes, and in part to the need for interpretation and judgment in the application of intellectual instruments. In any situation where actions involve extensive and significant consequences for the population affected, it is wise, and even essential, to assume that the initial effort to guide action will prove inadequate, even with competent application.

The element of interpretation that is unavoidable in policy applications tends to strengthen that assumption. In the circumstances, it is necessary to create an apparatus able to monitor the effects of action *before* action is taken; events can then be set in motion and adjusted over time by reference to consequences actually produced. Organized monitoring of this character involves much more than simple collection of pre-specified data; it implies a system that is sensitized to significant, not fully anticipated, and even never-before-encountered effects. The capacity for that kind of monitoring is, so far as is presently known, found only in competent, living humans, suitably trained. Again, the clearest illustrations are found in medicine. The post-operative monitoring facilities installed in quality hospitals exemplify the requirement perfectly. There, sophisticated mechanical-electronic monitoring is supplemented by the use of highly trained and experienced observers with considerable success. Of course, hospitals have the advantage of dealing with only one aspect of human life, but the principle is applicable to any type of activity that impacts human lives in normatively significant ways.

The need for monitoring tends to be masked in individual affairs by the combination of action-taking and consequence-monitoring in a single person. No additional machinery is needed, in personal affairs at least, although individuals may have to be sensitized to the need for monitoring and habituated to using the information gathered to modify future behavior (to learning how to learn and how to use what has been learned), and that may well be the most difficult part of human socialization. Hospital practice again provides a good emulation model because the need to keep close track of a patient's condition following a serious operation is too obvious to generate much argument. The equipment used in hospitals is designed both to warn of dangers and to provide evidence of success in achieving the preferred outcome. The hospital's monitoring capacity is limited by existing knowledge and technology, and the system must be installed prior to the patient's arrival; the need to supplement formal apparatus by informal observation using trained persons is easy to justify. In effect, that procedure takes advantage of the unarticulated human capacity generated by using the whole person as a monitoring device, accessing knowledge not self-consciously available to the person. In a hospital context, the relation between the various intellectual instruments is easy to see, and the use of information provided by such monitoring systems has been institutionalized to a remarkable extent. It is very unlikely that monitoring the effects of collective actions, public or private, could be raised to the same level, particularly over the short run, if only because hospitals need deal with but one major dimension of a life (health) while public agencies are, or should be, concerned with the life as a whole. Indeed, failure to recognize the inadequacy of a single-dimension focus has been responsible for some of the major failures in past public performance—efforts to deal with housing the poor that ignore subcultural traditions, the real purchasing power of income, or the effects of age, for example.[3]

Because actions require the use of a number of different intellectual tools, design of a monitoring system able to supply the information needed to maintain and improve each element may be a formidable task, for the monitor must be able to separate the effects of the delivery system from the other effects of the policy or program if the policy is to be improved over time. Nevertheless, because the intellectual apparatus used to guide actions is no stronger than its weakest element, there is no avoiding the problem. Some of the complexities are worth underscoring. Assuming that a priority has been justified, a policy can be tested by comparing the outcome desired and the outcome actually achieved. That entails the collection of detailed information about the normatively significant effects of action on a large enough sample of persons to allow an acceptable generalization to the whole of the *affected* population—the information gathered cannot refer to the "target" population alone. Even under ideal conditions, the design requirements for such a monitoring system are formidable and more likely to be worked out over time through action than generated full-blown from discussion and planning.

One potential escape route from the design dilemma, monitoring social features rather than individuals, might seem to be more efficient and simpler to create and manage. However, that procedure is only acceptable if changes in social features can be translated fairly accurately into changes in the conditions of life of specific populations. At present, such translations are rarely possible. In general, the use of aggregate data as an indicator of the the quality of performance of collective bodies amounts to making a grossly untenable analogy between human society and such mechanical systems as watches or automobiles. A watch can be evaluated by monitoring its time-keeping ability, by comparing performance to purpose. But at least two partially suppressed assumptions are required, and neither can be maintained with respect to human society. First, the process implies an external evaluation point, a user and purpose that is external to the watch; second, a watch is a logical structure, like all mechanical systems, hence if the time-telling feature is functioning properly it can be inferred that each of its elements is also performing correctly, assuming that the watch is well designed and constructed. Society, on the other hand, must be assessed by reference to its effects on its own parts and not in terms of its value to someone or some "thing" external to the society. Further, the elements of society are not related formally or logically; they are linked empirically and in ways that are often uncertain and perhaps subject to change. There is no overall design that reflects the priorities and purposes of an external "user." Therefore the assumption that the design is adequate and contains no redundancies, which is essential for assessing the performance of a watch, cannot be made with respect to human affairs. Since both errors in process and failure to include significant factors can produce discrepancies from anticipated outcomes, the characteristics of an adequate monitoring system for human society will differ radically from those of a system intended to apply to a mechanical or logical apparatus. At best, information about social features can suggest that something is amiss, and thus lead to further inquiry. At worst, collective "functioning," defined by reference to social features, can hide immense amounts of malfunctioning within the interstices of the aggregated information.

3

Theoretical Assumptions

The intellectual requirements for directing human actions on defensible grounds are very formidable indeed. At a minimum, the available knowledge must allow the user to: (1) predict certain future conditions to be expected if the natural flow of events is allowed to continue uninterrupted; (2) project the future implications of each of the actions lying within the capacity of a given actor at a particular time and place, either using concepts that capture the normatively significant dimensions of each outcome or subsequently translating projected outcomes into such normative concepts; (3) identify the preferred outcome within the set available for choice; (4) generate an action program (policy) that will lead to the preferred outcome with some degree of reliability; and (5) create an adequate monitoring system. Each instrument used to fulfill these purposes must be justifiable prior to application or use if actions are to be defended rather than rationalized. In addition, the support structure needed for creating and applying such intellectual instruments (concepts, indicators, measurements, descriptive accounts, language, logic, and so on) must already be in place and functioning, and a body of human experience must have been assembled in the past that is adequate for testing and justifying each of the instruments, and for supporting the judgments involved in their applications.

The central concern in this chapter is to identify a set of assumptions that makes it possible to create an intellectual apparatus that is adequate for performing all of those functions. The fundamental normative premise, which serves as a check on the various elements in the intellectual structure, is that knowledge must be adequate to maintain and/or improve the conditions of life of some human population. That overall purpose is achieved by creating the kind of knowledge needed to direct human actions—by the use of human intellectual capacity. One set of assumptions adequate for producing such knowledge is sketched below. It is valid only with respect to the purpose specified; assumptions meant for achieving other purposes need not be adequate for the purposes sought here, and those employed here may not suffice in other cases. The set must be treated as a whole; even if *some* assumptions are shared, the overall structures in which the shared assumptions appear may not be interchangeable, for the same reasons that a theory of play that is valid in one sport does not transfer automatically to another, even if the sports involved are quite similar and some of the basic rules, and strategies of play, are shared. A theoretical apparatus must be assessed holistically; the validity of the selection of elements it includes is determined by the overall normative purpose the apparatus is intended to achieve.

To develop the necessary intellectual apparatus, the ultimate purpose that controls the enterprise must be analyzed further seeking to identify the second- and third-order purposes whose fulfillment is necessary to achieve it. The analysis follows the same pattern as the development of a theory of play in athletics: it begins with the ultimate goal or purpose (winning the game while satisfying certain limits or restrictions) and then moves to such secondary goals as scoring points and preventing the opponent from scoring points. They in turn make possible more detailed analyses able to show the specific activities required for achieving those more limited purposes. Several levels of analysis may be incorporated into the theory of play used in quite simple games. In more complex sports such as professional football, the analytic apparatus used for preparatory coaching and for directing play during the course of the game becomes extremely sophisticated, leading usually to the development of specialists who focus on only one part of the total structure. Overall development is constrained and directed in fairly obvious ways by past experience generated by real games.

The primary assumptions that must be made before the knowledge needed for directing human actions can be created must refer to two major points: first, the set of human capacities and limitations that determine what can be accomplished using the intellect and how production and justification of knowledge must be approached; second, those characteristics of the natural universe that limit or facilitate knowledge development. In both cases, the limits and possibilities will reflect current understanding, or best knowledge, and that can change over time. Taken as a whole, the basic assumptions are tested first by seeing if they can account for past success in maintaining and improving the human situation, and second, by acting in accordance with them and comparing the results that are produced with the results to be expected if any of the available competing alternatives were employed instead. Such judgments are contingent, of course, on the availability of some capacity to assess the conditions of life of the human population affected by the actions.

Sensory Dependence: The Induction Problem

So far as is presently known, the human individual is wholly dependent upon the sensory apparatus, on the operation of the nervous system, for information about the world and its contents, including the self, and therefore for the knowledge that is created from such basic information. Most of the obstacles encountered in efforts to create and apply knowledge, well summarized in the so-called "induction problem," (which can be stated in a number of different ways) are a function of the need to depend on the senses for information. Accepting sensory dependence does not entail a denial of the existence of an external world; indeed, unless an external world is assumed that is in some degree independent of the observer, knowledge claims based on sensory perceptions would remain untestable.

The effects of sensory dependence are felt most strongly in efforts to provide a justification for knowledge claims. Because the sensory apparatus mediates between consciousness and the "external" (to consciousness) world, the information received in consciousness is always an inseparable fusion of the characteristics of external reality (which remain unknown), the effects of the transmitting medium (light waves, for example) on that unknown external factor, and the operation of the sensory apparatus. Direct access to reality is effectively ruled out. Put another way, the "black box" analogy fits perfectly the situation confronting sensory-dependent entities who seek knowledge that can be used to direct actions. It follows that knowledge claims cannot be tested by direct comparisons with the content of reality, and a correspondence theory of truth or validity is unacceptable. Some alternative means of testing or verifying claims to know must be produced.

A working solution can be created by accepting pragmatic criteria of adequacy or validity; they will refer to the relation between purposes sought through the use of knowledge and results actually achieved. In effect, the quality of knowledge can be judged in terms of its usefulness for achieving specified purposes within known limits of accuracy, reliability, and so on. By implication, knowledge must be linked to *some* purpose, either directly or indirectly, before it can be tested. Further, the relative significance of that purpose must be assessed as well, therefore the overall apparatus is contingent on the development and justification of an acceptable normative purpose as well as the knowledge required to achieve it. Within the overall set of assumptions from which knowledge develops, the normative assumptions always take precedence.

Sensory dependence affects both the kinds of knowledge that can be created, and the way in which it can be be produced and tested, in some very fundamental ways. For one thing, the information that reaches the central nervous system is "packaged" as a sequence of singular, static, units analogous to a set of snapshots, each taken at a specific time and place using a set of lenses that may vary greatly from time to time, and from one person to the next. The information that is contained in the snapshots is always partial and incomplete. Selectivity is controlled by (a) the design and functioning of the sensors that link the central nervous system to the external world, (b) the content and structure of the conceptual apparatus that has been incorporated into the central nervous system over time, and the way in which use of the various elements in the apparatus is cued, and (c) the functioning of the central nervous system proper. More important still, the incoming flow of information refers always to past events; the sensory system cannot, so far as is known, acquire information about events that have not yet occurred. Of course, the total intellectual apparatus can generate projections about future information, and justify accepting them, but that is a different matter entirely.

The basic dilemma to be overcome or evaded by members of the species seeking to create knowledge useful for directing action is a function of the two primary characteristics of sensory-based data (they are partial or selective and refer only to the past) taken in conjunction with the intellectual requirements developed earlier for controlling human actions. Human life is lived out in a time-driven system, a dynamic and ongoing flow of events. A good metaphor for the human predicament is an individual floating down a river of time, living at the juncture of present and past but driven inexorably toward the future, unable to stem the flow of time yet unable to turn toward the future and see what it contains. The primary limitation on the knowledge-producing potential of the species is found in the disjunction between the time focus of the information available to knowledge producers and the time focus of the knowledge required for fulfilling human purposes. All of the sensory data that are available to the central nervous system refer to the past; but both practically and intellectually, human life is oriented toward the future. The locus of present hopes, fears, and aspirations is in the future; if life is to be maintained and improved, the future must be anticipated and controlled; choices and preferences refer to the relative desirability of different, alternative, future states; the effects of action lie in the future; and the quality of the intellectual apparatus used to direct action is tested in the future. But knowledge must be at least partly justified prior to use or application, else the knowledge system is no more than a set of post hoc rationalizations. Assuming sensory dependence, the data available for justification are always singular, static, particular, and referenced to the past. The knowledge that is to be justified, however, must refer to the future as well if it is to be used to direct actions.

Somehow, then, knowledge created from information about the past must be used to justify efforts to achieve human purposes in the future, purposes that must themselves be justified, again by reference to information relating to past events. That raises the formal induction problem, a limit enforced by the kind of calculating capacity available to members of the species, by the characteristics of the formal logical or mathematical structures that supply the dynamics of systematic human reasoning. There is no alternative to using formal logic for exploring the implications of accepting any generalized statement or proposition. And for reasons to be examined in due course, there is also no alternative to accepting generalized statements and exploring their implications as a basic procedure for testing knowledge claims. Formal calculation is an essential part of the overall process. But formal calculation does allow inferences from statements about the past to statements about the future, from static propositions to dynamic propositions, from particular statements to generalized statements, or from empirical statements (what was the case) to normative statements (what is preferable). The elements in these pairings may be related in and through experience but the relations cannot be formal and calculable—propositions that refer to one set of factors are not "contained in" propositions that refer to the other.

The impact of the induction problem on justification of knowledge claims in a sensory-based knowledge system is potentially devastating. Nothing about the future can be inferred from statements about the past; nothing about preferences or priorities can be inferred from empirical statements, singular or generalized. Yet past experience provides the only available point of departure for creating the knowledge used to deal with future events, and formal logic provides the only available "engine" for moving the human intellectual apparatus. There is no alternative to proceeding "inductively," to beginning with specific, concrete experience, in both empirical and normative affairs. The procedure is not and cannot be wholly formal or logical; there can be no "logic of induction" within the present meaning of logic.

An evasion of the induction problem, a way of justifying knowledge claims relating to the future using evidence that refers solely to the past, can be arranged. The question how, and under what conditions evasion is possible will be examined in the remainder of this volume. The price of the evasion, however, is an irreducible and variable element of uncertainty that attaches to all of the knowledge produced by employing it. The assumptions that are required for the evasion, which refer to the attributes or capacities of members of the species as well as certain features of the general human situation, are relatively uncontentious. Not every assumption in the underlying apparatus can be identified and articulated, of course, but the principal elements are known and they suffice as a point of departure for criticism and improvement. Disagreement and discussion can be expected to refine and improve the apparatus in due course, or lead to rejection and replacement.

In the remainder of the chapter, those human capacities that contribute most to human intellectual performance are sketched briefly, followed by an examination of the two characteristics of the human situation that play a major role in determining intellectual achievement. Human capacities are then combined with the salient conditions of human existence in a summary statement of an overall procedure that can be used for evading the induction problem, and thus for achieving human purposes in the environment. That procedure will be examined more fully in chapter 4 as it applies to empirical knowledge. The remainder of the volume is then devoted to a systematic examination of its implications for developing, justifying, and applying normative knowledge.

ORGANIZING AN EVASION OF THE INDUCTION PROBLEM

The principal impediment to creating and justifying knowledge that is useful for maintaining and improving the conditions of life of some human population is the sensory dependence of the species. If "reality" could be directly perceived, and knowledge could be tested by direct correspondence to reality, intellectual life would be immeasurably simpler. However, a range of other attributes, all well-established for the species as a whole, makes it possible to overcome that handicap and create an adequate if imperfect base for human knowledge. Three of those attributes, taken in conjunction with two basic characteristics of the situation in which systematic inquiry is conducted, suffice for evading the induction problem, allow humans to provide an adequate justification for knowledge claims in advance of use or application. First, and most important, the human individual can and must "care," or have preferences. Second, given a creature that prefers some situations or conditions rather than others, no more is required than the capacity to: (a) organize or generalize perceptions, or experience of various kinds, into patterns; (b) calculate the implications of such generalized patterns, explore their full content, either alone or in combination with particular statements; and (c) compare the results produced with the products of experience. Third, the individual must have the capacity to perform the various acts of judgment required for fitting patterns to experience, to perform translogical operations in a "reasonably systematic manner" that allows the results to be tested against the performance of another "instrument" (person) capable of performing the same functions, a process that can also be generalized and tested over time. Each of these capacities or attributes is well established for the species as a whole, although the extent to which the full set is available in any given case may vary. They can therefore be stated as commonplaces, without trying to provide a detailed justification for accepting them.

Preferring or Caring

If knowledge useful for directing actions is to be created and justified, members of the human species must react differently to different environmental conditions; individuals must "care" about differences, must "prefer" some conditions to others—the flow of events, and particularly the changes that take place in the conditions of life of the self and other humans, cannot be regarded with indifference or unconcern. The basis for concern may be either affective or intellectual, although the latter is far more important over the long run. The capacity for caring is well established and can safely be assumed. Indeed, it may seem too obvious to require explicit articulation. Nevertheless, that human characteristic provides a bedrock on which knowledge can be built and tested. A knowledge system is basically a way of expressing, justifying, and achieving preferences; without preferences, there would be no reason to seek knowledge. The minimum requirement for continued existence, which is shared with every living thing, is for a system of differentiated reactions coupled to a Darwinian-style environmental-individual linkage. Human predominance is due mainly to possession of an intellectual apparatus that is driven by built-in differential reactions yet is able to condition or modify the response patterns built into the organism by organizing and applying past experience, by learning or creating knowledge. The ability to alter behavior through learning is far more efficient and less wasteful of life and resources than Darwinian adaptation; the latter modifies the species by killing the "unsuited"—no learning is required in an evolution-controlled process, only a differentiated rate of survival.

If affective reactions can be overridden or controlled by intellectual or "cognitive" concerns, as is the case with humans, the survival potential of the species is increased enormously. And the preferences that are expressed in action become a human creation rather than a genetic endowment or a gift of nature. In that sense at least, humans can "make" their own future. Priorities that are human creations can be modified to reflect changes in human perceptions of human conditions, and to take advantage of expanded human capacity to alter the human condition by deliberate action and thus extend the conception of what constitutes an "improvement." In those circumstances, the primary normative task is to create a system of priorities that takes the fullest possible advantage of improvements in human capacity or modifications in environmental conditions generated by natural change or human intervention. The primary function of science is to provide the means for extending and reifying the normative apparatus. Both factors are in constant flux. Changes in human capacity, in knowledge and resources, open the way to modifications in priorities; experience with a set of priorities can suggest the kind of additional capacity that should be pursued by showing the alternative preferences that could be implemented if the augmented capacity were available. Out of an ongoing interaction between preferences and possibilities, between capacity and willingness to live with the different conditions that capacity makes available, can come improvements in the human condition that are defensible as "improvements," in terms of the body of experience available to members of the species at any given point in time.

If the search for empirical and normative knowledge was well integrated, very little additional machinery would be needed to account for improvements in performance, and for improvements in the conception of "improvement" used to render judgment on changes made. A fairly simple apparatus, able to generate learning from trial and error, could over time produce the knowledge needed to make improvements in both areas, although improvements could not be guaranteed because they require creativity. If, however, the two types of inquiry are separated into essentially independent enterprises, as has usually been the case, the probability of improvement is much decreased. In those terms, one of the prime functions of the present discussion is to show why such integration is needed and to provide a base from which it could proceed.

Organization/Generalization

The central nervous system (CNS) of the human individual is literally bombarded with an endless flow of impulses from the receptors in the sensory system, stimulated by events external to the body, or by "events" within the body. In a sense, that flow has been "organized" in various ways prior to entering the CNS: by the character of an external event or object, by the transmitting medium, and finally by the operating properties of the sensory receptors. From the perspective of "consciousness," however, the incoming flow is inchoate and meaningless. Before any part of it can have meaning or significance for the individual, it must be organized *within* the CNS and linked to previously stored information in an appropriate way. The individual must, at a minimum

(a) discriminate among different parts of the flow, (b) organize some portions of the flow into patterns, some cross-sectional in time and others longitudinal through time, and (c) link particular patterns, or sets of patterns, to the content of past experience, previously organized and stored using a variety of similar patterns. In effect, the individual must have the capacity to create generalized patterns that can be imposed on the incoming flow of perceptions and used to direct reactions in appropriate ways. Knowledge, in that context, is comprised in the sets of calculable patterns that serve to organize human perceptions or experience in ways that are useful for either modifying the environment or conforming the individual to it, following some set of established preferences.

The patterns used to identify the "things" that are observed in the external environment (or within the person), and to capture the various empirical and normative relations that hold among the things that are either observed or projected, must be created within the neural structure. A large number of specific patterns is used to make everyday observations (to identify the things observed and to state the relations that hold among them) and to process the results. Analytically, they can be subsumed under a fairly small number of types of structures: concepts, relational terms, forecasts, theories, priorities, and formal patterns incorporated into logic and mathematics make up the greater part of them. Taken as a whole, such patterns provide the lenses through which the individual observes the world, the receptacles in which experience is stored, and the apparatus used to determine, and deal with, the implications of what has been observed. Summarily, the intellectual direction of action is a matter of combining the results of particular observations or experiences with relevant patterns of stored information generated out of past experience to create action programs for adapting individual to environment or environment to individual. The overall process requires the use of both empirical and normative patterns.

Before proceeding to a closer examination of the kinds of patterns that organization or generalization must produce, two points about the relationship between the patterns created within the neural system and the content of the experienced world bear additional emphasis. First, since the lenses or spectacles used for observing the external world are created by the observer, or inherited from a surrogate, they can, in principle, be ground to the wishes, preferences, or whims of the individual. Some means of limiting discretion, of restricting patterns within manageable grounds, is therefore essential. The "naturalist" assumption that there is "something" external to the human perceiver that is independent of the perceptive apparatus provides the needed check *if* (and it is a very big "if" indeed) knowledge patterns are linked ultimately to perceptions of that "something" and some at least of those patterns are used as a basis for human efforts to anticipate, control, or make choices in the real world. To illustrate, it is the observer who actually decides whether or not to include the tiger's tail with the rest of the beast in a single entity. But if the resulting pattern is used to deal with the tiger, that provides the tiger with an opportunity to influence the decision. Presumably at least, it can supply good reasons for including the tail with the teeth and the claws. That is the primary sense in which the naturalist assumption, combined with a pragmatic criterion for justifying knowledge claims, is an essential element in a testable knowledge system.

The one major area of intellectual effort that might appear to be exempt from the restriction is formal logic or mathematics. And so indeed it is. But the reason is found in the self-contained character of the formal logical enterprise, and the consequences of such isolation and self-containment are very severe. Logicians or mathematicians can assume entities with any attributes they please, and postulate any relations among them that the mind can conjure; the implications of such assumption and postulation can be explored formally in the same manner as any other set of general and particular propositions. However, the conclusions reached then have no necessary relation to human experience, they cannot be applied to the conduct of human affairs unless and until it can be demonstrated that the patterns used to reach the conclusion relate to past experience in definable ways.

The second aspect of the relation between "reality" and the human perception of reality that bears additional emphasis is the selectivity that characterizes the process of perceiving. Taken as a whole, the nervous system is flooded with information; much of it, clearly, does not reach individual consciousness, much less trigger a positive or conscious response. Most of the incoming flow is handled routinely (ignored or acted upon) by inherited or acquired mechanisms, and separating the two is in practice very difficult.[1] Without seeking to probe the specifics of the system, it is worth noting that relatively minor changes in the structures and processes used to organize experience can produce vast differences in the meaning or significance attached to particular perceptions, can lead to different assessments of future possibilities and consequently to very different human behavior. That is perhaps the major reason why conceptual modification or innovation plays such a dominant role in the expansion and improvement of knowledge and its application to human affairs. One need only examine the work of Albert Einstein in physics, or Karl Marx in social history, to see how conceptual changes can produce very dramatic shifts in the interpretation placed upon past events, and in the kinds of actions recommended for the future.

Types of Generalizations. In the most fundamental sense, organization or generalization refer to precisely the same process, although it is sometimes useful to differentiate process from product. Briefly, a generalization is a statement of a relationship between two or more entities (which can include an individual thing and its environment) that is not restricted with respect to time or place. A formal or logical general statement differs from an empirical or normative generalization in that the latter is necessarily isomorphic to past human experience and the former is not. Seen as process, generalization is the most important feature of human intellectual life. If descriptive accounts make up the basic building blocks from which knowledge is created, the primary statements of the content of human experience, their production is already contingent upon the availability of generalized patterns. Past experience is stored with the use of generalized patterns. Knowledge consists in patterned human experience and all of human experience that appears in a pattern has been generalized to some degree.

Generalizations, insofar as they can be defended or justified, provide the essential mechanism for evading the induction problem, for bridging the logical gap between past and future without losing calculability of implications. In an inductively based knowledge system, generalizations contain more information than the sets of particular propositions from which they are "induced." That additional content, if it can somehow be evaluated before it is applied, provides the necessary bridge between past and future, particular and general, or even empirical and normative experience. The relations contained in a generalized pattern are not limited with respect to time or place (although they may be restricted in various ways). Under certain conditions, they can be assumed to apply to the future as well as to the past. If that assumption can be justified, it provides the needed connection to expectations about future events, whether those events arise in nature or appear as a consequence of human action. Because the evidence for a generalized statement is never complete, its justification, and therefore its applications, remains problematic or uncertain. There is always a possibility that future experience may not correspond to the expectations generated by the pattern. Nevertheless, such patterns provide a solution-in-principle to the nasty problem posed by the gap between intellectual needs and what can be created in a logic-driven intellectual system that is predicated on sensory information—a way of evading the induction problem.

Five basic types of generalizations, five patterns of organized human experience, are needed to fulfill the second-order purposes involved in the directing actions. Development and justification of the four patterns used to express empirical relations are examined in chapter 4; the remainder of the text is devoted to a detailed study of the one primary normative pattern, the priority or preference-ordering. Each of the five basic patterns is relatively simple in structure, and the evidence needed to justify accepting a claim to know expressed in empirical terms can be established fairly precisely.

1. Patterns that state the attributes of particular entities or things—technically, the attributes of classes that have only one member. They are exemplified by such propositions as "My mother is a kindly person," or "That is a very gentle dog," and can be used to predict the class member's behavior.

2. Patterns that contain the attributes or distributed properties of classes of things, such as "Every house has a roof," or parts of classes of things, as in "Some houses are built of wood." This form of generalization plays a major role in structuring incoming perceptions, for it identifies class membership (which is based on a comparison of class properties and the content of observation); that process is an essential feature of every description, and descriptions are the fundamental elements on which the entire knowledge system is constructed.

3. Patterns, or generalizations, that assert the empirical or observed relations that hold among two or more classes of events or things. Two major sub-types, both already touched upon briefly, can be identified. The first, labeled a forecast, asserts that two or more events covary within time or over time in a particular way if certain limiting conditions are satisfied—"Crocuses bloom earlier in the year than daisies if weather conditions are normal," for example. The pattern generalizes past experience, and by doing so projects a relationship observed in the past onto events as yet unobserved, whether past or future. There is no implication that the events contained in the pattern are related causally, or that the relation can serve as a basis for action, although both may in fact be the case.

4. The second type of pattern used to generalize empirical relations states the necessary and/or sufficient conditions for a particular event to occur, and includes an assumed causal relation between two or more events. The causal assumption has the effect of forcing the implication that if one of the events included in the pattern occurs, however it may be produced, the second event can be expected to follow. That meaning of "causal" is quite restricted; no more than a constant conjunction plus a linking assumption, is required. But once established, such a pattern provides a justification for acting on the basis of its content. The "law" in science which asserts that water freezes at a temperature of 32 degrees Fahrenheit (0 degrees Centigrade) states a sufficient condition for changing the physical state of water from liquid to solid, other things equal, *if* it includes a causal assumption. Without that assumption, there would be no justification for expecting that water *placed* in an environment where the temperature is maintained below 32 degrees F. would change its physical state from liquid to solid. What separates patterns that contain a causal assumption from those that do not is the evidence that is obtained by use or application. If a pattern can be acted upon with confidence, then the causal assumption has been tested, whether or not it is recognized in analytic terms by the user.

5. "Normative" patterns or generalizations which assert that one outcome, stated in terms of a set of normative variables that refer to the conditions of life of the human individual(s) included in the projection, is preferable to any member of a specified set of alternatives, each containing a projection of a different set of conditions of life for some or all that same group of persons. Both a child's priority in the form "Prefer strawberry ice cream to any other flavor," and the politician's "Higher taxes are preferable to a reduction in social service programs," illustrate that type of pattern.

With minor modifications, all of the general propositions generated by real-world efforts to create knowledge useful for directing actions can be analyzed into these five basic patterns. A simple notation system can be used to state each pattern, regardless of its type. The elements in a pattern, which are mainly concepts or classifications, are called *variables*, and written (V). A pattern is enclosed in square brackets [] to show that it consists of a *selection* of elements; the content of such patterns is a function of the rules of selection. A set of two or more variables whose values are linked by rule and can therefore be calculated under specified conditions is indicated by the use of round brackets or parentheses (). In both types of patterns, a variable will have a "value," determined by measuring or calculating the denoted attribute. Thus the variable "physical state" may take the values "solid," "liquid," or "gas." In a description, the same notation is used, but the values of the variables are set by direct observation or measurement. No calculation is involved or required in a description, and nothing can be inferred from it.

The rules used to link the values of the variables found in other types of patterns will assert one of three kinds of relations: (a) for a classification, they will state the range of values that may be taken by a given set of variables that define the class—a robin is a bird between seven and nine inches in height, colored dark grey to black on top, and so on; (b) for a theory or forecast, the rules will link the values of the variables into a calculable relation—if the sky is red at dusk, it will rain before dawn; (c) in a priority or preference-ordering, the rules will identify the preferred outcome within a given set—prefer living with total deafness to living in total blindness, for example. In each case, application of the rules will usually be restricted in a specific ways; a *ceteris paribus* clause is always part of the overall structure, and the pattern can be applied only if the specified limiting conditions are met.

Calculation

The capacity to calculate, to manipulate patterns of nominally defined symbols in accordance with rigorous rules, provides the dynamic force that drives human knowledge systems. Without inquiring into either the nature of logic or the foundations of mathematics, it can be said that one basic function of calculation is to explore the particular implications of accepting a general proposition, or of accepting combinations of general and particular propositions. Put another way, the function of calculation is to articulate the content of sets of propositions, some of which must be generalized. Particular or descriptive propositions cannot be explored in this way; a description already states its own content. The implications of accepting two or more descriptions can be calculated, but that is a different matter. For example, the proposition "There is a chair in that room," is incompatible with the proposition "That room is empty," providing, of course, that the room intended is the same in both cases. Calculation makes it possible to assert that accepting a certain general proposition forces acceptance of certain particular propositions on pain of self-contradiction. Without that capacity, there would be no way to make use of general statements because there was no way to test or justify them. And it is calculation that forces a particular choice or action if a specified condition or event has been observed and a given set of general propositions has been accepted. Finally, calculation serves to convert the results of action into a test of the assumptions that forced or required it by providing a formal link between them.

Most of the problems that arise out of the use of calculation in human affairs are due to mistaken applications rather than calculating errors. To apply a formal logic or calculus to real-world affairs, to transfer the results of calculations made within a logic to the real world, each of the elements or symbols in the logic must be fitted to observation; abstract symbols, which are nominally defined, must be translated into concepts or classifications that are defined in real terms. Further, the sets of relations specified within the calculus must be isomorphic to "observed" interactions in the real world, with due regard for Hume's strictures on the limits of observation. Only if both conditions are satisfied can the results of calculation be transferred to real-world affairs. Thus the calculus that is labeled "arithmetic," which amounts in practice to counting units that are members of some common class (they may be counted forward or backward, alone or in groups of varying size), can be applied only to those situations in which all of the things to be counted can be specified as units and each of the units is a member of the same class of things. That is why "apples" cannot be added to "pears." The requirements for applying formal logics are exceptionally difficult to satisfy in many aspects of human affairs. It is relatively easy to add "votes," for example, if the vote is defined in formal terms within a particular decision system. But if the meaning of "vote" is extended to include the intentions of the voter, then identification of the members of a particular class of votes is an almost impossible task.

Judgment

Beyond purely formal calculations, reasoned direction of actions requires the individual to perform various other functions that are difficult to identify precisely but may usefully be grouped together under the rubric "exercise judgment." These functions or processes are translogical; they cannot be formalized or produced by rule, although useful rules may be developed from past judgments and applied. Judgments amount to using the total individual as a measuring instrument, and they are essential at various points in the development and use of knowledge. Even such relatively simple operations as describing what has been observed (I saw a cow in that field) depend on judgments: a member of the class "cows" and a member of the class "fields" must be identified, and the observed relation between those two class members must fit the definitional requirements of the logical/relational term "within," and none of these conclusions is a function of calculation alone. Another common form of judgment appears when the adequacy of a given body of evidence to support a theory or forecast is evaluated or assessed. Even in those cases where formal conventions have been developed for handling such matters, the question whether or not the formal convention ought to be accepted remains a matter for judgment.

The meaning of judgment can be clarified further using a context supplied by the techniques humans use to reach conclusions, for if the results must be justified, then only three fundamental procedures are available for use. First, conclusions can be based upon direct observation and measurement, but only if they refer to descriptive propositions, statements in the form "X was (or was not) the case." Second, conclusions can be generated inferentially, by logical calculation from an established or assumed set of propositions, some of which must be generalized in form. In all other cases, conclusions are based on the functioning of the total neural apparatus, but the specific content of the constituent elements of the process (assumptions) remains unknown. In judgment, the neural system is equivalent to a "black box": inputs and outputs can be observed but the intervening processes remain opaque to the observer, and often to the individual concerned. Ultimately, every human conclusion is based upon judgments of this kind. Technically, the process cannot be formalized, but if inquiry focuses on the observable dimensions of black box performance, seeking to create patterns that replicate its behavior and disregarding internal processes, the judgmental process can be at least partially stabilized.

Essentially, all of human knowledge partakes of this character, is usefully regarded as the product of human efforts to deal with "black box" performance.

The ways in which individual judgments can be tested and improved are as elusive as the process by which they are made. Very broadly, combining within a single person a suitable body of particular and generalized experience creates a decision tool whose capacity, in some cases at least, transcends the limitations of formal logic and thus makes possible the resolution of a range of formally insoluble problems, such as induction. The individual *creates* solutions to such problems. Whatever the precise basis for judgments, there is little doubt about human capacity to produce them. Further, the quality of acts of judgment can also be judged, presumably using the same capacities. Ultimately, such judgments will rest on the ability to replicate black box performance under specified limiting conditions. The only available check on human judgment is another human judgment, made by an equally competent judge. Conflicts among competent judges are resolved, if at all, by further reasoning and argument. Ultimately, there is no alternative to relying on the "best judgment" of the community of informed and competent persons in the field of inquiry where the judgment occurs for all qualitative assessments. If informed and competent judges differ, and the differences cannot be resolved by examining support arguments, the matter must remain moot unless and until time and experience produce a resolution—an event that may not occur.

Conditions of Application

For developing the knowledge required for directing human actions on defensible grounds, the human capacity for preferring, for organizing or generalizing, and for calculating must function under appropriate limiting conditions. In particular, the intellectual environment must have certain attributes or characteristics if the effort is to succeed. Two are particularly important. First, the quest for knowledge must take place in an ongoing enterprise that has been at least partly successful. If inquiry had to begin with a blank slate, very little could be written upon it. Some part of the available store of knowledge must be adequate for directing actions, and must be accepted as adequate for directing actions. Perhaps the most important function of any recommended analytic apparatus is to locate and isolate the valid elements in the knowledge supply and discover ways of justifying their claim to validity.

The second characteristic required of the intellectual environment is perhaps less obvious but ranks equally in importance: the overall goal of inquiry must be attainable given a capacity for dealing with recurring events. Put differently, one major limit on the intellectual enterprise is the inability of the human individual to do more than create the apparatus needed for dealing with an event on the occasion of its second appearance. Faced with an event wholly divorced from prior experience, the human intellect can only proceed by trial and error; in such conditions, neither extrapolation nor reasoning by analogy would be possible. Trial and error functioning can, under some limiting conditions, create the apparatus needed to learn from the flow of events, but in the total absence of information, the process is likely to be slow, painful, and costly.

Since nature has restricted human capacity to dealing with recurring events yet humans have managed to succeed at least partly in both improving the conditions of life for some of the population and improving the capacity to justify the judgment that an improvement has been made, it seems reasonable to assume that the capacity to deal with recurring events is adequate for the task. An event wholly detached from everything in past experience would have to be dealt with by trial and error. Events not expected to recur would not be worth worrying about, but the species does not have the capacity to identify them. Practically speaking, the problem is academic; in real-world affairs, nearly every event is in some respects unique and in some respects similar to other events. The critical question is whether events are sufficiently alike that knowledge gained from studying one can be used for dealing with the other, and under what circumstances such transfers can safely take place. Historically, at least, the question has been answered affirmatively in a great many cases, enough to maintain and improve the human condition in very significant ways. Of course, that does not *guarantee* the future. But such guarantees simply lie beyond human capacity and that is all that can be said on the matter.

Summary

Given individual humans whose endowed capacities include those enumerated in the basic assumptions, functioning in an ongoing intellectual system that contains at least some knowledge that is adequate for directing actions, a simple four-step procedure can be used to fulfill the ultimate purpose for which the present system was designed, and its various ancillaries, at least to the extent that they can be satisfied using an apparatus capable of dealing only with recurring events:

First, the purpose(s) sought in the environment must be identified within the boundaries of an adequate analytic framework.

Second, patterns of generalized experience, organized in the form needed for achieving the purpose in hand (as determined within the same analytic framework), are located within the existing store of knowledge, or created for the occasion.

Third, the pattern is applied to the particular situation. In all cases, application means combining a formal pattern with specific observations. The implications of the combination are then calculated and the results used to pursue the purpose at hand. If the pattern is valid, the diagnosis or application is correct (the observed situation is isomorphic to the elements and processes in the pattern), and the calculations are properly made, the purpose should be fulfilled within the limits of reliability assigned to the pattern.

Fourth, a comparison of purposes sought (expectations) and results achieved, with due regard for the seriousness of the problem under consideration, provides the evidence needed to reinforce the patterns and processes employed, suggest modifications, or enjoin rejection.

So conceived, knowledge evolves out of unending cycles of observation, generalization, calculation, action, and observation/testing/reaction. A classic illustration of the process is found in agriculture, where ongoing cycles of planting, tilling, harvesting, and consuming/evaluating/adjusting can over time produce improvements in what is produced, in the methods of production used, and in the criteria of evaluation applied to the outcome. Curiously enough the stage in the process most commonly ignored, particularly in societies that are heavily oriented toward production of goods and services, is consumption and evaluation by a human user, yet that is the only point in the process where learning, and therefore improvement, can occur.

The key to the evolution of knowledge, and to the evasion of the "induction problem," is generalization, the creation of patterns of relations that are not restricted in time and place. That such structures are created, in both empirical and normative matters, is well established. How and why creativity occurs remains a mystery. Once created, however, knowledge patterns can be tested in action by reference to the purposes of the user. If the purposes to be fulfilled have been identified, the requirements for fulfilling them can be determined, and criteria for assessing quality can be devised. The details of the major types of empirical or scientific patterns required for directing actions, and some of the ways in which they are developed and tested, are examined in the following chapter. Discussion then turns to a systematic examination of the normative requirements for directing actions, and the way in which those requirements can be fulfilled within the limits of human capacity.

4

Empirical Knowledge

Efforts to create the kinds of knowledge required for directing human action in ways that maintain and improve the conditions of life of some human population depend for their success on the human capacity to organize and generalize past experience into empirical and normative patterns. Those patterns are then combined with current observations to fulfill the various ancillary purposes involved in achieving the overall goal. Very little can be said about the way in which such patterns are created, although good reasons can in some cases be offered for preferring one strategy of development to another. Broadly speaking, the empirical purposes to be fulfilled are readily specified; the forms in which experience must be generalized to fulfill them are well established; the limitations and pitfalls commonly encountered in developing and applying such patterns have been charted; and with respect to empirical knowledge at least, methods of testing and justifying them have for the most part been agreed. There is nothing magical or mysterious about either the functions that the various patterns perform or the reasons why they are able to perform them. The situation with regard to normative knowledge is less clear, as will be apparent from the discussion to follow.

Fulfillment of the overall normative purpose set for the inquiry entails satisfying five major second-order purposes: past events must be described; events not yet observed must be predicted; the effects of action must be projected on the future; a preference must be established for one of the outcomes available to a given actor; and an action program (policy) must be devised for achieving the preferred outcome. The first three purposes (descriptions, predictions, and projections of the future consequences of action) depend on empirical knowledge or patterns;

preferences are based on normative knowledge; action programs or policies require both.

This chapter contains a brief summary of the structures and processes involved in the achievement of the three primary empirical purposes; the apparatus used to satisfy the more narrowly normative purpose of creating and justifying a priority or preference-ordering is examined in detail in the remainder of the text. The discussion of empirical knowledge centers on the basic characteristics of the patterns involved and the kinds of evidence and argument required to justify them. The treatment is brief; the aim is to provide an overview, an adequate point of departure for following the detailed discussion of normative structures and processes set forth in chapters 5, 6, and 7. A fuller account of the empirical apparatus and its applications is available elsewhere.[1] The relation between empirical and normative knowledge is given special consideration throughout the discussion, for much has been made of the so-called "gap" between "facts" and "values," and an action framework provides a way of linking or integrating these elements (Makes it possible to integrate these logically disparate elements within or through an analytic framework) and thus creates one escape route around the formal disjunction between them.

DESCRIPTION

Descriptions are the basic elements in every knowledge system; they contain the information from which all other forms of knowledge are created. Even affective reactions, which can play a major role in preferences or normative judgments, are reported as descriptive accounts by those who experience them. Beyond providing the raw materials from which knowledge is generated, descriptions also play a major role in testing the patterns or instruments used in the fulfillment of intellectual purposes. A prediction, for example, asserts that an observer located at a particular place and time will produce, or would have produced, a specific description of what was observed from that vantage point. The prediction is tested by comparing the projected description with a real description, made according to agreed procedures using established measures. The quality of the knowledge supply depends fundamentally on the quality of the descriptive accounts from which it was created. In principle, descriptions are the strongest and most reliable form of knowledge available, but quality can and does vary, for description involves both selectivity and judgment and each can lead to controversy under some circumstances.

Descriptions are created by organizing some portion of the flow of perceptions streaming into the central nervous system. From a slightly different perspective, descriptions are conclusions, embedded in propositions that assert what is the case, or was the case, at a particular time and place, that can be justified by reference to observations or measurements. Beyond the basic requirements of language, two major types of patterns are needed to produce a description: *concepts* or *classifications*, which serve to organize perceptions into the "things" observed—colors, tigers, typewriters, and so on; and *relational terms* or *logical terms* that identify and record the various ways in which the things observed are related or linked. Usage varies to some extent, and relational terms can be considered a particular type of concept rather than a different kind of pattern altogether, but the separation is useful for clarifying the structure and content of descriptions and is retained here.

The meaning of a concept, or classification, is found in the shared or "distributed" properties of the members of the class of things referred to. Classes range from single-factor "simples" like the primary colors, which cannot be analyzed into constituent elements, to very complex structures comprising a number of concepts or variables which in turn can be analyzed into substructures that are themselves complex concepts. Structurally, a concept consists of a selection of one or more variables (which are also concepts) that identify the shared attributes of class members, and a set of rules that stipulate the range of values those variables can take. The variables used in the classification include both the "indicators" of class membership (the variables that tell the user when it is appropriate to apply the classification) and the observables that are used to measure the value of the variable used to denote the concept as a whole. Relational or logical terms may refer to observable features of the environment, such as distance or shape, or to inferential relations such as "dominates" or "is more viscous." In either case, the term or concept must be supplied with an appropriate set of indicators, and the limits that control use or application must be stated.

Descriptive Quality

All descriptions are in some degree problematic, partly by reason of the instruments used to produce them and partly because of the way in which they are produced. Both the meaning of concepts and relational terms and the conditions limiting their applications are potential sources of uncertainty and disagreement in description. Since concepts and relational terms are generalized in form, their application or use requires an act of judgment and judgments cannot be validated in absolute terms. Strictly speaking, a descriptive statement is a conclusion, generated inductively from direct observations. The justification, which also depends on observation, is subject to the same uncertainties. Various techniques are available for limiting the scope of the judgments involved, and thus reducing risk. In physical science, the values of variables (concepts) are measured using carefully defined indicators, precise scales and accurate instruments—and the measurements may be read with the use of other instruments. Such techniques can strengthen the justification for a description, and can reduce, though not eliminate entirely, the level of uncertainty attached to it.

Descriptive quality is assessed in terms of two factors: first, and most obvious, accuracy and reliability; second, the adequacy of the description for the purpose in hand. In a knowledge system meant for directing human actions, both factors must be taken into account; descriptions are not produced for the sake of producing descriptions. The importance of descriptive adequacy is a function of the selectivity that characterizes the descriptive process. In principle, any set of perceptions can be organized in an infinite number of different ways by varying the selection of concepts and relational terms applied to them. It follows that every description is partial, even for very simple situations. The quality of the selection is therefore an important part of overall assessment, and that quality is a function of the purpose for which the description is to be employed.

Accuracy. The accuracy of a description depends on three main factors: the quality of the concepts and relational terms used to create it; the validity of the judgments made when those concepts and relational terms are applied; and the precision of the observations or measurements made. The validity of the judgments used for developing and applying knowledge is extremely difficult to treat in general terms; basically, validity is controlled by criticism produced within the relevant field of inquiry. In some cases, useful conventions are available for making the routine judgments encountered frequently by those engaged in specific inquiries, but ultimately the quality of the judgments made is tested against the parallel judgments of other competent and informed persons in the field of specialization, and that consensus extends to the established conventions that govern judgments.

Two of the more common problems encountered in conceptualization relate to the meaning of concepts or relational terms: some concepts are vague (the meaning is not clearly stated), while others are ambiguous (the meaning is open to more than one interpretation, each quite precise). A vague concept reduces the quality of the descriptions in which it appears, but the flaw need not be fatal. Indeed, vagueness may actually be useful in the early stages of development of a new area of inquiry. Ambiguity is a more serious problem, for it requires the reader or listener to choose among different, alternative meanings without providing adequate grounds for choice.

Two other conceptual errors common in descriptive accounts are (a) the failure to provide adequate indicators for concepts or relational terms and (b) the use of esthetic or normative terms as if they referred to observables. Inadequate indicators are a far more serious problem than the use of esthetic terms in "descriptions," other things equal. Unless some set of observables is available to serve as a continuum for measuring the value of a concept, or for determining when that concept can be applied to observations, the concept cannot be used. Quality varies enormously: such concepts as viscosity are supplied with very precise indicators, closely linked to a well-defined meaning; in other cases, such as schizophrenia, the theoretical apparatus used to link indicators to meaning is relatively weak, and conclusions based on the use of the concept are therefore easily disputed. The use of esthetic or normative terms produces propositions that are descriptive in form but evaluative in content—"That is a beautiful house," for example. Although propositions of that kind are also partly justified by referring to observations, additional assumptions that are quite different from those used in descriptions must be accepted before the conclusion can be agreed. They are reserved for later discussion and will not be examined here in any detail.

The precision of the observations or measurements used to determine the values of the variables employed in a description depends on the concepts employed, the measures available for use with such concepts, and the procedures followed in making the observations. At one extreme, descriptions are based on narrowly defined, technical concepts that are supplied with precise indicators, and measured on carefully calibrated scales using mechanical or electronic instruments. At the other extreme, the meaning of concepts is uncertain, the link between concept and indicator is weak, there is no unit of measurement, and measurement procedures are informal or casual, or performed under conditions of stress likely to foster serious inaccuracies. The latter situation is encountered far more often than the former, whether in everyday discussion of individual or social affairs, or in the social (as against the physical) sciences.

Adequacy. Descriptive adequacy is a function of the purpose for which a descriptive account is to be used. Purpose serves to determine relevance of content, to provide grounds for selectivity, and therefore to provide a basis for criticizing particular selections. Thus a description of a wrecked automobile that is adequate for a police reporting system could be seriously inadequate for the purposes of a garage mechanic who must estimate the cost of repairs. More generally, the criteria of adequacy applied to descriptions depend on whether the purpose of the user is to locate a problem or to resolve it; a description that is adequate for one purpose need not be adequate for the other. To illustrate, a dilated eye pupil is a good indicator of concussion in an accident victim, but a physician treating the victim would ignore the dilated pupil and concentrate on the condition that it indicates. Finally, judgments of descriptive adequacy must refer to significant *omissions* in a description. A classic illustration is found in the Sherlock Holmes story in which the failure of a particular dog to bark in the night was the clue that unraveled the mystery. A very powerful theory is needed to criticize a description because of what is excluded or omitted, for omissions are a special case of counter-to-fact conditionals or counter-factuals, and they raise serious problems for theorists, particularly in the social sciences, where theories with the required capacity are scarce.[2]

PREDICTION

A prediction states the content of a description that has not yet been produced. The event predicted may not have taken place, or it may have already occurred but was not observed. In most cases, the predicted event will lie in the future, but it is sometimes useful to predict past events, to conclude, for example, that yesterday's blizzard has blocked a mountain road. If a past event has already been observed by the "predictor," it is in fact a descriptive account and not a prediction. The procedures for making and justifying predictions are the same wherever the predicted event may be located in time. A pattern is created from past experience in which the event to be predicted is linked systematically to some other observable event, either directly or indirectly—a recurring relationship between two or more events is generalized. That pattern is combined with current observations, and the implications of the combination are calculated. The calculations are transferred to the world of experience as a prediction. The pattern is tested, in combination with the calculation, by comparing the predicted description with a description of real-world events as they actually appear to a competent observer.

So long as the need for testability is left aside, there are many ways of producing a projected description of the future, sometimes quite successfully—the local weather "expert" may have a good track record, for example, and prophecy is sometimes surprisingly accurate. But, unless a known instrument is combined with specific observations to generate the prediction formally or logically, there can be no testing, for there is no pattern to test. Neither conclusions reached this way nor the instruments used to reach them, can be justified; there is no basis for dealing with prophecy except faith (or the lack of it) in the prophet. The products of prophecy and prediction are identical in form; they are differentiated by the justification that is offered for accepting them. Patterns used to predict can be criticized in advance of use, and they can be improved over time out of experience; prophecies can be assessed only by reference to the past performance of the prophet. To obtain corrigibility and justification, the intellectual foundations of the prediction, the set of assumptions used to create it, must be isolated and identified. The products of application cannot be separated from the instruments applied, as the reasons for a judgment are an essential part of the judgment. Further, the knowledge and skills used to make the prediction cannot be transferred to another person unless they have been articulated. A valid instrument should be available for use by any competent person and should produce the same outcome when applied, regardless of the attributes of the individual who applies it.

Three different kinds of instruments or patterns, three forms of knowledge, can be used to make défensible predictions: classifications, forecasts, and theories. Although each pattern is a form of generalized past experience, the kinds of events that can be predicted, and the kinds of justifications that can be offered for accepting those predictions, will differ significantly from one case to another.

Predicting with Classifications

The simplest method of predicting events makes use of a classification, a pattern that states the shared or distributed characteristics of some class of things. The principle involved is quite simple: information relating to the attributes and behavior of a particular class of things is collected and generalized. That generalization can then be used to predict the future (or unobserved past) behavior of class members. To be useful for prediction, classifications must include at least two attributes, the members of the class must share at least two characteristics; single variable classifications (not classes with one member) have no predictive capacity.

Structurally, a classification consists of a set of variables, each identifying one of the defining attributes of class members, a set of rules that stipulate the range of values that each variable may take for class members, and any limiting conditions governing applications of the pattern. The variables used to classify swans, for example, include such things as size and shape, color, eating habits, and various behavioral characteristics. The rules stipulate physical dimensions, range of coloration, normal food preferences, and so on. And in the case of swans, one of the limits imposed on application informs the user that in Australia, and in certain zoos as well, some members of the class will be black rather than the usual white. Abstracted, classifications take the form: If A, then b,c,d . . . n, unless L where A is the class label or name, the lower case letters designate the distributed properties of class members, and L designates the limits that govern application or use.

Given an established classification, predictions are generated by a simple two-step process: (a) on the basis of observations made, it is concluded or assumed (a judgment is made) that a member of the class has been located; (b) the content of the observation is deducted from the total set of attributes established for the class; and (c) the remainder of the distributed properties of the class becomes the substance of the prediction. The logic of the process is straightforward:

a. All members of class C have attributes a,b,c,d,e...n (The content of the classification).
b. Thing T is a member of class C (an assumption or conclusion, based on observations that show thing T possesses attributes a,b, and c).
c. Thing T is predicted to have attributes d,e,f...n.

The predictive capacity of a classification is limited to the distributed attributes of the class that remain *after* a member of the class has been identified or assumed. That judgment, clearly, must be based on a partial enumeration of class attributes, otherwise there would be nothing left to predict. The judgment of class membership is therefore both crucial and problematic; it cannot be formalized perfectly unless the list of distributed attributes of class members is exhausted, in which case there is nothing left to predict. Since each application tests the quality of the classification and the validity of the assumption in combination, some fairly complex reasoning may be needed to establish the source of error if a prediction fails. Either the classification or the diagnosis (or both) may be faulty: if the class is wrongly diagnosed, the classification remains untested; if a fault is found in the classification, its content will have to be modified, or additional limitations will have to be imposed on applications.

The reason why classifications can generate defensible predictions is found in the way in which they are created and tested. A classification is simply a repository for summarized or generalized observed attributes or characteristics of the members of a particular class of things. The observer begins with a particular "thing" and describes it; continued observation produces a set of distributed attributes for that one thing, a class with but one member. If other things appear that seem to be "the same" kind of thing as the first, they can be observed and shared attributes identified. Suitably generalized, those share attributes become the defining attributes of a class. To illustrate, a child usually generalizes the day-to-day behavioral characteristics of its own mother (mother is gentle and kind, for example), producing a classification with but one member. The pattern has limited usefulness but satisfies all of the requirements for predicting. If the one-member class is extended to include all mothers, applicability is expanded but at a price in precision and richness. In any case, observations of a number of things that are members of "the same" class serve as the basis for generalization. If significant differences emerge from observation, the tentative assumption that all the things observed belonged to the same class may be modified, either by subdividing the overall class or by creating a new one. In either case, classifications only summarize the attributes or characteristics observed in *all* class members. A prediction based on a classification is a simple extrapolation from past experience with class members. The suppressed assumption, of course, is that class members will in future continue to display the same characteristic, a safer assumption with respect to genetically transmitted attributes than to acquired behavior traits where living things are concerned.

Predictions based on classifications, like predictions based on any other instrument, can be expected to fail occasionally. There are aberrations and exceptions to every pattern, cats without tails and wealthy Americans who do not contribute to the Republican party. If the frequency with which predictions fail is unacceptable, a question to be decided on normative grounds, the instrument must be improved or abandoned. To improve the classification, the user returns to direct experience with the individual things from which the pattern was generated, seeking to augment the structure by more tightly focused observations. In some cases, attributes may have to be added or dropped; in others, the limits on application may have to be increased. In extreme cases, the classification may be abandoned altogether.

A wide range of everyday purposes, from purchasing meat for the family dinner to prescribing a treatment for common ailments, can be satisfied using predictions based on classifications. The procedure used to make such predictions satisfies the requirements for testing in use; hence, both justification of the prediction, and improvement of predictive capacity over time, are possible in principle. However, such predictions have only limited value in the reasoned direction of actions (policymaking). More commonly, they are used to forewarn of situations that will require remedial action in future rather than to deal with such situations, although they may assist in the direction of actions when combined with other instruments.

Predicting with Forecasts or Theories

A more powerful, and flexible, type of instrument for making predictions can be produced by generalizing correlations among events that have appeared in real-world experience in the past. A structure created in this way consists of two or more variables or observables whose values are linked by rule under stipulated limiting conditions. If the variables included in the pattern are assumed to be linked causally, the resulting pattern is labeled a *theory* and it can be used as a basis for action. If no causal relation is assumed, the instrument is labeled a *forecast* and can be used for making predictions of the "natural" flow of events. Both instruments generate predictions in the same way. The discussion here will concentrate on prediction using forecasts, reserving the discussion of theories and their applications to the latter part of the chapter. Of course, those who do forecasting, who construct and apply such instruments, prefer to make use of variables that are known or suspected to be causally or theoretically linked, but any set of observables whose values correlate systematically can be used for predicting. To illustrate, it may be preferable, other things equal, to predict sales of particular kinds of clothing using such related factors as seasonal changes or demographic data, but if a more accurate prediction could be made by linking clothing sales to the number of ships arriving in New York harbor in a given month, that relation would surely be exploited. Any kind of covariance is potential grist for the forecaster's mill.

Once an instrument has been created, prediction is a very simple process. If the limiting conditions controlling use of the forecast are satisfied, observation is used to determine the value of one or more of the variables in the pattern. The value(s) of the other variables, which becomes the substance of the prediction, can be calculated using rules of interaction that have been generalized from experience (the heart of a forecast, or indeed of any pattern of organized relations, is contained in its rules of interactions). Similarly, if successive observations show that the value of one or more of the variables included in the pattern has changed, the rule can be used to calculate, and predict, the amount of change that has taken place in the others. In most cases, forecasts consist of two-variable sets, but complex patterns can be created by combining a number of dyads; so long as each pair shares a common or linking variable, such combinations can be treated as a single unit.

The principle involved in forecasting is readily illustrated using the same everyday example employed earlier. If the dates on which two species of flowers bloom each year are observed and recorded, and inspection shows that every case in the historical record fits a rule in the form "Flower A blooms 13–15 days after flower B," all the requirements for a sound forecast have been met. Testing is relatively simple: first, had the rule been applied in the past, would it have predicted the blooming date of flower A correctly for each year that has been recorded?; second, are there any established patterns of relations that would preclude or inhibit the event that is forecast? Once it is assumed that the pattern will continue to hold in the future, observing that flower B has bloomed leads logically to the conclusion that flower A will bloom in 13–15 days time. The structure of the forecast is simple: $X = Y + $

13 to 15 days, where X is the blooming date of flower A and Y is the blooming date of flower B. The logic is rudimentary:

$$\begin{aligned} \text{Assume:} \quad & X = Y + 13\text{--}15 \\ \text{Observe:} \quad & Y = \text{May 1st} \\ \text{Expect:} \quad & X = \text{May 13th} - \text{15th} \end{aligned}$$

A simple correlation, located in past history, has been generalized and then transposed from the past to the future; the implications of the transfer were calculated within the logic and the results translated into everyday terms—in most cases, the two operations are simply collapsed. If the forecast is not sufficiently accurate for the purpose in hand, it may be possible to tighten the rule, but that is a function of the content of history and not of the wishes of the forecaster. If the time margin in the rule can be reduced to a single day without affecting the reliability of the forecast, judged in terms of historical applications, well and good. More commonly, however, what is gained in precision will be lost in reliability; a smaller percentage of valid forecasts is produced if a more precise rule is employed.

The absence of a causal assumption in a forecast much simplifies the justification required for the pattern, but it also reduces its usefulness in human affairs. Any historical correlation can serve as a forecasting base, but the only evidence that can be offered to support a forecast is further historical correlation; experimental evidence is ruled out because that requires a causal assumption. In fact, efforts to use forecasts as an action base, such as trying to hasten the blooming of one flower by force-feeding the other, will usually destroy their predictive capacity.

The strength of the justification provided for a forecast, which must be estimated prior to application, is difficult to assess. The only evidence available is the degree of fit between the correlations contained in the instrument and the content of recorded experience and the presence or absence of knowledge that makes the forecast unlikely. Of course, such things as the time period covered by the available data, the range of conditions under which the forecast has functioned adequately in the past, and the frequency with which predictive errors have appeared in other applications will influence the confidence level attached to the prediction. Various techniques have been developed for improving the reliability of forecasts; most are a variant of the practice of making a number of predictions of the same event using different sets of correlations.[3] Coincidence in prediction, plus the past success record of the forecasting devices employed, then serves as an index to validity. A variant on that procedure seeks to eliminate factors known to affect the outcome of the events being forecast by restricting application in different ways. It should be noted, however, that if an entirely new element enters the picture, if the flow of events is altered by a factor not present in the historical record, the forecaster is at least momentarily helpless, as those who predict elections learn to their sorrow from time to time.

A theory is structurally identical to a forecast, and it generates predictions in precisely the same way as a forecast. The evidence for a theory, however, must include the results of deliberate actions or experimentation, making it very much stronger than the evidence usually available to support a forecast. Since theories can also be used to project the effects of action, and the procedure is precisely the same in either case, the use of theories to make predictions is examined in that context.

Projecting the Consequences of Actions

An instrument able to project the consequences of human action on the future must include an assumed causal relation between action and outcome. At a minimum, such an instrument will identify the necessary and/or the sufficient conditions for a particular event to occur. If an outcome is to be produced by human action, the sufficient conditions for the event to occur must be known; if the event is to be prevented, knowing the necessary conditions for occurrence may, in principle at least, provide adequate grounds for action. Instruments able to perform those functions are here labeled *theories*. They correspond fairly closely to the kinds of theories produced by experimental science, but even in the physical sciences, usage varies widely; not all of the structures labeled "theories" in physical science are in fact capable of projecting the effects of action, and in social science that capacity is rare. A theory, once it has been properly tested and validated, can be combined with observations to generate a prediction of future events in precisely the same manner as a forecast. If it is to be used in that way, no more supporting evidence is needed than any other forecast requires but in that case the instrument *is* a forecast and not a theory—the kind of justification required for any pattern or instrument is a function of the use made of the instrument as the quality of the available justification determines the nature of the instrument. Theories can also be combined with the first-order effects of deliberate human actions to generate a projection of the consequences expected to follow from that action, or more precisely, from the initial change produced by the action.

Structurally, theories are identical to forecasts, comprising two or more variables, one or more interaction rules, and a set of limiting conditions governing application. The limiting conditions provide a "ground" against which the variables interact according to the rules.

If the rules specify successive interactions among the variables (what is commonly and somewhat inaccurately called "feedback"), only two or three variables are likely to be included in the theory. A four-variable system in which there is feedback among all of the variables is practically incalculable; if there are as many as five such interacting variables, the structure is in principle beyond calculation. In the strong form of theory, the rule(s) assert that if specified conditions are met, a given event will occur (If A then B given C); the weaker form of theory states that an event will *not* occur unless some specified event takes place, or some set of conditions is met. (No A unless B given C.) The strong form of theory has greater potential usefulness, of course, but is correspondingly more difficult to create and justify.

The evidence needed to support or justify a theory goes beyond historical correlation because a causal assumption (in the limited sense of the term used here) must be justified. There must be reason to believe that the relations expressed by the pattern will hold whether they are triggered by deliberate human actions or merely occur in nature. Otherwise, the structure will not be able to fulfill the purpose required of it in the reasoned direction of human action. The historical evidence must show, either directly or indirectly, that the pattern can be acted upon, and not merely that it has held in the past during the natural flow of events. Since the causal assumption fulfills the logical requirements for systematic experimentation, that makes it possible to create the needed evidence by acting deliberately in ways implied by the theoretical structure under controlled conditions. Such evidence is probably the most important element in the justification of theories, particularly in the less well-developed disciplines. In a field of inquiry that is richly endowed with well-established theories of this kind, logical compatibility with the main body of accepted theory is often the primary form of justification offered for and demanded of proposed new theories.

The importance of the limiting conditions attached to every theory is worth underscoring, particularly since they tend to be ignored in discussions of theorizing, even in the physical sciences. No theory will function perfectly under all conditions, but in the sciences the limits may be so well established, and so well integrated into professional training, that they can be ignored without any serious side effects. In the theoretically weaker disciplines, the limiting conditions have a more important role to play. In principle, any theory can be improved, be made more precise and reliable, by increasing the number of variables it includes and/or by extending and elaborating the rules of interaction. However, either procedure greatly multiplies the complexity of the structure, making the theory more difficult to develop, to calculate, and to apply. An alternative strategy is to limit the number of variables included in the pattern and increase the complexity of the limiting conditions, of the "ground" against which the variables interact—in practice, to search for two- or three-variable patterns that hold under limited conditions. That strategy can in some cases provide a way around the impasse created by increasing to excess the number of variables in the pattern or by over-elaborating the rules of interaction.

Finally, the special problems that arise in every effort to apply a formal calculus to real-world observations need to be taken into account. It is useful to think of a theory as a way of isolating a selection of variables from the rest of the observed world so completely that any changes that take place in the values of the variables in the set can be accounted for perfectly given the rules of interaction. However, that implies a perfect fit between theory and observation, and a perfect fit cannot be achieved, or more precisely, cannot be known to be achieved. Indeed, if experimental results fit too perfectly, that may actually cast suspicion on the theory. A theory can also be construed as a pattern or overlay that can be imposed on the world of observation under specified conditions. And again, the pattern must be both structurally and dynamically isomorphic to observation, and the isomorphism must be perfect. The reason for insisting on a perfect fit is the need to know in advance that all the theory's implications are valid. If some of the expectations generated out of the pattern turn out to be valid and others do not, there must be some way to differentiate one from the other in advance of events, otherwise the structure is worthless. That is the main reason why patterns that incorporate false assumptions are not acceptable in disciplines that purport to provide guidance for policymakers, despite the claims that have been made on their behalf, particularly within the field of economic theorizing.[4] Even though *some* of the projections made using such theories are validated by subsequent events, that is unimportant unless it is known in advance which of the critical variables will project accurately. In the latter case it would be possible to restrict applications to those aspects of the projection; otherwise, the user is employing a random terror machine.

Unfortunately, it is impossible in principle to separate any selection of variables from the rest of the observed world perfectly and completely, or to know that such a separation had been achieved, so long as the sensory apparatus is taken as a limit on human knowledge. As measurement accuracy increases, every theory eventually breaks down and the results become indeterminate. Discrepancies between theory and observation can pose a serious analytic problem for the theorist. If they are included in the set of general propositions or assumptions that make up the theory, then those propositions are converted from nomic generalizations (form: All A is B) into probabilistic generalizations (form: Some A is B). Even if the portion of A that is B remains very large (approaches 100 percent), the logical effect is catastrophic, for the capacity to calculate implications from the theory nearly vanishes. The range of conclusions that can be drawn from a set of probabilistic statements, the amount of information that can be extracted from such statements logically or formally, is trivial compared to the amount of information available in nomic generalizations.

A relatively simple device will resolve most of the difficulty without any serious loss in either applicability or usefulness. A *ceteris paribus* clause, or fudge-factor, is added to the apparatus, but placed *between* the theory and its applications and not inside the structure. The rules of interaction can then be stated in nomic terms, and the restrictions on calculation imposed by the use of probabilistic generalizations can be avoided. The influence of *all* of the external variables on any of the elements of the theory is lumped together in the fudge-factor. The reliability of the theory, which can be determined from successive applications, then serves as a measure of the influence of these external factors, taken as a whole. Since *every* theory, in every field of study, has a reliability of less than 100 percent, nothing is lost by the procedure, and the increased analytic clarity and greatly augmented calculability obtained by using it are clear profit.

The use of a fudge-factor of this kind is particularly important in disciplines that are unable to produce generalized propositions of the form or strength available in some of the physical sciences. Adopting the technique allows the use of very weak theories as a basis for action— the physician is able to use a mode of treatment that is successful only ten percent of the time if the alternative is normatively unacceptable, if it involves the death of the patient, for example. Even in fields such as physics, where theories are fairly powerful (approach closely 100 percent reliability), use of the fudge-factor provides a better representation of the theorizing process than does a purely nomic model that ignores minor (and even major) discrepancies between the pattern and observed events.

5

Significance: The Normative Concepts

For reasoned direction of human actions, "normative" knowledge must be able to perform two basic functions: first, to identify the normatively significant dimensions of the outcomes available for choice, and second, to select the preferred outcome from within that set. The first of these functions requires an adequate set of normative concepts or variables; the second depends on the availability of a set of priorities or preference—orderings that can be defended out of experience. The remainder of this volume is devoted to a detailed examination of the assumptions, structures, and processes involved in creating and justifying these two types of instruments.

In the world of experience, concepts and priorities are very closely related and usually develop together. But analytic separation is essential, particularly for clarifying the kinds of assumptions on which an acceptable justification of such instruments depends, and for identifying the various limitations that must be imposed on their uses or applications. The nature of the required conceptual apparatus is discussed in the present chapter; the three chapters to follow are devoted to the development and justification of priorities or preference-orderings and the effects of the social context or environment on the overall apparatus. The amount of overlap among the chapters has been minimized, but some repetition is unavoidable.

Introductory: Assumptions and Limitations

Development of the conceptual apparatus needed to show the normatively significant dimensions of choice is directed, and constrained, by a number of fundamental assumptions about the nature of the normative enterprise. A brief summary will serve as an introduction to the discussion of content and structure; a fuller treatment is available in chapter 6.

Perhaps the most influential initial assumption is also the most difficult to manage properly: the development and justification of normative knowledge are controlled by the same criteria of legitimacy, and are subject to the same methodological limitations, as those that apply to the creation, testing, and justification of empirical or "scientific" knowledge. Each is a product of the same intellectual machinery; the neural system functions in the same manner, analytically at least, in both domains. However, the content of the two systems is different, they serve different purposes, and the criteria of adequacy applied are different; as a result of such differences, normative inquiry and justification are subject to limits not encountered in the quest for empirical knowledge, even though the overall process remains the same.

Assuming a common apparatus for empirical and normative inquiry has three first-order implications for the kinds of inquiries undertaken here. First, the normative instruments, the concepts and priorities used to direct actions or make choices, must be generated inductively from specific cases occurring within human experience, analytically if not historically. It follows that such instruments are justified by reference to the available body of past human experience in much the same manner as any other form of knowledge; only the aspects of experience taken into consideration will differ. Second, the ultimate basis for "testing" every form of knowledge is pragmatic usefulness in fulfilling specified human purposes; in the end, the apparatus is judged by its use in attaining the overall normative purpose for which the knowledge system was designed. Third, the final court of appeal in normative inquiry, as in any other field, is the judgment of the community of well-informed and competent persons, of "informed opinion." That group may be difficult to identify, for it is not limited to academics or members of any particular profession (and may not be organized), nor are members of any particular group automatically part of informed opinion. Membership is based on the quality of the arguments produced in real-world cases, on the kind of justification that is provided for the successive layers of assumptions and evidence used to support a normative position. When informed opinion is unanimous, or nearly so, its judgments will be decisive and authoritative, although only tentatively and temporarily. If there is a serious, irresolvable disagreement, the question at issue must remain undecided pending additional information or stronger argument—to be adjudicated by the same group.

The qualifications for membership within the body of "informed opinion" are relatively severe. They include, *inter alia*, five major requirements: (a) first-hand experience with the empirical situations to which the knowledge claim refers—familiarity with the phenomena treated by the subject field; (b) reasonably full possession of the body of relevant, recorded, human experience, of the knowledge available in the field, (c) awareness of the criteria of criticism/evaluation currently accepted in the field; (d) possession of the analytic/methodological competence, including logical skill, needed for assessing the assumptions, procedures, and evidentiary support on which knowledge claims depend; and (e) the kind of absolute intellectual integrity needed to make the system operate effectively.

Every claim to knowledge must satisfy methodological and normative as well as substantive criteria of adequacy before it can be accepted, but the need for analytic/methodological competence is particularly significant in normative inquiry. The rate of growth of knowledge within a field, and the level of reliability attached to the knowledge patterns currently accepted there, is closely linked to the size and level of sophistication of the current body of informed opinion; that in turn depends on the extent to which there is agreement on a body of fundamental assumptions, including both normative purposes and cannons of argument, that is adequate for directing and controlling inquiry. Those assumptions both reflect and influence the size and quality of the body of available knowledge. In normative inquiry generally, the foundation of agreed assumptions, and the body of established knowledge, is quite small and seems likely to remain so for the near future. The rate of cumulation of normative knowledge is therefore likely to be low, and a high level of disagreement among the "informed" can be expected to characterize the field. In the circumstances, the prime need is to develop a consensus on such methodological fundamentals as the nature of the normative enterprise, and the criteria of argument that should be accepted at the present time. Otherwise, a rapidly-changing real-world situation is more likely to produce deterioration than improvements in the quality of the normative apparatus (measured against human needs), especially in the short run. For that reason, among others, this volume is concerned first with identification of the major purposes to be fulfilled by normative knowledge, and then with articulating a set of basic assumptions that are adequate for satisfying them; no effort will be made to produce an argument for any specific substantive position.

Of course, every approach to normative inquiry depends on some substantive assumptions, and two of those employed here are sufficiently important to bear reiteration. First, the primacy of human life in normative judgment, its role as the basic unit of significance in deciding preferences, is taken as given. The principal reasons for making the assumption are negative: if it is rejected, the criteria used to direct or criticize human actions would have to come from an extra-human source (to which humans have no access) and/or human affairs would lose their significance for humans. Either outcome is absurd. More positively, there seems to be no feasible alternative available. In any event, if anything intellectually accessible to the species is to have significance for species members, human life will have to be included on the list. That does not require a denial of the possibility of developing other alternatives, although at present that seems unlikely. The second substantive assumption, a corollary to the first, is that with respect to life itself, one human life is the equal of any other. This amounts in practice to saying that if nothing is known of two lives beyond their humanness, there is no way to justify attaching greater significance to one than to the other. That assumption turns out to be exceedingly powerful and it plays a central role in the justification of actions, particularly by collective bodies, as will be made clear in chapters 6 and 7. Neither assumption is particularly contentious and both are essential if the purposes set for the inquiry are to be fulfilled.

One last preliminary: the conventional terminology of ethics or moral philosophy has, for the most part, been avoided or abandoned.[1] Such concepts as "good" or "right," which are often held to be the essential elements in an acceptable ethical apparatus, do not appear in the text, nor does the discussion make use of such concepts as "justice," "equity," or "fairness," or their various corollaries. The reason for this somewhat radical departure from current usage is found in the purposes set for the inquiry and the criteria of adequacy they entail. The question to be answered here is not "How should situation S be evaluated?" but "Is there a preferable alternative to S among the set available to the actor in the situation?" For reasons that have already been given, there is no feasible alternative to an action focus, and a normative apparatus that is adequate for guiding real-world actions within the limits of human capacity must function by *comparing* the outcomes available to a specific actor at a given time or place. Actions in turn are judged by reference to their human consequences and not their intrinsic properties. It follows that the normative apparatus used to direct actions must include either (a) a way of weighting each of the available outcomes in absolute terms, using a standard unit of measurement; (b) a way of making direct comparisons (ordinal measurements), and utilizing the results to produce defensible judgments; or (c) some other viable alternative. Neither of the first two of these options is actually feasible, for reasons that will be explored in due course, barring acceptance of an untenable set of assumptions such as those commonly employed in "welfare" economics—which are both empirically unacceptable and analytically question-begging.[2] A different procedure, and appropriate criteria, must be created and applied if choices and actions are to be made on defensible grounds.

Although it may appear that the normative apparatus outlined below can and does provide answers to such questions as "Is this the right thing to do?" or "Has that action produced a good or just result?" that is not really the case. Questions relating to the "rightness," "goodness," or "justice" of either actions or outcomes are not and cannot be answered within the analytic framework used here for making reasoned choices; such terms have no meaning there. Taken at face value, such concepts require assessments of specific human states; they are not designed for making comparisons. Propositions in the form "Prefer outcome A to outcome B," which are necessary for directing actions, need not imply such propositions as "A is better than B," not to say "A is good." Outcome A need not be judged "good" to be preferred to outcome B, and outcome B need not be preferred to outcome A even if B is judged "good." Within the critical apparatus, the proposition "Prefer A to B" where A and B are the projected consequences of action, means only that some justification can be offered based on past human experience, suitably generalized, for acting to produce A rather than B. The meaning of "preference" is to be found in the content of the justification. Of course, the overall critical apparatus is subject to criticism on both experiential and methodological grounds, but that involves the use of an alternative overall framework meant either to fulfill the same fundamental purpose or to pursue a wholly different purpose.

THE NORMATIVE CONCEPTS

In normative affairs, as in the sciences, the selection of concepts or variables used for structuring the outcomes from which choices are made is controlled by two major factors: first, the content of past human experience, which does not require a commitment to any particular set of concepts but does restrict the kind of apparatus that can be created (in part because the content has already been organized using a set of concepts); second, the overall purpose for which knowledge will be used—the initial normative commitment. These limits function in precisely the same manner that the purposes of games such as football, and experience gained through seeking to achieve them, provide the basic criteria for assessing the conceptual apparatus employed in coaching. In a knowledge system meant for maintaining and improving the conditions of life of some human population by directing human actions, the normative concepts will refer to the attributes of human life that are the prime determinants of the relative preferability of different conditions or states of life, and will be linked by the very complex concept "the quality of human life" on which the validity of the selection depends. The information that is produced by applying normative concepts must suffice to allow a user to judge that the anticipated conditions of life of some population that appear in one of the outcomes available for choice are preferable to the conditions of life of the same population projected for any of the available alternatives or that the choice is a matter of indifference given the accepted normative system.

In principle, any concept can be a normative variable, and including trivial dimensions of individual life in the projected outcomes poses no special problems because the process of establishing a preference will separate the significant from the trivial. The first important requirement to be imposed on a normative conceptual apparatus is for comprehensiveness; the second is measurability. Comprehensiveness is prime, for any aspect of the available outcomes that is not captured by the conceptual network will not be taken into account when a judgment is made. Otiose information is easy to eliminate; sins of omission cannot be remedied. The situation is precisely equivalent to the problem encountered in efforts to use John Stuart Mill's "Methods" for locating causal relations: the final judgment is limited qualitatively by the selection of variables used in the analysis. The need to measure the value taken by the normative variables, which must be satisfied before comparisons are possible, is the major reason for the complexity of the apparatus needed to structure the outcomes available for choice.

"The Quality of Life" as a Normative Concept

Given the set of initial assumptions accepted here, the central normative concept, the continuum on which the outcomes available for choice are compared producing the evidence on which judgments of preference are based, is the "condition," "qualitative state," or "preferability" of an individual human life. Preferences depend on a systematic comparison or measurement of the value of that overall normative variable for each person affected by action in each of two or more outcomes. But a human life is a very complex configuration of attributes that varies, often significantly, from one person to another. The life whose different states are to be compared begins at the point where action occurs and extends to termination, or to the limits of projective capacity at the time of decision. It has both a longitudinal and a cross-sectional dimension, a subjective as well as an objective aspect, and so on; each of its facets may play a significant role in preference. Even within a single culture, an almost infinite variety of different lives can be found, each open to some kinds of modifications through human action, and each to some extent differentially affected by given actions. The conceptual apparatus included in the normative system must suffice for handling the changes induced when the lives of large and diverse populations are altered by human actions.

Most of the major difficulties encountered in efforts to create an adequate set of normative concepts, to measure their values in particular cases, and to justify a particular preference out of past experience, can be traced to the peculiar character of the concept "quality of individual life" and to the measurement and other problems associated with it. Priorities, or preference orderings, must be stated in terms of complex configurations of already complex normative variables. Viewed analytically, the conceptual apparatus required for choice is exceptionally complicated, which may suggest the reasons why normative inquiry must begin with a normative system, however faulty, already in place. A precisely analogous situation appears in the field of medicine where physicians must compare the "state of health," of an individual at different points in time, or of two or more individuals concurrently. Four types of problems that arise during efforts to develop and apply or measure normative concepts or variables, which can be traced directly to the need to make comparisons of the qualitative state of different human lives at different points in time, are particularly important here: (a) what is best termed the basic "measurement" problem; (b) the "microscope-telescope" problem; (c) the "multi-function" problem; and (d) the "holism" problem. Each contributes to the overall complexity of the required apparatus.

The "Measurement" Problem. With respect to any human life, various attributes or dimensions can be identified that are generally agreed to be significant determinants of its overall quality or preferability under certain stipulated circumstances. The dimensions of life that influence its quality, the normative concepts or variables, include such things as the state of the individual's health, access to resources, relations with others, types of subjective feelings, and so on. The character of the normative variables must be such that if the value of one of them differs measurably in two or more of the available outcomes, the result will make at least some potentially significant difference in the value taken by the overall normative variable, the quality of the individual life. Such differences provide the grounds on which judgments of preference are based. In due course, then, the relation between the value of any normative variable, and the quality of the life as a whole, must somehow be assessed. That already requires a complex structure of rules, variables, and limitations. And the problem is further confused by the common practice of basing judgments on the values taken by particular variables, ignoring the overall construct needed for defensible judgments—a practice that amounts to using such concepts as "condition of eyesight" as a surrogate for the overall "state of health" concept that actually controls, or should control, decisions in medicine.

The source of the error involved is readily demonstrated. The effect of a difference in the value of any normative variable on the total life of the individual depends on the other attributes of that life, on the values of other variables (some of which at least may also be regarded as normative). But an individual life is not completely represented by any finite configuration of normative variables; the relative preferability of any given condition of life is a function of the configuration *as a whole*. There can be no standard unit for measuring the overall "quality" of an individual life, for there is no single, well-defined, homogeneous continuum on which to make such a measurement. Further, no rule can be created that will generate a value for the "quality of life" variable from the values taken by a finite set of normative or other variables. Yet the comparisons needed for justifying preferences must refer to the overall concept. Much the same limitation holds for other concepts that are clearly normative in character: "health," for example, is precisely analogous to the concept "life"; its full meaning cannot be fixed, and therefore its relative value (as a variable) cannot be stated in terms of standard units or calculated by rule from the values taken by some fixed set of other variables (Indicators and Buffers).

So long as the meaning of the continuum used to make the comparison remains in some degree unclear and uncertain, preferences cannot be based on direct comparisons. That does not mean that comparisons that make use of such concepts as "condition of life" or "quality of life" are entirely useless. But the elimination of direct comparisons, whether or not they employ standard units of measurement, forces reliance on other procedures and evidence for justification. One way of dealing with the problem is set forth in chapter 6; others may in due course be forthcoming. What is encouraging, all things considered, is that the measurement problem is soluble in practice within the limits of human capacity; the solution may be crude, but it is corrigible over time out of experience, and that is all that can reasonably be demanded of any intellectual system.

The "Microscope-Telescope" Effect. Use of the concept "life" as the basic continuum for making and justifying preferences creates a second type of problem, a microscope-telescope effect, that is also cause for concern, particularly in the management of collective affairs. The term "life" usually refers to both the aspects of individual life that are accessible to an observer functioning at close range with a familiar subject, such as a family member, and to those available to a distant observer, as exemplified by bureaucratic surveillance from a national center, and the two can differ quite fundamentally. Far more is involved than conceptual bias. Bias in the observer affects what is seen from among the things that *could be* seen if the observer were not biased, or more precisely, had a different bias. The microscope-telescope problem, on the other hand, refers to what *can be* seen from each perspective. Much of the information that is available at short range to a competent observer cannot be accessed through a "telescope," despite competent efforts. Similarly, a distant perspective can make available information, say about the relation between individual lives and social institutions, that is either not readily obtained or is wholly inaccessible from close up.

Given the differences in accessibility that follow from perspective differences, the question "What kind of information is needed to make decisions?" will tend to determine the locus of decision-making in a well-designed organization. But historically, such functional assignments have in many cases already been made, and not always in an appropriate manner. The problem is particularly acute in societies where the role of government in the lives of its individual members is substantial and increasing, as seems to hold in most of the industrial nations. That trend should, in due course, underscore the need for information about details of individual life that can only be collected locally, that cannot be aggregated and then disaggregated without losing validity. The relation between medical diagnosis and individual symptoms illustrates the point well; the results of diagnosis are often usefully summed, but an aggregation of symptoms observed in a range of different patients would be meaningless.

In contemporary industrial society, detailed information relating to specific individuals seems likely to increase in importance in future, if only as a necessary prerequisite to improvements in institutional design. The significance of the difference between a long-range and close-up perspective will depend on the meaning of the normative concepts considered essential for an adequate justification of actions, and their relative accessibility from different physical and social "distances." If the dimensions of life that contribute most to the relative preferability of a given life are discernable exclusively, or even preeminently from a close-up or "microscopic" position, that will greatly influence the information-gathering system that is installed by a society seeking to perform at an optimal normative level. There is no abstract way of deciding such matters; they must be resolved within the context of a real normative structure functioning in an ongoing society.

Multi-Functional Concepts. In an action-oriented field of inquiry, normative concepts serve a number of related functions, a requirement that further complicates the problem of conceptual development. Their prime function is to capture the normatively significant dimensions of the outcomes available for choice; that purpose provides the basic criterion for judging conceptual adequacy. However, such concepts also serve as the basic units of organization in the kinds of population inventories (descriptive accounts of specific populations) that corrigible policymaking demands. Population inventories are needed to locate situations that are considered normatively unacceptable in terms of current standards and which therefore require individual and/or collective actions to improve them. They are also needed to monitor the effects of action and supply the information used to correct and improve the policies that produced them. Finally, population inventories identify and define the fortunate and unfortunate members of society, measured in terms of current standards, and thus produce working models of the conditions of life to be eschewed or sought after. They serve, indirectly at least, to establish the parameters of minimum performance applied to existing social institutions. Concepts able to perform these functions must be more or less interchangeable: propositions that use one set of concepts must be fully translatable into propositions that employ the others. Otherwise, none of the necessary functions can be performed, and the inquirer is faced with a problem akin to the policymaker whose theories make use of concepts that cannot be translated into the normative concepts needed for establishing preferences or priorities.

"Normative" concepts, which refer to the significant dimensions of individual life and are used to structure outcomes projected to follow from human actions, or to inventory the members of society, need to be separated sharply from "early warning devices," from concepts that can serve as useful indicators of impending disaster in individual or collective affairs. The separation will depend on the situation, for concepts that are "early warning devices" in one context may be "normative" in another. In some cases, the separation is easily made: "infant mortality rate" is a feature of society and not an attribute of individual human life; it can therefore function only as an early warning device. But in Third World health programs, one of the more useful indicators of impending health problems in infants is to register the weight of the child, week by week, after birth, and check for "normal" progression. Is "infant weight" therefore a normative variable?

In practical terms, how a variable is labeled matters less than how it is used. Concepts that serve as warning signals relate to normative concepts in much the same way that a flashing light on the dashboard of an automobile relates to the absence of oil in the automobile's engine. The light has no intrinsic normative significance; its importance is derived from the condition that it indicates. Such devices depend absolutely on the prior availability of a normative apparatus able to identify the conditions to be warned against; they can neither substitute for such an apparatus nor function without it. Further, their uses are severely restricted: they can be used to call attention to normative problems but not to deal with them. It is unlikely that anyone familiar with automobiles would try to fix the problem indicated by the oil warning light by seeking ways of putting the light out. But overfeeding of infants in an effort to maintain normal development, triggered by a weekly weight recording program, can and does occur. And when legislators seek to remedy such serious problems as poverty by income modification alone, or economists seek to improve economic conditions by controlling the "money supply," or "interest rate," something very close to the same kind of conceptual error has occurred—with potentially tragic results.

The "Holism" Problem. Very little of the conceptual apparatus needed for directing human actions is presently available. In part that is due to the handicaps noted earlier; in part, progress is and has been slow because the central thrust of contemporary normative inquiry tends to take a different direction. What is particularly unfortunate is that improvement seems unlikely in the near future, whether in philosophy, in the so-called "policy sciences," or in everyday affairs. Most of the impedimentia to conceptual improvement, or conceptual development, are effects of the need to deal with individual human lives, and to treat each life holistically, as an integrated unit. In reasoned action or choice, the object of preference is always a complete outcome, projected as fully as existing theory permits; the outcome in turn is stated in terms that refer to individual lives, taken as a whole. Each outcome, and each life, must be treated as an entity. Specifying the kind and amount of change that has been introduced into an individual life by human action does not provide an adequate basis for preference, nor can specific dimensions of individual life be isolated and evaluated apart from the whole life—although the practice is commonplace. To use a reasonably accurate metaphor, a human life resembles in some respects a journey; it has both instantaneous and extended characteristics, either of which can be important depending upon the particular circumstances. What is compared in reasoned action or choice is the foreseeable remainder of the whole journey, beginning at the point where action occurs; the past cannot, so far as is known, be erased, although it may be taken into account in planning the future. A number of human attributes, all well established for the species as a whole, serve to complicate the task of producing the conceptual apparatus needed for life-as-a-whole comparisons of the required order.

First in importance is the enormous diversity among individual human lives that appears within every society, and even within each life over relatively short periods of time. A conceptual apparatus able to capture the major effects of specific actions on such diverse and changing populations is much more difficult to create than an apparatus that will function effectively with a simple and relatively homogeneous population. The structure of the kinds of normative concepts adequate for fulfilling real world purposes is thereby complicated to a considerable degree, as will be made clear in due course. Measurements and applications of such concepts are correspondingly more difficult than might otherwise be the case.

Second, human life has duration as well as breadth and intensity, and each dimension influences the relative preferability of a life in significant ways. An adequate conceptual apparatus must be able to capture both. The most difficult task is to create concepts that refer to the attributes of life over an extended period of time; those needed for cross-sectional accounts are much easier to produce or apply, and perhaps for that reason, the available supply is much larger. Absent a set of concepts that refer to longitudinal factors, an extended narrative, hedged with reservations and contingencies, is needed to state the effects of action on human life over time. That much complicates the systematic comparisons needed for justifying preferences. At present, the resulting conceptual problem is handled by the use of modifiers like "permanent" disability, or "momentary" pain, but the effectiveness of that technique is clearly limited. Reconceptualization, or the creation of new concepts able to handle complex conditions over extended time periods, is one obvious solution to the problem, but it is far easier to articulate than to achieve in defensible terms.

A third source of complexity in efforts to create a conceptual apparatus adequate for dealing with human life holistically is the need to take into account both life's subjective and objective dimensions. The problem can be narrowed somewhat by extending the meaning of "objective" to "life as directly experienced by another sentient person," and assuming that everything about the individual which is accessible in principle to an observer (who may be the self) is part of the objective world—including both individual attributes and the relations between individual and the external environment. That procedure, however, leaves some serious problems unresolved, particularly those that relate to controlling the quality of the knowledge that is produced when data relating to the subjective aspects of individual life are employed.

Subjectivity implies a dimension of life that is normatively significant yet restricted to access by the individual concerned. There is no way to be certain that the content of subjective experience is being articulated accurately by the individual with direct access to that experience, although there are procedures that can reduce the risk of serious error. Validity is therefore a major problem, potentially at least, even with respect to simple, descriptive accounts of, say, affective reactions. Indeed, even the meaning of concepts that refer to subjective experience, leaving aside the need for appropriate indicators and measures, is difficult to stabilize and assess. In one sense, subjective experience is "observed" and recorded by the experiencing person in the same way as any objective phenomenon, but the procedures commonly employed for limiting uncertainty and increasing descriptive accuracy with respect to objective phenomena cannot be applied. Further, the extent to which subjective descriptions are influenced by bias and operant conditioning is exceptionally hard to determine, even by the individual involved. Of course, inquiries into the objective conditions of individual life are subject to many of the same constraints, but procedures can usually be devised for limiting their impact on conclusions reached, for narrowing the range of potential error.

Whatever the risks and uncertainties involved, the normative conceptual apparatus must be able to deal with the subjective as well as the objective dimensions of life. To ignore the subjective would open the way to creating objective heavens that were hell in subjectivity; to reverse the emphasis and ignore objective information would make it possible for the "happy hog" to resist criticism. And the existence of a concept such as "happy hog" already suggests the extent to which the subjective and objective dimensions of life are intermingled in assessments of relative preferability.

One last point, already touched upon briefly, remains to be made about the conceptual apparatus used in reasoned action: if the quality of individual life is the central concept used to assess significance, and its meaning cannot be fully captured by any finite configuration of normative variables, there is no possibility of identifying concepts that are "intrinsically" rather than "instrumentally" significant. Aspects of human life that are considered intrinsically important in one context may be only instrumentally important in another. Neither term is required by the analytic framework being developed here. In the circumstances, the distinction can simply be ignored. The overall adequacy of the normative conceptual apparatus does, however, have to be questioned systematically in all cases. The principal danger to be avoided is omission of significant aspects of the human condition; otiose concepts may create inefficiencies in processing, but they will not alter the validity of the preference-ordering or impugn its justification. A sound working strategy is to regard the set of concepts in use as a tentative selection and be sensitized to the importance of omissions, to the possibility that something important has been or is being overlooked— assuming, of course, that the necessary time and resources are available.

Structural Complexity: Measuring the Normative Concepts

Structurally, a conceptual apparatus adequate for capturing the effects of action on individual life is complex but manageable. The nature of the complexity is most readily clarified by focusing on a single concept and tracing the evolution of an apparatus that is able to capture the impact of specific actions on the person and transform them into normative terms. One primary requirement of such an apparatus is that it provide an unbroken chain of causal linkages between an action (or a change that is introduced by action), and the projected value of the normative concept or variable. In effect, projecting the value of a normative concept requires a miniature theory. The structure will include two or more variables, a set of rules linking their values to the value of the normative variable, a causal assumption, and appropriate limiting conditions. Despite their structural complexity, such projections are commonplace in everyday affairs, which is at least encouraging. Stripped to essentials, the apparatus must show the effects of some action or change on the value taken by a normative concept, and ultimately on the value of the overall normative concept accepted by the inquirer—here, on the quality of individual life. Ideally, it should provide a basis for measuring the values of the normative variables.

The Descriptive Base. Development of the apparatus begins with the particular life affected by human action, tracing the connection between the change produced in the condition of life and the originating cause. At any given point in time, an individual life can be described, incompletely but adequately, by stipulating the values taken by some finite set of variables; not all of those variables will have normative significance, obviously. Such a descriptive account will be an "open" selection; there will not be any rules linking the values of the variables; the values are set by direct observation. The concepts employed can refer to either the objective or the subjective dimensions of life, depending on the observer. Subjective statements also refer to objective phenomena, to events that are accessible to the sensory apparatus, but only for the person making the observations. For all other persons, statements about subjectivity are only inferences and not part of a descriptive account.

Schematically, each individual can be described by using a selection of concepts or variables, establishing their values by direct observation or measurement. Ignoring for the moment the grounds on which the variables are selected, the structure will take the following basic form:

$$[V_1\ V_2\ V_3\ V_4 \ldots V_n]$$
Description

The square brackets surrounding the set indicate that it is only a selection of variables, an open set, that the values of the individual variables are not rule-connected and calculable one from the others.

The "Input" Variables. There are two ways in which an action can affect the life of an individual: first, by producing a change in the value of one of the variables used to describe the person; second, by preventing a change in the value of one of those variables that would otherwise occur. (Rather than continue the practice of referring to both change and the absence of expected change each time the effects of action are discussed, "change" will henceforth refer to both types of outcomes.) For example, action may add to the amount of resoures available to the person (by gift), subtract from the available resource supply (theft), prevent an addition to those resources (interfere with the bestowal of a gift), or prevent a subtraction from resources (interdict a robbery). Whatever the effect produced, the value of at least one of the variables used to describe the person must be altered before it can be said that a change has occurred or an action has taken place. More generally, the immediate or proximate effect of action can be stated in the form: action A changed the descriptive account of person P between time t_1 and time t_2 from state X to state Y, on the understanding that states X and Y differ with respect to the value of at least one variable—that variable need not be normative.

In most if not all cases, introducing a change into the environment, however slight, triggers a sequence of further changes, creating a "ripple effect" that may extend over considerable periods of time and involve a great many persons. In principle, the full effects of action include all of these repercussions. In practice, the limits of human capacity to project such ripple effects is reached fairly quickly, and the projections are often both crude and highly uncertain. All that can reasonably be demanded of the justification for an action is the fullest possible projection of these repercussions given the knowledge, resources, and time available for the task, with due regard for the best assessment currently possible of the potential significance of the action. It need hardly be said that the limits of human potential are rarely achieved, particularly in day-to-day affairs. On the other hand, human experience over time does tend to identify actions that have in the past had significant human consequences and are likely to do so again in future; therefore, the process is not wholly random or mindless. The normative variables must be sufficiently rich and varied to articulate the projected effects of action fully enough to provide the information needed to make choices in ways that will, at a minimum, make possible human survival. Such richness is achieved by creating theoretical chains (assumed causal linkages) connecting the original action to the conditions of life of specific individuals or classes of individuals. Whatever the connecting linkages located in the environment may be, at the level of the individual the result of action is always a change in the value of one or more of the variables that describe the affected person at the time of impact.

The variables that register the initial change in a human individual induced by action, whether internal or external to the person, can now be separated from the remainder of the descriptive account and labeled *Input* variables (IV). In those terms, the first intellectual requirement for reasoned action is a causal linkage connecting the action taken (which can be represented as a change in the value of some variable external to the individual affected by the action) to some set of Input variables. Input variables need not refer to aspects of the individual that have normative significance; they serve as connectors in the theoretical apparatus, linking actions to their normative consequences. Structurally, they can be depicted as a subset of the selection of variables used to produce the initial description of the impacted individual:

$$[IV_1\ IV_2\ IV_3 \ldots IV_n] \qquad [V_1\ V_2\ V_3 \ldots V_n]$$
$$\text{\textit{Inputs}} \qquad\qquad \text{\textit{Description}}$$

From the perspective of the individual who serves as object, the initial effect of action is either a change in the value of one or more of the Input variables or the absence of such a change when it would otherwise (on theoretical grounds) be expected to occur. To have any effect, indeed, to be an action, at least one such change in the descriptive account of one or more persons must be produced. The amount of change that is expected, which has to be projected on the future by an adequate theory, is always to some degree uncertain or problematic: that uncertainty will influence judgments of preference to some degree, depending on the nature of the change that is projected and the amount of significance that is attached to it.

The "Buffer" Variables. The initial impact of action, the change(s) in the value of one or more Input variables, must now be translated into normative terms, into the value of some normative concept such as "state of health." That requires a further extension of the theoretical apparatus. The immediate effect of introducing a new and different species of germs or viruses into the human body, for example, will be a change in the composition of the blood (IV = "blood content"). The effect of that change on the individual's state of health will depend on various other aspects of the total situation: (a) the kind of germ or virus that is introduced into the blood; (b) other attributes of the individual (antibodies already produced by vaccination or prior contact with the germ, body capacity for producing antibodies, and so on); and (c) the nature of the concept used to state the normative impact on the person, the meaning assigned to the concept "health." Clearly, only a very few changes are likely to produce exactly the same effect on every individual; the introduction of a particular germ may produce death in one case and have no effect whatever in another. The mediating effect of individual attributes can vary enormously, depending on the initial change in the Input variable, the value of the mediating variable, and the full configuration of variables that make up the attributes of the individual.

The analytic structure must therefore be extended to include the individual attributes that mediate the effects of action on individual life. Those attributes will be labeled *Buffer* variables and symbolized

(BV). The set of variables that actually perform a buffering function in any particular case depends on the nature of the action and other characteristics of the situation. A strong body can mediate the impact of physical change, for example, but may do nothing to moderate the effect of monetary loss, while economic capacity may moderate the effects of economic losses yet be useless for mediating the effects of physical damage.

The need to take into account the values of the variables that "buffer" the effects of action serves to complicate the structure of the normative apparatus substantially. First, the Buffer variables will have to be included in the descriptive account of the individual from which analysis begins. More generally, the selection of variables used to inventory the conditions of life of any set of individuals in ways that can be used to project the effects of action, or monitor the impact of policy, will include both Inputs and Buffers. The Buffers may serve as part of the theoretical linkage connecting action to consequences, but are more likely to form part of the set of limiting conditions governing the operation of a particular set of causal relations—introduction of germs of type A will produce effect X in the presence of Buffer attributes B and C, for example.

When the Buffer variables are separated from the remainder of the descriptive account of an individual, the analytic structure becomes:

$$[IV_1 \ IV_2 \ldots IV_n] \qquad [BV_1 \ BV_2 \ldots BV_n] \qquad [V_1 \ V_2 \ldots V_n]$$

Inputs $\qquad\qquad$ *Buffers* $\qquad\qquad$ *Description*

To this point, the apparatus is purely descriptive; no rules of interaction are required beyond the linkage between the original action and the change in the value of one of the Input variables. But in practice, it would probably be impossible to identify the Buffer variables without taking into account the theoretically projected effects of combining particular changes in the values of specified Input variables with known or assumed values for a given set of Buffer variables.

Identifying the Buffer variables, and separating them from the remainder of the descriptive account, creates an invaluable characteristic in the overall structure. Taken as a whole, a set of Buffer variables whose values (or range of values) can be specified in ways that determine the normative impact of a given change in some Input variable, identifies a *class* of individuals that will be affected normatively in the same way by a given change in the value of that Input variable. For example, the effect of a given monetary loss will be trivial for all persons whose incomes exceed a given amount (which can be determined out of experience), leaving aside psychic differences in the response to losses, and so on. That characteristic of the analytic structure is particularly useful for creating the kind of inventory of the population needed for making collective decisions or calculating/monitoring the effects of collective actions. A social policy meant to produce a particular outcome in human individuals can succeed only if it is applied to persons who share the same set of Buffer variables, each taking an appropriate value, since the value of the normative variable will depend on both the change induced in an Input variable and the value taken by the Buffers. One of the more challenging tasks facing those responsible for directing the use of collective authority, and those who seek to provide them with the knowledge and information needed to perform adequately, is to determine the sets of Buffer variables, and their range of values, that identify critical target populations in terms that provide an adequate basis for developing policies able to modify their condition of life in predictable and desirable ways. Thus far, success has been extremely limited, and the use of crude single-variable classes such as income level to identify target populations for public programs is common.

Measuring the Value of a Normative Variable. The value of a normative variable is a function of the interaction of Input variables and Buffer variables. To obtain a measurement, a dynamic factor must be added to what is thus far a purely descriptive structure. A rule or set of rules is required that will link the values of specific Input and Buffer variables in such manner that the value of the normative variable can be calculated. The rules must express an assumed causal relation, and in that sense, the structure required qualifies as a full-fledged theory. For all practical purposes, the apparatus used to measure the value of a normative variable is identical in character and function to the internal structure of an adequate theory in the sense in which that term is used here.

The analytic apparatus required to link actions taken to changes in the value of a single normative variable is now complete. The change induced by action is shown with the use of Input variables; the mediating effects of the Buffer variables, which may either mitigate or exacerbate the initial change, are incorporated into a set of rules that link the values of the Inputs and Buffers to the value of the normative variable. Those rules need not state arithmetical relations, but they must allow calculation or inference. Relative terms such as "more" or "less" are often a sufficient basis for decision; in other cases, it may be enough to establish unacceptable values for particular variables, or cut-off points at which the significance of a given variable diminishes or expands very rapidly. So long as the normative variables refer to the longitudinal as well as the cross-sectional aspects of life, and take into account both the duration and the intensity of the impact of change in a context supplied by *all* of life's salient attributes, an apparatus adequate as a point of departure has been created.

The overall structure used to measure the value of a normative variable can be depicted fairly accurately; for simplicity, the otiose descriptive variables have been dropped from the diagram below. Although the structure may appear unwieldy, particularly when it is recalled that a single decision may involve small differences in a number of those variables, it is actually used regularly and frequently in everyday affairs, sometimes quite accurately. The skeptical reader need only pause to consider the intellectual processes that are followed when working out the effect on the self of a large and wholly unexpected expense, or a temporary but disabling accident, to see how the structure is fleshed out in real cases. In the process of determining intellectual requirements and their implications for everyday custom and practice, one acquires a genuine respect for the built-in capacity of the intellectual apparatus employed in daily life, as well as some appreciation of the positive role played by the knowledge embedded in custom and tradition—often wholly beyond individual awareness or consciousness—and not just an increased sensitivity to the potential for error that the system implies.

The Measuring Apparatus: One Normative Variable

$$([IV_1\ IV_2\ldots IV_n] \qquad [BV_1\ BV_2\ldots BV_n] \qquad [R_1\ R_2\ldots R_n])$$

| Inputs | Buffers | Rules |

Since the value of the normative variable can, in principle, be calculated by applying the rules, the overall structure is enclosed in parentheses.

The substance of the normative variables, the dimensions of individual life that determine its relative preferability (the "quality" of the life), cannot be identified in abstract terms; they are created out of human experience, direct or vicarious, and will include health, various psychic states, access to resources, and so on. The substance of the Input and Buffer variables, which depends on the normative variables in use, must likewise be created out of experience gained from efforts to deal with real cases. It is useful to lay out the procedure in wholly general terms because of the almost universal availability of *some* conceptual apparatus for use in almost any conceivable situation. There is neither need nor capacity for beginning with a blank slate. The most serious problem likely to be encountered in real situations, aside from testing the acceptability of the justification that can be offered for a particular preference or priority, is the need to translate from the conceptual apparatus used in the theories that project the outcomes into the concepts used to identify normative attributes. The structure of the particular normative variable provides the essential mechanism linking actions (changes in the values of Input variables) to normative consequences.

Measuring the Quality of Life. One more element is needed to complete the apparatus needed for directing human actions: differences in the values taken by one or more normative variables must be linked to the overall normative variable used to establish preferences, to the relative preferability of the condition of life of the individual. In effect, a structure must be created in which each of the particular normative variables becomes an element and some basis is available for comparing overall configurations of normative variables. The relation between the values taken by a configuration of Normative variables (NV) and the relative preferability of a condition of life, or state of existence, is precisely equivalent to the relation between the values taken by a set of Input and Buffer variables and the value of a particular normative variable.

Measuring the quality of individual life
$$([NV_1, NV_2. \ldots .NV_n] [R_1, R_2 \ldots R_n])$$

Overall preferability is a function of a configuration of normative variables and not a single variable, although the value of one normative variable may be decisive in particular cases. Health, for example, is only one factor to be considered when assessing the relative desirability of different conditions of life. Another set of rules is needed, then, that will link the values of the specific variables in a configuration to an overall value for the relative desirability of the set. As it turns out, "relative preferability" defies measurement and cannot be calculated directly from the values of any selection of normative variables. A different approach to preference is required, but that problem is best left to chapters 6, 7, and 8, where the development and justification of priorities or preference-orderings is examined in detail.

6

Preferences and Priorities: Introductory

The analysis and discussion of the justification of preferences is most effective if it is broken into three distinct stages, each focused on one aspect of the overall process. The overlapping and repetition produced by the analytic separation, which may be somewhat accentuated by the physical separation of the materials into three chapters, is probably advantageous, serving to clarify an admittedly complex yet somewhat vague and unfamiliar set of procedures and criteria. The first task, which occupies the remainder of this chapter, is to summarize the relevant limitations on normative inquiry, the major intellectual problems encountered in efforts to produce a justification for a preference—to enumerate the principal obstacles and impediments to be overcome and their implications for justification. In chapter 7, a way of justifying preferences that circumvents these restrictions is suggested and illustrated; in effect, it shows how the "best solution" to a justification problem can be produced within the limits of human capacity as presently understood. The major complications that emerge when the social context is factored into the justification of preferences are reserved for discussion in chapter 8.

The analysis is only sparsely illustrated, and most of the illustrations are taken from either medicine or agriculture. There are compelling reasons for restricting exemplifications to such fields. First, very few cogent and uncontentious examples are available in other areas of inquiry. Further, the kinds of intellectual problems that appear in normative justification are in most cases precisely exemplified within medicine or agriculture. Negatively, there is no identifiable body of informed and competent opinion presently in place from which authoritative illustrations might be obtained. Contemporary ethics or moral philosophy has not established the normative requirements for directing human actions on defensible grounds; philosophers have not, for the most part, concerned themselves with that question. And the normative systems actually in place have not been organized and evaluated in the ways that an action-based approach to normative affairs requires. Indeed, that kind of systematic assessment, which is contingent upon the availability of a body of informed and competent critics, emerges as one of the primary additions to normative inquiry needed in the immediate future. In short, examples of normative justification agreed to be valid and competent are at present very hard to find outside of medicine and agriculture. In the absence of agreement on fundamental criteria of argument, demonstrating the validity and competence of justifications offered as illustrations would be an almost impossible task. And efforts to exemplify the argument from within either classical or contemporary ethics, or from social science/social practice, are more likely to produce disagreement and confusion than to clarify the criteria needed to justify preferences.

In the present chapter, a brief overview of the structures and processes involved in justification is followed by a preliminary distinction between the kinds of evidence and argument that can be adduced to support knowledge claims in the sciences and in the normative realm, for this is a prime source of disagreements about normative conclusions. Three major types of constraints on inquiry are then examined serially: first, those shared with empirical inquiries—particularly those arising from the need to agree on fundamental assumptions, to develop and apply theories, to generalize, and to rely upon induction; second, limits that are peculiar to normative inquiry, such as the need for cut-off points or "benchmarks" to indicate unacceptable conditions of life, the kinds of measurement problems created by the use of normative concepts, and so on; and third, the special problems that appear in normative justification because of: (a) the forced reliance on argument rather than testing and in particular, the need to create a "discipline" that can serve as a base for the assessment of arguments; (b) the conditionality of normative conclusions; and (c) the central role of human judgments in preference. The chapter concludes with a brief account of four simplifications that can be used to bring the overall process under better control.

Overview: Structures and Processes

The structures and processes involved in systematic efforts to direct human actions on defensible grounds are captured in global terms within a deceptively simple five-step progression. First, a human actor is identified who has the capacity to produce some change in the environment by voluntary action. Whether analysis begins with a specific actor or with a situation in the environment that is considered unacceptable on normative grounds, the actor who *will* alter those conditions must be stipulated before the options available for choice can be determined and the process of establishing a preference can begin. Second, each of the outcomes lying within the actor's capacity at the time of action, plus the outcome to be expected if events are allowed to follow their present course uninterrupted (if the capacity is not used) is projected on the future as fully as the available time and resources, as well as knowledge, permit. Third, the content of the outcomes, specified as a set of values for some selection of normative variables, is compared in an appropriate context and either a preference is established for one outcome or the choice is judged a matter of indifference. The focus of comparison is the conditions of life of the human population that appears within the outcomes, of the individuals whose lives are altered by the action; the basic task is to find reasons in experience for preferring one of those life situations to any of the others. Fourth, the solution to the particular choice (here labeled a *preference*) is then generalized to create a *priority*, is transformed from a statement about particulars into a statement about classes of events. Fifth, the generalized statement, the priority, is accepted and applied. (Its implications for the situation in hand are calculated formally and then acted upon.) The priority must be clear and precise enough to force selection of the preferred outcome as a logical entailment once accepted. In effect, a solution to a particular choice is produced first; priorities are created by generalizing such solutions. The justification for a priority is always contingent upon the prior justification that can be provided for a particular preference.

In structural terms, each choice can be depicted as a matrix in which the projected conditions of life of each of the populations affected by action are arrayed for each of the available outcomes. (A simple matrix containing a two-option choice is shown below.)

TWO-OPTION MATRIX

Individual/group	Option A	Option B
one	Condition A-1	Condition B-1
two	" A-2	" B-2
three	" A-3	" B-3
———	———	———
"n"	" A-n	" B-n

Regardless of the number of options that are available and the size of the affected population, the matrix will retain certain basic characteristics. Two are particularly important in the present context: first, each option is treated as an entity and must be selected in its entirety; second, within any option, each person or group that is affected significantly but differently by the action must be separated from the others. Understandably, the structure expands very rapidly as the actor's capacity increases, but the conditions of life depicted by a given symbol can be quite complex so long as they hold for each of the persons to whom the symbol applies.

The priorities used for dealing with recurring choices are also simple structures. Because each outcome is compared to the others *as a whole*, it can be represented by a single element or symbol. For any n-option choice, if each complete option is symbolized by a single letter, the resulting priority will take the following form:

$$\text{Prefer A to B, C, D} \ldots \text{N unless X}$$
$$\text{or} \quad \text{A} > \text{B, C, D} \ldots \text{N unless X}$$

Once accepted, that pattern *forces* selection of option A in any situation where a choice must be made between options A,B,C,D...N, unless condition X is satisfied.

The crucial element in reasoned and defensible choice, the primary concern in normative inquiry, is the justification that can be offered for a particular preference. For that reason, the principal goal in the kind of epistemological/methodological inquiry undertaken here is to determine what sort of justification can be offered (and should be accepted) for a preference, under what set of limiting conditions—to show how the best justification possible can be produced and recognized, given the limits and possibilities that control normative inquiry. The substance of a justification, the reasons that support the preference, cannot be stated in general terms, for they combine the results of a systematic comparison of the available options, with the content of the relevant body of organized prior experience—suitably augmented by extrapolations and projections.

THE SHARED CONSTRAINTS

Caution suggests that discussion of the question proposed here as a focus for normative inquiry ("What is the best possible argument that can be offered to support a preference?") should begin with a brief examination of the two principal sources of infinite regress that plague all forms of argument. First, before any argument can be assessed, an argument about the factors that determine the quality of an argument must be created and evaluated. In some discussions, the two points are collapsed and considered together, and more commonly, such second-order questions are simply ignored. Yet, without a high level of agreement among those active in the field on (a) the more fundamental assumptions about the nature of inquiry that control and direct the production of evidence, and (b) the sets of expectations relating to the form and content of arguments that can be derived from them, arguments about justification of preferences will not intersect. Strictly speaking, neither agreement nor disagreement is possible under those conditions. Second, no argument in an inductive knowledge system can begin in a vacuum; some body of assumptions must be accepted before the search for knowledge can proceed.

The importance of reaching agreement on fundamentals, and in consequence of sharing common expectations about the use of evidence and argument, and the problems that emerge if there is no agreement, are well illustrated by the old and derisory apothegm about a mountain that "labored mightily" but gave birth to a mouse. The suppressed assumption, that the mountain could have made much better use of its time and energy, whether or not it is true, is in any case not obvious. It is at least possible that the mountain should be lauded for a major accomplishment rather than derided for indulging an exercise in futility. Judgments in such matters depend on the significance of the outcome, and the limits and possibilities that constrain the actor's efforts. Until those factors are made known and agreed among the protagonists (to the extent that they have been articulated), systematic efforts to reach an agreed assessment of performance are out of the question.

The point is particularly important with respect to normative inquiry of the kind undertaken here, for although there may be little disagreement about the significance of the preference being justified, there are profound and often unarticulated differences in fundamental assumptions, and in the kinds of expectations about justification derived from them, that frame discussion. Such differences tend to rule out productive argument about preferences or the priorities generalized from them. In most cases, assumptions relating to the canons of argument and their implications remain unstated, but they tend to be based upon the set of methodological assumptions commonly accepted in the physical sciences—which may be a reason why "humanists," who attack as "positivism" almost any effort to deal systematically with such questions, dislike them. And in fact, borrowing from physical science is in this case an error, leading to excessive expectations about the kind of arguments needed to justify a judgment or conclusion. Indeed, those who move from traditional philosophic inquiries to a practical concern with the justification of real-world actions on the basis of past human experience, find themselves forced by the conditions of inquiry to make successive reductions in their aspirations with respect to expected achievements. The small "mouse" of limited improvements on current practice, or the even smaller "mouse" of achieving some measure of clarification in basic tools and procedures, tends to be assessed more and more favorably as experience with practical problems cumulates—which may be no more than a rationalization of failure.

Scientific and Normative Argument

The common assumption that criteria of argument derived from the physical sciences should apply unaltered to normative discussions is as least as common, and just as pernicious, as the opposing assumption that such criteria have no role whatever to play in normative affairs. The differences between the methodological criteria to be applied to inquiries seeking to justify real world preferences, and the canons of inquiry accepted in the sciences, are profound but specific and fairly limited. Those that matter most are due to the differences in the content or substance of the conclusions that each seeks to justify.

It has already been argued that the same intellectual apparatus and the same fundamental procedures or strategies, are employed in each field. Each must deal with the logical gap between the knowledge needed to fulfill its basic purposes and the kind of information that the sensory apparatus can provide. But the escape route that is available given the questions that the sciences seek to answer (testing in use against pragmatic criteria of effectiveness) is closed to those seeking justifications for preferences. To satisfy its requirements, science can organize and generalize past experience, create formal patterns or models of the processes and relationships observed in experience that will account for the past and allow prediction of future events, including the effects of deliberate human actions, under specified limiting conditions. Normative inquiry, however, is not concerned to organize the past in order to predict or control the future, but to organize the past in ways that allow *selection* from among alternative futures, some of which may not have been experienced in the past. That requires assessment or preference, for in principle humans have the capacity to tailor the future to their own preferences or aspirations. Although scientific inquiry contributes greatly to that capacity, it does not, and cannot, given its canons of inquiry, control all of the judgments or decisions involved—although it can and should deal with those that fall within the province bounded by its own set of purposes.

The key to limiting the use of scientific canons of inquiry in normative argument lies in the differences in the kinds of conclusions or statements to be justified in the two areas. Such differences are reflected in the kinds of questions that are asked, and the kinds of evidence and argument that can be adduced as answers, given accepted limits on human capacity and on the functioning of the natural universe. As noted earlier, scientists seek answers to questions in the form: "What is the case?" or "What is likely to be the case if specified events occur under stipulated conditions?" To generate answers, they create and test classifications, forecasts, and theories, among other instruments. The underlying assumptions that direct scientific justification were, for the most part, developed with those questions or purposes in view.

In contrast, the central question in normative inquiry is: "Which of these outcomes should be preferred or chosen?" As the term is used here, the meaning of "preferred outcome" is purely normative. It is the outcome that is valued more than any of the others, the outcome that *should be* chosen by an informed and (normatively) competent actor. It is not necessarily the option that *will be* chosen by a given actor; that is an empirical matter falling within the purview of the psychologist or the student of socialization. Nor is it the option that would be selected if those affected by the action were to make the decision using their "revealed" preferences, extrapolated from past performance, as in welfare economics. Finally, the preferred outcome cannot be identified by reference to the procedure used to make the selection, even if the process has been labeled *rational choice* (and the meaning attached to that term, particularly by economists, has made it virtually useless for normative inquiry); the defensibility of a preference is independent of the process used to produce it. Such formulations are adequate within the mode of justification accepted within the sciences, and in some cases were adopted for that reason; they cannot be used to deal with normative conclusions, or to answer normative questions of the kind being considered here.

If agreement on the kind of argument that should be deployed and accepted for preferences or priorities is essential, then the only reasonable course of action available to normative inquirers is to make accessible to the reader or critic as much of the information required for assessment of performance as possible—on the understanding that complete articulation is out of the question. Agreement is needed first on the limits and possibilities that empower and constrain the prospective chooser. Some of the limiting assumptions here accepted as controlling normative argument have already been touched upon and can be summarized briefly; others are peculiar to normative inquiry, a function of the real-world meaning of the points that are being argued, and need to be treated in some detail.

The effects of not having a body of informed and competent critics in place are felt most strongly with respect to such fundamentals. The situation is particularly unfortunate because the justification of preferences is primarily an intellectual function, marked by complex and abstract reasoning. It is not now and is unlikely in future to be widely available to the public at large. True, the general public is often affected profoundly by normative decisions, and in the "representative self-governing" societies in particular, the agreement of at least the major part of the citizenry is usually assumed to be an essential prerequisite to the "legitimate" exercise of public authority. But ordinary citizens of "democratic" social organizations, however well-intended their behavior, are not very likely to produce valid justifications for preferences, or to be able to distinguish between spurious and competent justifications when exposed to both. As in medicine, they must rely on the consensus produced within a body of informed and competent persons to protect the quality of judgments. That is reasonably regarded as "elitism," and therefore a serious fault in the approach (although that criticism is not applied to physics or medicine yet both are elitist in that sense). But the conclusion cannot be avoided (presently at least) if the intellectual integrity of the justification process is to be preserved. Access to the skills required for competent normative argument can and should be opened to everyone; an equal opportunity to acquire the necessary knowledge and competence can at least be approximated. But if there is no agreement among the already well informed, little would be gained from the effort to extend competence beyond an increase in the number of voices on each side of numerous pointless arguments. The first order of business is to obtain agreement on the fundamental assumptions essential for stabilizing arguments in the field, and that requires technical competence. An effort can then be made to create an educated public opinion that is competent to render judgment in such matters—an outcome that may be difficult in practice, but is certainly possible in principle and has already been achieved experimentally on a small scale.[1]

That judgment, which seems inescapable, leaves a field of inquiry that can and does regularly have human consequences of enormous human significance virtually immune to criticism by "outsiders," at least for the present. Even if agreement can be reached within the community of "informed and competent" persons, they will then share an enormous burden of responsibility, of the kind best exemplified in the medical profession. Those responsibilities can be, and have been, abused; that may suggest the urgency of trying to educate the public in competent argument, with respect to normative as well as scientific matters, but does not alter the present situation. Obviously, agreement at the intellectual level is not always followed by appropriate behavior, even if everyone, including the general public, is convinced by the reasoning and evidence offered to support the conclusion—cigarette smoking illustrates the point precisely. But when the "informed and competent" disagree among themselves, as is presently the rule and not the exception, third parties (including governments) are left to choose among contentious advocates, or to rely on their instincts or hunches; the likelihood of significant improvements emerging from the field of inquiry, or from current practice, tends to diminish rapidly and dramatically.

Empirical Limitations

At the level of the five-step procedure set forth earlier in the chapter, various limits on normative intellectual performance are shared with physical science. Briefly summarized, they can serve to introduce the more specialized, and far more serious, limits that constrain the kinds of justification that can be provided for normative preferences. Comparisons of the sort needed to generate a preference, which are the most difficult part of normative justification, do not appear in the empirical disciplines except in a purely technical context (as a way of estimating the relative efficiency of alternative solutions to technical problems), and are examined separately.

Determining the Actor's Capacity. Even in the case of the single person, it may be difficult to determine the actual capacity of an actor, yet that is an essential prerequisite to justification. The person who is technically "capable" of performing a particular action but is psychologically unable to do so illustrates one kind of problem that plagues the normative inquirer; when the capacity of collective actors such as parliaments or legislatures is to be estimated, the complexities are greatly multiplied. If the search for a preferred outcome begins with a "normatively unacceptable" human situation, still other limitations appear. In some cases, such as the onset of a new disease like AIDS, no human actor may be competent to deal with the problem. In others, the actor with the requisite capacity may not be known to those actively concerned with the problem, or may not be personally aware of it and thus unable to volunteer. And finally, an actor may be aware of the undesirable situation, and capable of improving it, yet be "unable" to change it because other outcomes that lie within his or her capacity are judged to have even greater significance.

Projecting the Outcomes. Two basic types of difficulties arise with respect to the projections of outcomes, one shared with the sciences and the other peculiar to normative justification. The accuracy and adequacy of the concepts, theories, and other empirical instruments used to project the outcomes are assessed first; the reliability of the projections is then estimated as accurately as possible. Each of these factors may determine the judgment of preference. Very summarily, the empirical base on which normative operations are to be performed is stabilized as fully as existing knowledge, and the available time and resources, allows. The projections, which are analytically prior to normative decision in all cases, are here assumed to be agreed, but in everyday affairs disagreements ostensibly relating to "values" refer more often than not to empirical questions. That is, "What is likely to happen if action X is taken?" rather than "Is outcome A preferable to outcome B?" is the more common focus of normative disagreements, particularly in public discussion of public issues.

The second problem arising out of the need to project future outcomes is unique to normative inquiry: because the theories used to make the projections will rarely if ever employ concepts that refer directly to the normatively significant dimensions of human life, the projected outcomes must usually be translated into normative concepts after the projection has been completed. At a minimum, that creates yet another opportunity for errors of judgment to creep into the results; at worst, translation may turn out to be an impossible task. In effect, the concepts incorporated in the theories used to make future projections must serve as indicators for the set of normative concepts used to structure those outcomes for comparison. If theories make use of such concepts as "income level," the user must translate the projected income level into normative concepts relating to the conditions of individual life that can be used to assess the available outcomes. "Income level" may translate reasonably well into such normative concepts as levels of nourishment, or even adequacy of housing facilities, although both are likely to be disputed by at least some authorities, but the relation between income level and such aspects of life as psychic states may be difficult or even impossible to establish with confidence. The still more narrowly normative question relating to the projected outcomes, the adequacy of the selection of normative variables used to structure content, which is of prime importance for those seeking to justify preferences, does not appear in empirical or scientific inquiries. It will be discussed in chapter 7.

Generalization and Application. The potential difficulties associated with the process of generalizing, which transforms singular and particular propositions into statements about classes of events that are not restricted with respect to time or place, are common to all forms of inquiry. In effect, the process requires the generalizer to treat the particular case as an exemplar of a class of cases. The points where errors can appear are fairly obvious: aspects of the particular situation may be omitted that are essential for accurate classification; the elements selected as a basis for the classification may be unique to the particular case, and so on. Such errors create a more serious problem for normative inquirers than for those engaged in empirical inquiry because of the inability of the former to conduct the kinds of testing-in-use that is commonly employed in empirical inquiries to refine the conceptual apparatus.

The application of a pattern or logic to the world of experience or observation creates difficulties of the same order for both empirical and normative inquirers. Assuming that calculations are correct, the question whether or not the results should be accepted, and with that degree of confidence, depends fundamentally on the strength of the pattern; that in turn is a function of (a) correspondence with other established patterns that deal with the same or related phenomena; (b) the extent to which the limiting conditions for use can be stipulated precisely and extensively; and (c) the accuracy of the application, the degree of fit between the pattern (including its limiting conditions for use) and the situation to which it is applied. Given the vagueness, not to say ambiguity, of the concepts that are commonly employed in normative inquiry, and the undeveloped state of the field as a whole, it is probably reasonable to assume that application is in practice a much more hazardous enterprise in normative affairs than in the physical or even the social sciences.

Inductive Inquiry. Both the sciences and normative inquiry proceed "inductively," begin with particulars and only subsequently develop or create generalized patterns that can be used to achieve their respective purposes. The importance of induction in normative development tends to be masked by the fact that every choice occurs in a world that already contains a great many priorities, created in all manner of different ways and based on a wide range of different, and often incompatible assumptions. For reasons to be examined below, there is no alternative to using the available apparatus as a point of departure in justification, and then proceeding inductively to correct, improve, and extend the inherited structure.

Three points relating to the overall characteristics of inductively based knowledge systems are particularly important for normative inquiry. First, it is essential to note that the term does *not* refer to the way in which priorities are produced but only to the relation between conclusions and evidence, to the way in which conclusions are justified or "tested." No logic of creation need be implied. In its most useful sense, "induction" means an approach to inquiry in which the general is contingent on the specific, in which knowledge, whether normative or empirical, is not derived from first principles, and therefore cannot be tested by reference to its correspondence with some set of basic assumptions. In effect, a commitment to induction establishes the direction of contingency between experience and generalized propositions: a generalized priority is contingent upon particulars and not on some "higher" principle; in the event of conflict, the general and not the particular must yield. The critical element in the argument or justification offered for a priority is the relation between the results produced by accepting it and the content of past experience, and the latter is always decisive.

Second, the elements in any inductively based system of priorities *must* be ordered transitively where they intersect; otherwise, the overall structure is ambiguous and has no coercive power—it cannot be applied. In principle, transitivity makes possible the "reduction" or integration of the theoretical apparatus in the sciences, and of the priority system in normative affairs. In practice, formal reduction or integration may be extremely difficult to achieve and is very unlikely to progress very far in normative affairs given the present state of development of the field. Nevertheless, the transitivity assumption is a requirement in an inductive knowledge system and it greatly facilitates the justification of preferences.

Third, inductively based knowledge cannot be produced in a void, whether that knowledge is empirical or normative. There must be some body of knowledge already in place before inquiry can proceed; the larger the supply of available knowledge, the easier it becomes to generate and assess further claims to know. Very briefly, inductive inquiries are concerned almost exclusively with assessing, integrating, and augmenting an already established body of knowledge; they cannot begin with a tabula rasa.

To the extent that it has been created "inductively" from particular cases, a set of priorities will appear as a weakly linked collection and not as the kind of coherent structure that can be derived formally from a common body of axioms. Within the overall structure, some aspects of the human condition will be differentiated narrowly and carefully organized; others may be completely ignored or overlooked. Taken as a whole, the apparatus is roughly analogous to a road map that is full and detailed for some areas and nearly blank elsewhere. A sustained effort to create priorities using a common set of assumptions might in time produce a comprehensive and fully integrated structure, but in practice that seems very unlikely to occur, and may not be desirable—the assumptions employed are likely to change as human capacity, and human society, evolves. However, the apparatus can be systematized and integrated to a considerable extent, and that exercise is as necessary first step toward improving overall normative performance.

A note on nomenclature may be helpful at this point. The full set of priorities and benchmarks accepted by an individual is probably the best candidate available to be labeled an *ethic*. But labels are less important than meaning, and that meaning does not accord well with current usage, either in ethics and moral philosophy or in everyday affairs. The term "ethic" is therefore avoided. Instead, such terms as "preference-ordering" or "priority" and "priority system," will be used to designate elements in the apparatus and the overall apparatus respectively. Whatever the labels applied, everyone acquires a set of such basic tools over time; otherwise, there would be no way to deal systematically with everyday actions, and that would make life unbearable for both the actor and those affected by the actor's choices. However, the scope, content, and acceptability of the overall normative apparatus in use will vary widely. In those terms, a major problem for the inquirer is to find ways of assessing or evaluating the total apparatus as well as its individual elements. The problem is peculiarly difficult, in a way that is unique to normative inquiry, because the capacity to convince depends on the ability to argue rather than to demonstrate by test. In such arguments the assessment of elements is always to some degree contingent on prior acceptance of a whole in which the element plays an integral part, and the validity of the whole depends in turn on acceptance of the validity of its parts. The seeming impasse can be avoided in a system that functions in ongoing time with recurring events *if* the ability to deal with recurrences is adequate for the purposes of the knowledge user, but the conceptualization is complex and consistency in usage can be difficult to maintain.

CONSTRAINTS PECULIAR TO NORMATIVE INQUIRIES

In addition to these broad and very general limits or handicaps that normative inquirers must overcome and/or evade, limits shared to some extent with scientific and other disciplines, three types of requirements or constraints peculiar to normative affairs further restrict the kind of justification that can be offered for a preference. First, for both practical and analytic reasons, it is necessary to be able to identify outcomes that are assessed as either highly desirable or grossly unacceptable. Second, justification of preferences requires the capacity to make systematic comparisons of the content of the outcomes, focused on the desirability of the projected lives of the population affected by the action. Third, partly as a consequence of the first and second of these imperatives, the justification offered for a preference will depend on an unformalizable procedure best labeled a judgment. Conclusions based on judgments can be supported by evidence and systematic argument, but the process by which conclusions are reached cannot be formalized. Each of these requirements/constraints seriously limits the kind of justification that can be offered to support a preference. The reasons why they must be accepted, and the more important of their implications for the justification of preferences, are summarized briefly below. A more detailed discussion of the implications of forced dependence on the judgmental process, and the kinds of arguments that can be produced to support conclusions reached by that process, then follows.

The Need for "Benchmarks"

The need to be able to identify human situations that are regarded as grossly unacceptable or highly desirable can be argued on both practical and analytic grounds. Nearly every actor has the capacity to perform a variety of different actions at any given time; a "choice among choices" is therefore preliminary to virtually every action. Systematic comparison of successive pairs of outcomes within an adequate intellectual framework can, under some conditions at least, establish which outcome, if any, is *relatively* preferable to the others. But practically speaking, such judgments are inadequate for directing actions, for if all of the members of the set of choices from which the initial "choice of choices" is made are trivial, then efforts to achieve the preferred outcome, identified in relative terms, could be very costly, especially if they interfered with subsequent opportunities to achieve or avoid a far more significant outcome. An element of "future orientation," of holding capacity in reserve against future contingencies, is essential in human affairs as in warfare. In the absence of some capacity to identify conditions to be sought or avoided, such potential concerns may suffer. There are also compelling practical reasons for agreeing on a set of "cutoff" values of normative variables that identify conditions of life considered "grossly unacceptable" or "highly desirable" under specified limiting conditions (here labeled *benchmarks*). Much human activity is normatively trivial and can safely be ignored; only a very few of the total number of choices facing each individual in an ordinary day can be taken seriously. The use of such "benchmarks" makes it possible to concentrate on significant choices to the fullest extent possible by facilitating quick and efficient separation of trivial from grossly unacceptable (or very desirable) outcomes.

That much said, it should be emphasized that absolute judgments of significance are impossible in principle within the limits of human capacity. At most, the points of reference used to make judgments of extreme human situations can be stabilized, thus providing a practical tool that is very useful for making choices, and that can be corrected and improved out of experience over time. Human affairs probably could not proceed very far without creating some apparatus of this kind; every human actor needs, and develops, a set of such benchmarks or cut-off points, whether the actor is an isolated individual or a collectivity such as a family, tribe, or national state. Obviously, the more important benchmarks are those used in collective decisions that affect large populations in fundamental ways—those accepted by a national state, for example—but all normative systems in use contain them in some form, whether they are recognized or not. They are effective so long as they do not overlap with other incompatible systems of assumptions (a point to be examined more fully in chapter 8).

An obvious corollary to the need to be able to identify both unacceptable and highly desirable conditions of individual life is the need to locate those actions likely to produce them under specified environmental conditions. It cannot be assumed that every option available to an actor will be fully explored before a decision is made. Any number of factors can intervene: shortage of time, scarcity of resources, lack of awareness or sensitivity on the actor's part, or simply inadequate knowledge, among others. There are also practical limits on the demands that can be placed on the neural machinery; a substantial part of the total range of actions lying within real capacity must be ignored or regarded with indifference, otherwise the overall functioning of the intellectual apparatus may be affected adversely. The necessary selectivity can be achieved without serious detriment to performance if unacceptable or desirable conditions of human life can be identified at sight, or more commonly, if the actions that are liable to produce them have been located and tagged.

Assessments of the unacceptable and the highly desirable are incorporated into the overall apparatus employed here as benchmarks, cutoff points on the values taken by particular normative variables or combinations that separate the unacceptable and the desirable from the trivial. They perform an essential function in normative decisions and supporting arguments. For example, in many and perhaps in most cases, the impetus to normatively driven action flows from a judgment of the egregious character of specific conditions observed in the environment. Of course, agreeing that a situation is "unacceptable" does not mean that it can be improved at acceptable cost, any more than being able to identify highly desirable conditions implies that they should be sought at any price. But it does provide a vital focusing mechanism for inquiry and decision. The alternatives may be worse; a desirable condition may lie beyond reach. But without some capacity to identify the unacceptable and the desirable in concrete and specific terms, efforts to direct human behavior would be left in a position roughly equivalent to modern medicine shorn of its knowledge of both dangerous states of health and the attributes of a "normally healthy" person. Further, given the assumptions on which justification depends, judgments of preference in decisions involving serious consequences for large populations will be based, in most cases, on the size of the population placed in "grossly unacceptable" conditions of life in each of the outcomes, for reasons that will be explored more fully in due course.

The principle impediment to the development of universal benchmarks is the pluralist character of contemporary society. The various social organizations to which an individual belongs will each have some impact on the positioning of the normative benchmarks in the individual's priority system, on the assessment made of particular life states. And conversely, the set of benchmarks accepted and applied by the various social organizations, and particularly by the national states, will profoundly influence the conditions of life of very large human populations. When the benchmarks accepted by the individual and the society differ markedly, that can lead to nearly unbearable tensions. It is a commonplace that conditions of human life that are regarded as grossly unacceptable in one national state may be considered normal or treated with indifference in another. And within a national state, conditions of life that are ignored within one family may occasion alarm and concern in another. Further, the normative system actually applied within a national state, since it is usually combined with powerful social or cultural myths and vague historical traditions, tends to limit or define the scope of individual and collective responsibilities. That in turn will usually determine whether a remedy is sought mainly or entirely through self-help, the family, private voluntary associations, or some form of collective action by a public agency. Over the long run, such decisions can determine the conditions of life of major segments of the society. In any case, all such responses, whatever their character, are triggered by an initial recognition of the "unacceptability" of observed conditions of life in some part of the overall society. A normative apparatus that could not perform that function would be seriously inadequate for directing human actions.

The need to know which actions are particularly liable to produce such unacceptable outcomes is equally urgent, for that kind of knowledge plays a major role in both formal and informal socialization. Parents use it to instruct their children when to act with extreme caution because of the potential danger of serious injury to the self or to others. More generally, any actor with substantial capacity to produce change but limited decision time can probe only a very small part of capacity prior to action. Some basis for making a selection is essential, and knowing which actions are especially liable to produce highly undesirable (or highly desirable) outcomes can help to reduce the likelihood of serious error. Similarly, persons vested with the capacity to cause serious injury to the self or to others need to be aware of it, and to know which of the actions lying within capacity are most likely to result in such unwanted outcomes. Those newly appointed to positions that carry great potential to harm others, such as members of a police force, are commonly introduced to job performance from that perspective through various kinds of orientation and training programs.

Comparisons: The "Measurement" Problem

A second set of impediments to the justification of preferences is a function of the basic assumptions on which justification depends and the conceptual apparatus they enforce. The overall instrumental requirements for directing actions, and the limits on human capacity generally, have already been examined. The narrower and more specific limits that constrain normative justification are, for the most part, a function of the measurement and conceptual problems created by the commitment to using individual human life as the basic unit of significance in choice or preference, while at the same time relying on systematic comparisons as a basis for justification. They can be referred to collectively as "the measurement problem."

Four of the limits on the development of an adequate normative apparatus, which may be construed as different ways of looking at one basic problem in measurement and comparison, are particularly important. First, a standard unit for measuring the relative desirability of human lives lies beyond human capacity. Second, human life cannot be represented adequately (for normative purposes) by any single concept or variable. Third, human lives are not completely interchangeable; each human life follows a "track" through time that is in some respects unique, which tends to limit legitimate comparisons in quite significant ways. Finally, preferences or priorities cannot be tested using the procedures and criteria commonly employed to test empirical knowledge claims. Each of these constraints is a consequence of having to create an intellectual apparatus that is adequate for directing human actions on defensible grounds within the limits of human capacity. In combination, they create a "measurement" problem that parallels in many respects the induction problem that arises in empirical inquiry as a consequence of the need to depend on the sensory apparatus for information, although the former seems on the whole less tractable, much more difficult to evade.

The remainder of this volume is usefully regarded as a systematic examination of the extent to which the "measurement" and other related problems can be overcome within the limits of human capacity. The discussion begins with a closer look at the reasons why the limitations responsible for the "measurement" problem arise. They hinge on the meaning of two fundamental terms, "preference" and "a human life," and the consequent difficulties encountered in efforts to produce measures for the fundamental normative continuum or to test the normative assumptions used for directing actions. That will provide a framework for discussion of the manner and extent to which those difficulties can be evaded, and of the price to be paid for the evasion.

The Basic Continuum: Human Life. If the justification for a preference must be based on a systematic comparison of the outcomes available for choice, it follows that the quality of the justification is contingent on the kinds of measurements and comparisons that can be made. That in turn is a function of the nature of the continuum to be measured. One set of limits on the kind of justification that can be offered for any preference, hence on the kind of justification that must be accepted with respect to preferences, is a function of the kinds of measurements that are possible given the continuum enjoined by the basic assumptions accepted for inquiry. The information that can be produced within the limits of human capacity must be adequate to justify preferences. Or, to invert the point, the kind of evidence and argument that must be accepted as adequate justification for a preference is determined by the limits of human capacity as presently understood and the limits imposed by the conceptual apparatus presently available for dealing with the quality of an individual human life. Acceptance must, of course, be "knowing," aware of the limitations inherent in the best available justification.

Two basic modes of comparison—two ways of making measurements—are available to human inquirers; the analytic requirements are quite different for each case. The first, which can be labeled *indirect* comparison, requires that the continuum on which comparisons are made be of an order that allows development of a standard unit of measurement. Comparison proceeds by first measuring each of the things to be compared, using the standard unit, then making comparisons indirectly, using those measurements. The alternative is to specify a continuum for making comparisons and to compare two or more things *directly* on that continuum, avoiding the need to create a standard unit. In such direct measurements, one of the things measured serves as the "standard unit" used to make the comparison, but the unit itself can remain incompletely defined.

In statistical parlance, indirect measurements produce interval or ratio scaling, direct measurements generate only an ordinal scaling. Either process can be used to make comparisons of two or more things. The results of indirect measurements can be transitively ordered to show the kind and *amount* of difference among the ordered elements; direct comparisons, which can also produce a transitive ordering of a set of things, cannot, for obvious reasons, specify the amount of difference between any two of the ordered elements. Other things equal, more information is produced by the use of indirect measurements rather than direct measurements. And formal or mathematical treatment of the information produced by valid indirect measures can generate propositions relating to the range of differences among outcomes, and to the relations that hold among *all* of the things compared, that are impossible when direct measurements are employed.

For most purposes, indirect measures, and the kinds of comparisons they make possible, are highly desirable. Their availability, however, hinges upon the creation of a standard unit for measuring the continuum used to make the comparisons. That in turn depends on the meaning of the continuum being measured. In normative affairs, the things compared are in all cases individual human lives (the preferability of aggregates is determined by examining the status of individuals within the aggregate); the goal is a measure of the *relative preferability* of lives that differ in various ways. Thus far, efforts to produce a standard unit for measuring the relative preferability of different conditions of human life have proved futile. At a minimum, a standard unit is unlikely to appear in the near future, and there are some reasons to suppose such measures are unattainable in principle. That is unfortunate, for if the preferability of a human life could be measured indirectly, priorities could be stated and validated in the simple form, "choose the most preferable outcome." Absent a standard unit of measurement, priorities or rules of preference stated in that form (Choose the option that carries the highest "utility" value, for example) are effectively ruled out. The same reasoning serves to eliminate such formulations as "prefer the option that contains the greatest amount of good for the greatest number of persons" from use in directing human actions. The reason for the limitation is in both cases the same: each requires the capacity to measure individual states of life (indirectly) and sum the results, and that is not possible without a standard unit of measurement.

The data used for arguing or justifying preferences cannot, then, come from indirect comparisons. However, ordinal measurements could also supply the information needed to establish preferences, and little would be lost by the substitution. Indeed, reliance upon indirect measurements in the justification of preferences would probably be avoided in any event, since they introduce an unnecessary complication into a field of inquiry that is already quite difficult enough. All that is required for creating priorities is identification of the "preferred" outcome, the outcome that ranks highest on the "preferability" continuum used to compare individual lives—with due regard for what has already been said about the need for benchmarks. Ordinal measurements are quite adequate for that purpose.

Unfortunately, direct measures of the relative desirability of different states of human life also lie beyond human capacity. At a minimum, ordinal measures require an adequately specified continuum, a clear statement of "what is being measured," and that cannot be supplied at present. Much the same situation occurs in psychology with respect to such concepts as "intelligence." Although an organized structure can be created that makes possible defensible judgments of preference—at least to the same extent that a physician can judge one patient to be in much poorer health than another even though the precise meaning of the term "health" remains uncertain, or a psychologist can compare "intelligence" using a standardized test—the measurement problem remains insoluble in principle in all such cases. A practical working solution, an evasion of the difficulty, can be created, but the price of using it is a serious weakening of the argument or justification that can be offered to support the judgments on which conclusions depend and a consequent expansion of areas of potential disagreement that cannot be settled by reasoned argument.

Irreducibility. From a slightly different perspective, if the continuum used for making comparisons, the continuum to be measured, is the "relative preferability" of different conditions of individual human lives, and a strategy based on direct comparisons is unavoidable, the overall quality of a human life must be reducible to a single variable whose value can be "measured" by direct comparison—the same sort of reduction is necessary to meet the transitivity requirement imposed on priorities. That leads once again to the "measurement problem." Although a human life can be represented more or less accurately by a configuration of variables, the representation is always incomplete. The full meaning of the concept or continuum on which human lives can be measured or compared is not captured in any finite selection of variables. It follows that no rule can be produced linking the values of some set of variables to the value of a single variable that represents the overall preferability of an individual life. It can be agreed that a number of dimensions of individual life, each captured by a single variable, play an important part in determining the relative preferability of that life, and that allows the creation of benchmarks, but in principle "life" must be treated as a complex variable whose meaning cannot be specified fully in terms of the values taken by any finite selection of other variables. Technically, then, every measurement made on the "condition of life" continuum will be partial and incomplete, based on *some* of the sub-units in a complex set. Other aspects of life that might have been included in the measurement (had they been known) would therefore have to be regarded as statistically independent, as not affecting the measurement, before it could be used. That assumption, though pious, and perhaps necessary, opens the way for truly egregious errors of judgment. For that reason, among others, an alternative approach to justifying preference is essential. If none can be produced, partial configurations must be extended as fully as current knowledge permits before being applied, leaving it to experience to produce the limits to be enforced on use or application.

One of the best illustrations of the nature of the conceptual/measurement problem labeled "irreducibility" is found in the field of art. For purposes of measurement, the concept "quality of a painting" (not potential selling price) is precisely analogous to the concept "relative desirability of an individual life." The quality of a painting relates to the various factors that determine its quality in precisely the same way that the desirability of a human life relates to the factors that influence its desirability. As in normative judgments, the full set of factors at work in any particular case cannot be specified with assurance. Further, a painting's quality cannot be expressed fully and adequately by combining the values taken by each of the contributing elements through an appropriate rule, and efforts to do so are merely a special form of the composition fallacy. In effect, a valid rule linking the values of such particular elements or variables to the overall quality of the painting lies beyond human capacity. Comparisons of the overall quality of two or more paintings therefore cannot be carried out using such rules and configurations alone. Judgments of the value of a painting can be made, but they must employ an alternative or augmented set of structures and processes. Similar problems arise in any field of inquiry concerned with grading or qualitative assessment of two or more units or elements.

A painting, to put the matter differently, is valued holistically. Of course, knowing the factors that contribute to the quality of a painting (use of color, balance, brushwork, and so on) is essential for criticizing or assessing overall quality. Poor balance, for example, may reduce the quality of a painting, but it is also the case that the balance of a painting may be "wrong" without seriously affecting its quality. Indeed, imbalance may be introduced deliberately to produce a particular effect, thus enhancing the quality of the overall product.

The consequences of the holism requirement may be obvious, but they can be devastating for the kind of inquiry undertaken here. For it follows that no amount of observation or comparison of two paintings in isolation can supply *all* of the information needed to justify choosing or preferring one rather than the other. In art, as in normative affairs, preferences for one product of human actions rather than another require holistic comparisons, *made in terms of some external referrent,* some overall conception of what a painting, or a particular class of paintings, can be (a conception, needless to say, that is itself susceptible to change over time out of experience). Evaluations of two or more entities of the same order as paintings, or conditions of human life, depend absolutely on such an external frame of reference, an overall construction of what a painting, or a human life, can be. That apparatus must somehow be extrapolated from past experience before qualitative assessments are possible.

Incomparability. Thus far, the discussion has focused on the kind of measurement problem encountered in efforts to compare two or more states of a single human life. When more than one individual is affected by action or choice, a further complication emerges: the relative pre-

ferability of any given condition of life varies from one person to another. A life state that would be regarded as a disaster for one person
might be considered an improvement for another, even within a common culture. Each life follows a unique track, and preferences must be
established within its limits. In effect, no human situation can be assessed in absolute terms; each assessment is made by comparing the
different life states available to the particular individuals involved. Yet
human actions, and particularly collective actions, often affect a number of different lives in different ways, and some basis for preferring
complex configurations of different lives is essential if choices involving a number of different lives are to be justified.

Within the analytic framework, the problem of comparing different
states of individual lives is handled by the way in which alternatives
are projected, and by limiting statements of preference to specified sets
of alternatives. If the consequences of inaction, of allowing the free flow
of events to continue, are included among the set of options available
for choice, that effectively resolves the "incomparability" problem for
any choice involving a single individual. And if several lives can be
aggregated and then included in the outcomes, the apparatus remains
adequate in principle. However, only those individuals or groups whose
lives will have the same attributes if the course of events is allowed to
flow without interruption, those whose lives will be affected in the
same way by the introduction of a specific change (who share a common
set of Buffer variables that take specified values), can be aggregated.
Aggregation cannot, moreover, eliminate the need for an external reference point in the justification of preferences; the assessment system
must be anchored somewhere. But objective, additive measures that
could provide the needed baselines are beyond reach. An external point
of reference must therefore be found or created before preferences can
be supplied with an adequate justification.

A good illustration of the "incomparability" problem, and a sound
approach to resolving it, can be found within the field of medicine.
From an analytic perspective, the concept "state of health" is of precisely the same order as the concept "relative preferability" of different
life states. No standard unit can be developed for measuring either
concept; neither meaning can be captured fully by stating the values
of any finite set of variables. The state of a person's health, like the
relative preferability of two life states, is a complex concept whose
meaning and significance *depend on* the values taken by a number of
specific variables but are *not captured fully* by any finite configuration
of variables. When a physician compares two or more "states of health"
of a single person, or the "states of health" of two or more persons, he
or she is performing the same type of intellectual operation as an art
critic who argues for assessing the quality of one painting higher than

another, or an individual who expresses a preference for one condition of life rather than another.

Clearly, the evidence needed to assert either that patient P is "healthier" at time t_1 than at time t_2, or that patient P is "healthier" than patient Q at some fixed time, cannot be produced from direct observation of the two patients alone. Yet physicians make such judgments frequently, if crudely, and can justify doing so; the reasons why that is the case are explored in more detail in chapter 7. Further, in medicine, as in human action generally, some capacity for defensible multi-person comparisons is essential; no proposed approach to the justification of preferences would be regarded as adequate if it could not deal with that class of problems. A solution to the incomparability problem has been produced within medicine that seems to be adequate for physicians' purposes (for making needed judgments of preference); whether that solution can be adapted to human preferences generally, an equivalent apparatus must be created before an adequate field of inquiry can emerge.

Testing. Given the basic purpose pursued here (identifying the kind of knowledge required to maintain and/or improve the conditions of life of some human population), the "relative preferability" of different states of human life, singly and in combinations, must somehow be established and justified—some form of priority or preference-ordering is essential. The needed apparatus can certainly be created; the only limit functioning there is a failure of imagination. But the complexities generated by the peculiar character of the normative conceptual apparatus, combined with the need for justification, produce a "testing problem" with reference to priorities that is essentially insoluble. Neither particular preferences ("Situation A is preferable to situation B") nor generalized priorities ("Given a choice between outcome A and outcome B, choose outcome A") can be "tested" in the same sense that empirical propositions, whether particular or general, are testable. Even if all of the limitations that hold for testing empirical propositions are taken into account, the tests that have been developed for use in that area cannot be applied to normative propositions. In principle, that limitation rules out at least some approaches to the justification or improvement of priorities.

The nature of the limitation is readily stated. Empirical knowledge consists in sets of propositions that either (a) state the content (assumed) of observation (X is/was the case), (b) link the content of two or more observations (See X expect Y under condition C), or (c) link actions to their consequences (Do X under condition C, expect Y). Each such proposition implies a fairly obvious testing procedure: descriptions are tested against competent observations; forecasts are tested by first observing one event in nature under suitable conditions and then waiting for the appearance of the anticipated event; theories are tested by acting in a given way under appropriate conditions and comparing the events observed to follow to the events anticipated as a result of applying the theory. Of course, the adequacy of a justification based on such tests can be questioned, and the questioning, relentlessly pursued, will lead to an infinite regress. In practice, however, the regress can be headed off by stipulating, and justifying, pragmatic criteria of adequate performance or by developing conventions (from a pragmatic base) for determining whether performance is acceptable. The "justifications" produced in this way remain logically incomplete, but accepting pragmatic criteria of adequacy provides a practical and humanly useful way of evading the formal impasse.

With respect to propositions in the form "Prefer A to B," even that limited kind of testing is ruled out given the meaning of the term "prefer." The testing problem is not a function of uncertainty due to sensory dependence, as in the justification of empirical propositions, but an obstacle created by the absence of a "testable" meaning. The question whether or not a particular actor *prefers* A to B is readily tested. The question whether condition of life A *should be* preferred to condition of life B, irrespective of the actor concerned, which must be answered if action based on that preference is to be justified, cannot be "tested" by acting upon it. Such actions would produce evidence that could be used in the justification offered for the preference, but the evidence would not of itself be such a justification. Thus, an action based on a preference provides an opportunity to respond affectively to the situation created by applying the preference, and that reaction serves as a test of the empirical proposition that an individual's affective reaction to that outcome is of a particular order. But it does not and cannot test the normative proposition that the situation produced *should be* preferred to the available alternatives.

In normative justification, then, "testing" must be replaced by some alternative procedure. The best, and perhaps only, viable alternative available is *argument*, a process of giving reasons and evidence to support a particular conclusion or judgment. A priority must be assumed, in the same manner as any other intellectual instrument, before it can be acted upon; reasons and evidence are required to justify making the assumption. Those reasons, taken in conjunction with the content of past experience, become the focus for subsequent argument. The process of "pushing back" the argument step by step will lead eventually to: (a) agreement, (b) disagreement focused on an identifiable difference in assumptions, or (c) an irresolvable difference in judgment. The main analytic requirement is for an appropriate set of canons for controlling or assessing the conduct of the argument. That generates yet another set of problems or handicaps to be overcome in the process of justifying preferences—specifying criteria for judging arguments.

ARGUMENT: LIMITATIONS AND USES

The need to depend on argument rather than testing accounts for most of the primary differences between the justification of normative and empirical conclusions. Actions can produce evidence that is useful for arguing that one human situation should be preferred to another, but it is the argument, the use made of the evidence (the way it is linked to other aspects of human experience), and not the evidence per se, that is crucial. An argument in turn depends ultimately on a complex process conveniently labeled "an exercise of judgment." It amounts to using the overall intellectual capacity of the individual to perform a holistic measurement or comparison, to generate a value for a complex variable—to produce and defend a judgment of the value of a particular painting, or to justify a preference for one state of individual life rather than another, for example. Some element of judgment is found in all forms of intellectual activity; the quality of every proposition outside of formal logic depends ultimately on the competence with which judgments are made.

The judgments that enter into normative decisions differ in some very important respects from those required in empirical inquiries. Therefore, the justification that can be offered to support a preference for one human condition rather than another, or that can be required from those seeking to justify accepting such a preference, will differ from the justification that can be used, and should be accepted, in support of, say, a judgment to the effect that a given body of evidence warrants accepting a particular set of medical assumptions about the outcome to be expected from a mode of treatment given a patient in a particular state of health. The basic structures and processes will be very similar in both cases; the persuasiveness of the result may vary considerably. The principal determinant of persuasiveness will be the level of development of the field in which the argument occurs. Identifying the factors that determine or influence that "level of development" is an important part of creating the apparatus for assessing arguments, for deciding whether to be persuaded.

The transitivity requirement allows the justification of preferences, and the supporting argument, to proceed as if all choices consisted of only two elements or options. The actor or critic need only supply reasons for preferring one of two options, or for regarding the choice between them as a matter of indifference. Resolving successive two-element choices will in due course produce a solution to any choice problem. The key to success is the adequacy or power to convince a competent critic of the set of reasons adduced for preferring one outcome to another—the argument must convince the "right" persons (informed opinion) for the "right" reasons. Leaving aside frivolous assertions, almost any reason may be considered adequate in the absence of counter-argument; assertions of preference for which no argument is provided can be ignored. Arguments or justifications are targeted at actions or choices and do not transfer automatically or necessarily to the actor, whether the actor is an individual or a collectivity.

At present, little can be said about the substantive characteristics of an adequate or convincing reason for preferring one outcome to another, although some common characteristics of successful arguments can be identified; too much depends on the specific factors involved. The kinds of arguments that can be offered to support a preference emerge only in the course of serious efforts to deal with real cases—an indication of the relatively weak state of development of the field. That limits what can be accomplished in general inquiries such as this one rather severely. The best that can be hoped for is a summary account of the major limitations and possibilities that are associated with the process. A handbook for making decisions is effectively ruled out by the data-dependent nature of argument in undeveloped fields.

The Basic Apparatus: Overview and Illustration

Normative arguments are based upon comparisons; comparisons cannot be performed in the absence of a suitable context. A fairly complex set of assumptions is required for even the simplest comparison. The overall context required is roughly equivalent to the full set of assumptions and data, the body of established information and knowledge, combined with the relevant canons of inquiry and argument, that is generated within a competent physical scientist through training and experience and used in the justification of theoretical claims. That overall apparatus is what gives meaning to terms and force to arguments within the field. It will be labeled a *discipline*. The term is somewhat misleading, for a "discipline" (quotes used to indicate the special meaning attached to the term) need not be academic or even based on systematic inquiry and cumulation, for every form of human activity will in due course generate an overall apparatus of this kind, but it conveys the basic character of a very complex construct better than any other available label. A "discipline" that is adequate for informed, competent normative inquiry, that can be used to create and justify, criticize, and/or improve preferences and priorities, and the policies based on them, is not available at present. But some parts of an adequate "discipline" are always found in current usage, in normative inquiry as elsewhere, and the major constituent elements of an adequate "discipline" can be identified, the prime requirements that each major element in the "discipline" must satisfy can be established, and their implications for inquiry can be explored in quite useful ways.

Most of the essentials of the basic apparatus required for justifying and improving intellectual tools in an ongoing human situation have been captured at least implicitly by Norton E. Long in a simple, everyday illustration that deals with an empirical instrument, but incorporates a set of general principles that holds equally well for normative affairs:[2]

> We are not bemused by the fact that a hammer is an instrument devised in action for the purposes of action, and improved in action for purposes of action that themselves improve with the improved possibilities the hammer's improvement opens up. Sextus Empiricus' arguments on the criterion against the dogmatists hold no terrors of an infinite regress for the improver of hammers. Like Sextus the skeptic, the improver of hammers—quite undogmatically unconcerned with metaphysical impossibilities—goes on in a humanly meaningful way to improve his hammer.... And men by their practice agree that he has made an improvement.

The basic prerequisites to justification of preferences or improvement of normative performance are readily available in Long's illustration. First, a critic, or "improver of hammers," must have a well-defined purpose to be achieved by applying an instrument or tool, something must need to be "hammered" before an improvement can be made in hammers. Absent a purpose that could be fulfilled by hammering, there would be no hammer, no reason for seeking to produce a hammer, and no way of judging that the search had succeeded if, by accident or design, it proved to be "successful."

Second, a hammer must be available before hammering can begin or before hammers can be improved, although in the absence of a hammer, recognition of the need for an instrument able to fulfill the purposes of hammering could lead to the creation of a hammer. Since it can be assumed for purposes of normative inquiry that some apparatus is already in place, the special problems that arise in that process can safely be ignored here. The available normative structure may not be perfectly suited to the particular case in hand, but it can usually be adapted to fit, and that is generally, though not invariably, an easier task then beginning *de novo*. The prospective learner who must first "unlearn" before learning can commence illustrates the most common exception to the rule.

Third, a "discipline" is needed that summarizes, generalizes, and extends the knowledge available in the field. It includes, among other things, an overall construction of the targeted process or activity, a conception of "hammering" that encompasses the available knowledge of and past experience with hammering, of things that have been hammered, and of what has been used to do the hammering. Beyond such generalized historical experience, an adequate "discipline" will include both the criteria applied to argument and justification in the past, and the results produced by applying them—an integrated priority system that orders the various states of the world that have been produced in the past by hammering. And if the "discipline" is well-developed, it will also include a range of extrapolations and speculations relating to what "could be" hammered or what "could be" used to perform the hammering function.

Finally, a "discipline" implies "awareness" on the part of practitioners, particularly of principles developed in other fields that could be applied to hammering, and of the problems that have been encountered in the past and the way in which they have been solved. "Disciplines" of this order are essential for making qualitative judgments of the performance of those who hammer, of those who design hammers and/or suggest new ways of hammering or new things to be hammered, and for assessing the justifications offered to support the claim that an "improvement" has been made in either instrument or purpose. Such an evolving conception of the overall process of "hammering," which is a product of self-conscious efforts to hammer, is an essential tool for criticizing and improving the knowledge and instruments employed in hammering—and for improving the overall process itself and thus opening the ways for the creation of still further knowledge and even better instruments.

In addition to an integrated priority-system or preference-ordering, an adequate hammering "discipline" will include a set of benchmarks that can be used to identify the grossly unacceptable, the highly acceptable, and the trivial outcomes produced by hammering. Benchmarks, which are derived from a combination of the integrated priority system and the overall construction of "hammering" built into the discipline, perform such functions as suggesting that efforts to "hammer" likely to cause serious injury to the self or to others are unacceptable. They are derived from and depend for their validity upon the content of past experience, including judgments made of the content of that experience. Benchmarks are essential in any field that makes qualitative assessments of actions or outcomes but their function is perhaps more easily seen in the kinds of choices required for policymaking.

Finally, the "discipline" must include a body of informed and competent users, a collection of persons who by virtue of their knowledge of "hammering" will be able to judge, always tentatively, that an improvement in hammers or hammering, or a valuable extension of the process to another area of activity, has been produced. Since some of those informed and competent users will be engaged in hammering, at least some of their judgments may be expressed in actions rather than through verbal reactions or comments, thus producing real-world effects that become part of "relevant" experience. That serves to create or reinforce the connection to real-world affairs, and provides a potential channel for refining and improving the content of the overall "discipline."

An Adequate Normative "Discipline"

Transposing those intellectual prerequisites into normative terms, the minimum requirements for justifying or criticizing preferences are: (1) a real-world case in which one or more human lives are to be maintained and/or improved; (2) some capacity to identify the significant dimensions of individual life and to assign a preference-ordering to different configurations of those variables (a set of normative concepts and a set of more-or-less integrated priorities); (3) an intellectual apparatus in which the conditions of human life that have appeared in the past, the preference-orderings imposed upon them, and the arguments and evidence used to justify them are consolidated and integrated (in effect, a summary of the choice problems encountered in the past, of the instruments created to deal with them, and of the results obtained by applying those instruments, plus a range of extrapolations or speculations about the kinds of choice problems that could appear in the future and how they might be treated); (4) a set of benchmarks that indicate (a) conditions of human life considered so unacceptable that they suffice to eliminate an outcome from consideration, and (b) other conditions of life regarded as highly desirable; and (5) a number of informed and competent users or consumers of such knowledge, some of whom are engaged in real-world activity that employs or depends upon the results produced within the field.

A "discipline" that is adequate for generating, applying, and improving human knowledge, whether empirical or normative, consists of a number of closely interrelated, mutually reinforcing parts, each of them at least partly independent of the others. One of the basic elements in an adequate normative discipline, the conceptual apparatus (normative variables) used to state the normatively significant content of the outcomes available for choice or to identify the normatively significant dimensions of individual human lives, has already been discussed in some detail. The others, including the priority system used to locate the preferred outcome within a given set, have been treated only briefly and require further elaboration. That elaboration will provide the point of departure for a discussion of the conditionality of normative arguments and the role of judgments in the overall process.

Integration. The most obvious prerequisite to the justification of a preference is the availability of an "integrated" priority system, a collection of priorities or preference-orderings that has been used in the past to organize the recurring configurations or states in which human life has appeared to show their relative preferability. Absent a starting point, humanity would have no alternative to proceeding by trail-and-error methods—at enormous cost. The actual historical process by which priorities emerge remains uncertain, but, since they are found everywhere, that is not cause for concern. Future development, however, is contingent upon the availability of the other elements of an adequate "discipline"; priorities do not emerge alone and in isolation.

The transitivity requirement allows every complex choice to be broken into a sequence of two-element choices. If development of priorities begins with a single human life and each state in which that life appears is ordered, a priority system applicable to that one life will be created in due course—ignoring, for the moment, the problem of justification. The overall priority system must, however, be able to deal with the full range of life states available to *all* of the persons included in the options. Analytically, that is equivalent to creating an independent priority system for each person or class of persons and integrating them into a single, coherent whole. A structure of that kind can be produced by cumulating and integrating successive judgments of preference for one of the elements in two-element choices. That creates a set of life states, ordered to show preference, as in Figure A:

FIGURE A

Life #1	Life #2	Life #N
State AA	State CC	State OO
State BB	State GG	State GG
State H	State H	State H
State CC	State LL	State KK

Every individual will in time develop an overall pattern of this kind, whether from direct experience or vicariously. The quality of the justification that is offered for the pattern will vary, as will the quality of the pattern itself—its comprehensiveness and internal consistency, for example.

Because of the transitivity assumption, the sets of preferences can be integrated through shared life states. Thus in Figure A, Life #1 and

Life #2 are linked through shared state CC, allowing an inference to the effect that states AA and BB are preferable to LL. The link between Life #2 and Life #N through shared state GG makes possible the further inference that state OO is preferable to states KK and LL. The relative preferability of states AA/BB in Life #1, or GG/LL in Life #2 cannot be inferred from the information provided, but further choices may supply the needed connections. If not, a hypothetical state (H) can be inserted into each set and used as a reference point for producing the needed integration.

The analytic procedure employed for developing an integrated priority system has an additional advantage given the way in which preferences are to be made and justified: because of the transitivity assumption, in the overall structure created by ordering successive preferences from among two-element options, those states of life ("outcomes") that are rejected consistently in favor of others will tend to cluster at one end of the preference continuum, while those states of life that are consistently preferred to others will cluster at the opposite end. That polarized ordering can help to locate the conditions of life that are considered either grossly unacceptable or highly desirable given the accepted normative assumptions—to fix the benchmarks. Further, the procedure will over time contribute to the overall construction of human potential that is needed to develop justifications for preferences. In real life, the "ordered array" is likely to be a hodge podge, riddled with inconsistencies and ambiguities, but, however crude and inconsistent, it provides the essential point of departure for creating and justifying preferences.

In addition to a set of normative concepts, an integrated priority system, and a set of benchmarks, an adequate normative "discipline" will include a broad, generalized construction of human *potential*, an overall conception of what human life can be that parallels the conception of "health potential" used to make medical judgments. The conception of human potential, taken in conjunction with the integrated priority system and the set of accepted benchmarks, is based upon, or extrapolated from, past experience, broadly construed and systematically organized. It can be combined with present knowledge to provide a basis for making and justifying the judgments of human significance required for the direction of actions. Experience gained by making such judgments, and living with the consequences, makes it possible in principle at least to further develop the benchmarks, and elaborate the overall conception of human potential used to identify and defend them.

Beyond these basic instruments, an adequate normative "discipline" will incorporate: (a) a summary, which is at least partly integrated and generalized, of the available body of relevant knowledge and experience, and (b) the set of epistemological/methodological assumptions and practices that are presently accepted and applied within the field, plus a set of principles that control the use of evidence and argument. In sum, it must include all of the intellectual apparatus that a competent inquirer or critic needs to perform the functions involved in justifying preferences or priorities. That extends well beyond the available body of substantive knowledge, the sets of concepts and priorities established and accepted within the field. As noted earlier, the "discipline" must allow the separation of significant from trivial differences in the conditions of life of individuals, and supply a basis from which an adequate justification to support such judgments can be produced. More precisely, a "discipline" must enable a competent user to argue that certain conditions of life are grossly unacceptable and others are highly desirable—to identify the disasters to be avoided and the successes to be repeated, other things equal, by directing human actions in appropriate ways. Otherwise, the dilemma created by the "measurement problem" cannot be circumvented. And by facilitating the creation of benchmarks, a "discipline" can also make it possible to identify those human actions that are particularly liable, under stipulated conditions, to produce grossly unacceptable outcomes and should therefore be avoided, thus fulfilling another of the essential requirements of a defensible normative enterprise.

Conditionality

One major point to emerge from the discussion is that human judgments, normative or not, are always conditional or contingent, depend upon prior acceptance of a complex set of assumptions, some of them empirical, some methodological/epistemological, and some normative. The total apparatus, here labeled a "discipline," summarizes, integrates, and extrapolates from or extends the body of knowledge and experience available within the field. To recapitulate briefly, it will include, among other things, the set of concepts currently accepted within the field, the various instruments created with the use of those concepts, the body of evidence and argument that serves to justify both concepts and instruments, and the criteria of argument which control acceptance of proposed justifications for the instruments themselves and for conclusions based on their use. It can also include a variety of suppressed assumptions, speculations, and marginal beliefs that contribute to the creation and justification of judgments and preferences. Guiding the development of the overall apparatus will be a generalized conception of the nature of the object of inquiry—in empirical terms, an overview of how that aspect of dimension of the world "works," and even more important, how it could work, its potential; in normative terms, an overall construction of the use that could be made of that empirical potential, the kinds of lives that could be lived if that potential were properly exploited or applied. That composite overview serves as a point of departure for identifying and justifying concepts and other instruments. Construed in this way, the *content* of a "discipline" is the central element in the development and justification of intellectual tools. It does not, of course, provide those in the field with a set of absolute or incorrigible fundamental premises, or suggest that their inquiries should be directed to creating such an absolute foundation.

The conditionality of argument or justification is a function of the basic characteristics of the human intellectual enterprise. In an inductive knowledge system, every argument, whether it is concerned with preferences or empirical relations, will, if relentlessly pursued, lead to either indeterminacy or to an infinite regress. Inductively based arguments, to use a reasonably accurate metaphor, hang from "sky hooks," or rest on a foundation that is itself without a foundation. In the last analysis, the fundamental epistemological or substantive assumptions needed to pursue intellectual purposes find their justification in the use that can be made of the knowledge that is created by accepting them compared to the use that can be made of knowledge created by accepting any of the available, competing alternatives. Further, assessment of the "use" that can be made of such knowledge requires a judgment that will be based at least in part on the same set of assumptions. In those terms, all arguments, including the normative, verge unavoidably on circularity. That outcome is avoided, though only conditionally, by adding a time dimension and an external reference point (use or application in real-world affairs) to the apparatus.

What is meant by the "contingency" or "conditionality" of arguments is that no argument can be produced unless an intellectual apparatus with certain minimal characteristics is already in place. The implications of that contingency for normative argument are demonstrable in commonsense as well as epistemological terms. That is, preference begins with the set of options available within the capacity of a real-world actor. Those options must be projected on the future by appropriate theories. The projected content of the options is unavoidably partial and selective rather than exhaustive, and problematic or uncertain as well. Faced with a concrete case, the actor or critic must first check the accuracy and adequacy of the projections. Empirically, that involves an assessment of the validity of the theoretical apparatus used to make them, and a judgment of the degree of uncertainty that should be attached to each projection. Normatively, the principal concern is the adequacy of the conceptual apparatus used to state the outcomes. Three questions need to be answered: first, have all of the normative significant dimensions of each outcome been captured by the conceptual network?; second, what is the relative preferability of the normative content of the configuration of variables that defines one of the available choices, taken as a whole, compared with the content of every other option available to the actor? (each choice also involves a choice among choices); third, is the content of the preferred outcome trivial, or does it warrant attention? In sum, before actions can be justified, argument must serve to establish the normative significance of the variables used to structure the available outcomes, the relative preferability of the outcomes, and the human significance of the preferred outcome, especially at the extremes of urgency and triviality.

The first step in the justification of a preference is to establish the accuracy and adequacy of those projected outcomes. But to argue that the projections are adequate, to assert that the normatively significant dimensions of the anticipated future outcomes have been captured by the concepts employed, that they are humanly non-trivial, and that one outcome is preferable to any of the others, presumes the capacity to identify and order the normative dimensions of human life. Until some normative assumptions have been accepted, no preference can be justified and reasoned choice is effectively ruled out. A normative point of departure with certain basic features or characteristics is essential; there must be an at-least partly developed "discipline" in place. The primary problem is to find ways of assessing that point of departure, to provide criteria for improving it over time and for arguing subsequently that an improvement has been made. A basis for action can always be found (in a coin toss, for example), but the kind of systematic comparison of outcomes that is essential for justification of choices is a more difficult problem. Faced with a real choice but absent any established conception of the relative significance of different dimensions of human life, an actor or chooser would be unable to proceed. Happily, that situation rarely arises in human affairs. The world is, and has been, amply populated with normative tools. The principal handicap to be overcome stems from the disparities in their quality. How or why they first appeared is of no concern. As in empirical inquiry, the kind of justification or reasoning available for accepting or rejecting an assumption is important; its origins are not.

The need to accept one set of assumptions in order to argue for accepting another assumption or proposition is not peculiar to normative inquiry. The empirical sciences, because they are also inductively grounded, must satisfy the same requirement and are subject to the same limitations. Before a theory in science can be tested or justified, a number of assumptions, amounting to a minimal construction of the way events in the observed world interact, must be accepted. The apparatus required in science is precisely analogous to the kind of "discipline," the kind of established knowledge system, that is needed to justify choices or preferences, although the content and the organization of the two structures will be different. In both cases, a set of assumptions is taken as a point of departure, tested as far as possible against past experience, then used to guide future actions in ways that will generate the kind of information needed to strengthen, or refute, the initial assumptions. If there were no accepted body of knowledge to provide a point of departure for inquiry, there would be no alternative to proceeding blindly, generating experience that could, under some circumstances, produce the starting point needed for further progress. Without a minimal starting point, even a trial-and-error approach to justification would be ruled out, for it depends upon learning, which in turn requires the capacity to detect error and to identify success. Such judgments cannot be made until an initial set of assumptions, a "discipline" of the kind outlined above, is accepted at least tentatively. There is no possibility, and no need, to begin with a clean slate. The basic task in justification, the prime goal of argument, is to clarify, correct, extend, amplify, or amend an at-least partly established normative apparatus.

Put somewhat differently, success in normative inquiry is a function of the human ability to accept and apply a body of knowledge while retaining the capacity to criticize and to improve its elements. Useful working models for the undertaking are available in medicine (particularly teaching hospitals) and in agriculture (especially the traditional extension services provided for farmers), among other places. Those fields are characterized by the kind of well-defined, human-centered, real-world purposes that are particularly well-suited for developing pragmatically grounded performance criteria. In pedagogical terms, improvements in the quality of normative knowledge depend on the human ability to formulate knowledge claims in ways that attract and facilitate criticism and improvement out of experience, and to transmit such knowledge in ways that both stimulate awareness of the need for self-conscious and systematic criticism and contribute to the development of the intellectual capacity required to produce such criticism effectively and efficiently. The skills to be fostered will refer to the formulation and assessment (or appreciation) of competent and convincing arguments and not merely to the capacity for testing propositions, whether statistically or experimentally.

Argument and Justification: A Summary

The principal reason why those engaged in normative inquiry must focus on the capacity to formulate and appreciate compelling arguments is the basic "untestability" of normative propositions already noted. Argument, grounded in experience and linked to human actions in pursuit of human purposes, is the only available alternative to the kind of testing in use that provides the principal justification for accepting the results of empirical inquiries. Of course, neither testing nor argument can "prove" empirical or normative propositions in any inductively based knowledge system; in both cases, the end result is tentative acceptance or rejection by the community of informed and competent users. But it is essential to bear in mind that the justification of normative propositions through argument is not a simple matter of showing that real-world expectations generated from known assumptions, or particular conclusions deducible from some set of generalized assumptions, correspond well with experience.

The purpose of a normative argument is to convince an informed and competent listener or reader that one assumption is preferable to any of the available alternatives given certain other assumptions which are also preferable to any of *their* alternatives. Because the criteria applied by the informed and competent when making their judgments cannot be known fully and perfectly articulated, persuasiveness is always relative to the state of knowledge with respect to the point at issue, and to the availability of informed and competent critics. That creates a potentially dangerous situation, for in the land of the blind, one-eye is reasonably considered king, and by extension, competent. The extension may not be warranted. The question "What set of criteria should be applied to those thought to be, or seeking to be considered, competent" remains open, but the "informed and competent" must be more than a collection of self-aggrandizing mavens.

Perhaps the most important implication of the need to rely on argument for justification of preferences is that expectations must be tailored to fit a realistic assessment of human capacity. Although a number of simplifying assumptions can be made, the strongest justification that can presently be offered for a specific preference is likely to be weak and tenuous, even under the best of circumstances, particularly if it is compared to the kinds of reasons that can be provided for accepting empirical propositions. Quite extensive and fundamental differences and disagreements are to be expected, in the future as in the past. In part, the weakness that characterizes the justifications offered for preferences is due to the "life optimizing" focus of normative inquiry; further uncertainties are introduced by the need to rely on arguments, and therefore on the complex judgments needed to assess them, rather than on relatively clear and simple tests of the kind that can be produced for theories and forecasts. Of course, the simplicity of the "tests" used for assessing theories and forecasts is also deceptive; it is one thing to test an instrument and quite a different matter to decide whether a given body of evidence (including the results of such tests) is sufficient to justify accepting it. Nevertheless, developing or assessing an empirical argument is, and seems likely to remain, much easier than performing the same task in the normative arena.

Every argument, empirical or normative, is conditional or contingent; judgments of acceptability depend on a complex set of factors that cannot be formalized. Arguments about preferences, like arguments about the validity of scientific theories, will if pressed to extremes or approached from the position of the implacable skeptic, end in infinite regress. Reasons can always be found for refusing an argument, whether in science or in normative affairs. What is crucial, therefore, is the ability to assess an argument in positive terms, *to know when to be persuaded*, however tentatively. That is perhaps the main reason why the body of opinion used to support or reject such judgments must be "informed and competent." In part, what makes an argument persuasive depends on the current state of development of the field in which the argument occurs; in part it is a function of the urgency of the need to act. In effect, the need to act serves as a razoring device that much facilitates the assessment of normative arguments. For if some set of assumptions must be accepted in order to act, and action is unavoidable, the task of making and justifying a judgment is actually made easier. The critic need only decide which of the various sets of assumptions that could be used to direct action in the case at hand can be justified most effectively in terms of informed opinion as presently constituted. The best argument available may be considered quite weak and unconvincing without destroying the justification for relying on it if the need to act has been established. Absent an ultimate commitment to action, no argument outside the boundaries of formal logic can be brought to a satisfactory conclusion.

A FINAL COMPLICATION: THE ROLE OF JUDGMENTS

Every conclusion, and every argument in support of a conclusion, depends ultimately on a complex process already labeled "an exercise of judgment." The full meaning of "judgment" appears most clearly in a context supplied by the techniques available for reaching conclusions. Three basic procedures can be followed: first, direct observation or measurement can produce conclusions in the form "X was (or was not) the case"; second, conclusions can be obtained inferentially, by logical calculation from a set of general propositions; in all other cases, which can be aggregated and labeled *judgments*, conclusions remain based on the functioning of the neural apparatus, but the constituent elements of the decision process remain at least partly unknown. In judgment, the neural system functions like a "black box" in engineering, an apparatus whose inputs and outputs can be observed but whose processes remain hidden. A judgment can be regarded as a conclusion reached holistically, by the functioning of the total intellectual system. *All* human conclusions, and not normative decisions alone, depend ultimately on such judgments. Within the neural apparatus, they may well be created by formal processes, but if the assumptions from which inferences are drawn are unknown, the system cannot be formalized and evaluated in terms of its internal consistency. What appears as inconsistency at the outputs of such a structure may be only a reflection of a set of internal processes inadequately captured in the assumptions used to criticize the system.

The major difference between testing the products of a judgment and testing the products of other intellectual procedures is that more is required than comparing a conclusion derived formally from some set of known assumptions with a set of observations (the usual "testing" requirement for empirical structures). Judgments are based on some part of the full set of assumptions programmed into the neural machinery; neither the complete set, nor the selection actually used, can be specified with certainty for any particular case. Conclusions drawn from an unspecified set of assumptions are "untestable," or to be more precise—since it is the assumptions that are tested—an inability to identify those assumptions effectively precludes test. The products of intellectual activity are a function of neural process and substantive content operating in combination. If some of the substantive premises incorporated into a judgment remain concealed, knowing that the results were generated by formal processes does not constitute an adequate basis for evaluating the quality or acceptability of the judgment.

Regarding each individual as a "black box," an opaque functioning unit, provides a useful way around the impasse raised by the need to depend on judgments in human affairs. There are good reasons to assume that the operating axioms within any single "black box" are *not* wholly consistent, and that they are not competently applied in all cases. Nevertheless, there are also good historical and pragmatic reasons for regarding some human performances as more than adequate. The logical character of the human neural system, moreover, provides a crude but effective way of assessing the performance of the apparatus. The full set of assumptions and data built into any individual's neural system is hopelessly beyond reach. But if only part of that full set of assumptions is used on any one occasion, which seems likely in the light of the available knowledge of neural functioning, then in any specific case, if the results produced by one logical structure are compared to the results produced by another logical device of the same order, assuming that both have been programmed with approximately the same axioms and premises and provided with the same body of data, then at a minimum, agreement can be regarded as *some* reason

for accepting the judgment. The "test" is weak, but a decided improvement over no test at all. A stronger form of the same test occurs when
the operating axioms assumed to be relevant to a particular decision
are formalized and the results calculated and compared to human performance. What is proposed here is only a weaker form of the basic
process used to create human knowledge generally, whether empirical
or normative.

The Role of the "Discipline" in Judgment

The only logical device presently available that can equal the capacity
of a human neural system is, of course, another human brain, and
completely identical programming of two or more human individuals
is very unlikely if not impossible. Comparisons of the intellectual products of two or more total neural systems will, therefore, lead eventually
to indeterminacy, or to an endless regress if pressed. But if only part
of the total system is employed in particular cases, experience suggests
that a simple process, "pushing back" the reasoning step by step, seeking to articulate the assumptions on which judgment depends, can
stabilize the apparatus well enough for such "comparative testing" to
function effectively. Further, that process can in due course serve both
to create and to test the overall construction of the situation to which
argument refers by linking the assumptions employed in the judgment
into a more or less coherent whole. That is, forced articulation of reasoning can over time generate a "discipline" for use in farming, or for
dealing with the relative preferability of different states of human existence, that is able to serve its required function in justification.

Analytically, a "discipline" of that kind is needed in order to develop
criteria for assessing the particular configurations of life available for
choice through action. There are good reasons to suppose that such
"disciplines" are everywhere available, although their scope and quality may vary enormously. Unfortunately, they tend to remain unarticulated and incoherent, even in such highly developed fields as
medicine, but standardized training and systematic criticism can lead
to the articulation of a stable, useful, and reliable working apparatus.
Properly integrated, such a "discipline" provides a base that can be
used for assessing and improving judgments, and the arguments that
support them.

Within that context, three techniques are available for improving
critical quality: first, the programs introduced into the "black boxes"
concerned with particular classes of judgments can be systematized
and extended, in both substantive and methodological terms, on the
basis of performance—the substantive and methodological content of
the "discipline" can be stabilized, a process that is already well-ad-

vanced in physical science; second, the number of "black boxes" can be increased, and their performances integrated or averaged; third, pragmatic criteria of relevance and adequacy, generated from an initial normative commitment, can be included in the set of assumptions programmed into the "judgment-making" units, and modified as experience dictates. In effect, improvements in critical capacity require some ability to educate competent critics, and to learn in the process how to improve the quality of such education as measured by the performance of those previously educated. Ultimately, of course, improvement also depends on the capacity to argue convincingly for particular qualitative assessments of their performance. That in turn is a function of the adequacy of the available "discipline" and the level of competence of its practitioners. The process teeters unavoidably on the verge of circularity.

Obviously, both the validity of the inculcated program and the extent to which it is replicated and dominant in each of the "black boxes," will affect success. If, as in social science, there are serious ongoing disagreements or uncertainties regarding substantive premises, and if training is based on conflicting methodological/epistemological assumptions, levels of disagreement with respect to particular judgments will be much higher than in fields of study where the basic apparatus is widely agreed and stable (as in physical science). It must be granted that agreement and stability are not sufficient in and of themselves to establish validity; those limited requirements could be satisfied within such "fields" as witchcraft. The set of assumptions must also be credible in the light of overall human experience, and the results of use must be assessed favorably by informed opinion. Within those limits, an effective apparatus can be created and improved over time if a starting point can be agreed. Agreement is worth pursuing, for however weak the justification provided by such comparisons may be, it is a considerable improvement over the available alternatives, particularly those that lead to reliance on some form of elitism or authoritarianism, whether rooted in the culture or traditions of the society, or incorporated into the claims of arrogant individuals.

A successful effort to validate judgments by stabilizing the education and training of those required to make them depends, as noted earlier, on the development of a consensus among those who make up the present community of "fully-informed and competent" persons, among the available set of adequately programmed "black boxes." That criterion applies to all forms of intellectual activity, and not to scholarly inquiries alone. The members of the informed community may be hard to designate, particularly in new or poorly developed fields of inquiry, and there may be profound disagreements with respect to appropriate qualifications. But in general terms, the knowledge-validating body is comprised of all "competent" persons, meaning those who are thoroughly familiar with the relevant data in the field, and with the body of knowledge that has been created from those data, and who share an agreed set of methodological/epistemological assumptions of demonstrable adequacy for the accepted purposes of inquiry. More briefly, the body of "competent" persons comprises all those who share the best "discipline" currently available in the field. Honoring such a set of limiting conditions serves to differentiate the judgments of informed opinion from both current practice and from uninformed or unfounded judgments.

Within the body of informed opinion, development of a consensus is constrained by an extensive body of both substantive propositions and methodological requirements. Those limitations are commonly suppressed in everyday discussion and argument, sometimes deliberately but more often for lack of awareness; they surface quickly in the better-developed fields when differences in judgment arise. Absent such controls, the quality of judgments can and often does vary wildly, and disputes tend to remain unsettled, however significant the topic. Indeed, the presence of very many such major unsettled differences is usually an indication of serious inconsistencies within the fundamentals incorporated into the established empirical/normative apparatus, or of inadequacies in its application. However, even if all of the established constraints are satisfied, the possibility of serious ongoing disagreements within the community of informed opinion cannot be eliminated. For one thing, the articulated portion of the full set of premises or assumptions inculcated into a given "black box" is always incomplete, and the full set employed by two or more persons in a given activity cannot be known to be perfectly matched. Further, human individuals can and do differ greatly in their willingness to undertake risky ventures, or to accept given standards of adequacy with respect to evidence. Nevertheless, there is no good alternative to relying upon human judgment in such matters. The principal challenge to those in a field is to optimize the quality of the judgments made, and to optimize the likelihood that optimal quality will be achieved and recognized. For that purpose, there seems no good alternative, at least for the present, to systematic efforts to stabilize and improve the quality of the overall "discipline" along the lines suggested above.

SIMPLIFICATIONS

The crux of the normative enterprise, strictly construed, the key to its success or validity, is the justification that can be provided for a particular preference, for selecting one of the available options in a finite set. The justification in turn depends on the criteria that are applied to the supporting argument, including both the fundamental methodological/epistemological assumptions accepted by those engaged in assessing normative (or other) arguments, and the set of generalizations about the content of past human experience that is currently accepted. Unfortunately, an adequate approach to justification of preferences cannot be created by following the strategy employed in the philosophy of science to determine criteria for justification of empirical knowledge claims. The kinds of "successful" disciplines in physical science (most commonly physics) that were studied systematically in an effort to identify the reasons for their success (or discover "the logic of science") have no counterpart in the normative field. Although some part of the existing normative apparatus is surely "acceptable," whatever the criteria of adequacy that are employed, and some part of the apparatus *must* in fact be accepted before a justification can be produced for any normative assumption, no agreed normative equivalent to a "successful" mode of inquiry such as those found in the physical sciences is presently available. Indeed, the grounds on which those elements in ethics or moral philosophy that are useful for justifying preferences can be separated from the rest are perhaps the major point at issue. The full effects of the resulting "testing problem" emerge most clearly during systematic efforts to produce acceptable criteria of justification for real preferences.

The various impediments to creating justifications for preferences sum to a formidable intellectual challenge; there is a real and serious "problem of justification" in normative inquiry. But the effect need not be lethal, even though no formal resolution is possible. Put differently, the problem is insoluble only to the extent that it is logical; logics that can do more than replicate their own content are ruled out by the rules of logic, so far as can presently be determined. The "justification problem" can, however, be evaded in much the same way that the induction problem is circumvented, and at roughly the same cost. Normative structures adequate for dealing with real-world problems can be produced that will fulfill the requirements such knowledge must satisfy, and in an ongoing system of inquiry, they can be justified. Some evidence for that belief is found in the availability of a body of normative knowledge that has allowed the species to survive and prosper, however erratically, for so long. As in the case of induction, formal requirements can be transcended in an ongoing world by living systems that react differentially to environmental differences, and are capable of learning. The challenge is to find ways of separating adequate and inadequate solutions to such problems, to develop some capacity for both justifying preferences and for assessing the justification—and in due course, assessing the assessment. The importance of creating that capacity could hardly be greater, given the nature of the field. However, importance is not always a good indicator of the likelihood of success, or even of sustained and serious effort, in any field. And the inadequacies of the present body of normative knowledge, and particularly the absence of agreement on the criteria to be applied to arguments used to support preferences, despite the long history of normative inquiry, suggests that improvements are likely to be slow in coming and limited in scope.

Fortunately, the task of justifying preferences can be simplified in a number of ways without seriously reducing the quality or acceptability of the result. Four of them are particularly important here. First, there is no need to establish a preference-ordering for every outcome available for choice by a given actor. The actor or critic need only identify the preferred outcome within the available set. That task can be fulfilled, adequately if imperfectly, by combining priorities with relevant benchmarks, both of which are available in principle within the limits of human capacity.

A second simplification is achieved by assuming that the effect of most human actions, particularly in everyday affairs, is relatively minor or trivial pending evidence and argument to the contrary. Almost any action can, under certain conditions, produce significant consequences, but if experience does not suggest otherwise, the triviality of most actions is safely assumed. Measured against the whole of a human life, most of the actions taken in day-to-day affairs produce temporary and relatively minor effects on the self and others. What is more important, those actions that do impact major parts of an individual life in important ways are for the most part well known. The "triviality" assumption leaves systematic normative inquiry free to examine or seek justifications for already established preferences, and to concentrate on unresolved or disputed problems of agreed human significance, and that is a major advantage given the present state of development of the field. Further, areas where the cost of error is relatively low provide a useful site for learning or for improving procedures, and learning how to learn and improve seems far more important at present than creating solutions to specific choice problems. The old adage: "Give a man a fish, feed him for a day; teach a man how to fish, feed him for a lifetime," suitably modified, is usefully transferred to the conduct of normative affairs where it underscores the importance of learning how to exploit learning opportunities when they arise, and of regularly regarding applications of an established normative apparatus as learning opportunities as well as opportunities to validate the apparatus.

A third simplification of the task of justifying preferences is obtained by insisting that user expectations be realistic; people must be willing to accept tenuous and limited justifications for preferences and not demand absolute judgments supported by irrefutable evidence for every decision that must be made. In normative matters, the best available models for emulation are such fields as medicine or agriculture, where crude and imperfect knowledge is widely and successfully used for dealing with significant problems and some admittedly significant problems remain unresolved. There is no need for perfect and timeless statements of preference, or priorities that can be applied with complete confidence; justifications need not be fully convincing to serve as a basis for action in the present and a point of departure for argument and future improvement; not every problem of preference can be resolved. A normative system that can handle choices well enough to maintain the species is worth having. Any tool may be employed if the need is great, if the capacity and limits of the tool are known at least partially, and if the application is structured to allow for correction and improvement out of experience. The search for a normative apparatus that will function perfectly in every situation and will be accepted by every human actor is as badly misdirected as an effort to produce a single map that will serve all potential map-users in every imaginable circumstance. In normative affairs, all that can be demanded is a reasonably convincing justification for a modest instrument able to deal with basic problems in at least some cases. So long as it furthers the effort to deal with the major recurring choices that appear in the everyday lives of individual and society, the instrument is valuable. The crucial need is for widespread awareness of current criteria of acceptable argument, for that is what makes possible the justification of exceptions to current practice.

In effect, and it cannot be said too often, those who inquire into normative affairs, and those who seek to criticize their efforts, must function with an appreciation of the prime characteristics of the "state of the art," or the nature of the enterprise. Perhaps the most important of those features is the absolute need to act; life and action cannot cease pending normative development. As a physician will use willingly a mode of treatment known to work only five percent of the time if the situation is desperate, the user of a normative system that is known to be weak and faulty must employ it nonetheless if a decision is forced and nothing better is available. The major caveat is that some effort be made to learn from the application. Put differently, there is no quick and easy road to development of a normative system by "inductive" procedures, and no dramatic breakthrough can be expected. As in medicine, the best available strategy is a sustained, systematic, and relatively dispassionate effort to deal with major problems as they appear using the accepted normative structure, seeking meanwhile to clarify, adapt, and improve the normative system used to deal with them, and above all to improve the capacity to argue that an improvement has been made. History provides ample evidence to show that the practice of medicine is not improved merely by practicing medicine any more than the quality of play in a game such as football is improved merely by playing football. Something more, a deliberate and self-conscious effort to treat each action as a learning opportunity, and particularly as an opportunity to learn how to learn about how to coach the activity, is needed. The requirements for controlling and improving the quality of the normative enterprise are identical to those that control the extension and elaboration (or "improvement") of physical science, the operation of a self-governing political or social system, or the development and maintenance of a physically sound human body.

A cooperative effort to cumulate and improve knowledge, extending over considerable periods of time, seems unavoidable. Success is contingent upon the development of an agreed body of fundamentals, and on strict maintenance of the integrity of the reasoning employed in the arguments created from the agreed base. That simple-sounding requirement may in fact constitute the greatest single obstacle to success in the enterprise. For of all the performance criteria pursued by the species, persistence with integrity in the face of limited accomplishment and strong external pressures has been one of the more difficult to achieve and maintain. Metaphorically, experience suggests that it is usually pointless to shout "To the barricades!!!" if the barricades are more than a few blocks away. And should they be manned, it is even more futile to expect them to remain so for more than a short period of time by more than a small band of "true believers," and the latter are as likely to do harm to the cause that occasioned the march as to further it. The well-documented human propensity to excessive expectations, and gross impatience when such expectations are frustrated, may be the most serious obstacle to normative extension and improvement, at least to the extent that it weakens that capacity for persistence in relatively unrewarding drudgery on which intellectual improvement so largely depends. The most serious substantive obstacle to success is, of course, the pronounced tendency to extreme selfishness characteristic of species members.

The final simplification, and in some ways the most important one, flows from the requirement that all of the elements included in the priorities that comprise the overall system be ordered transitively where they intersect. The principal implication of that requirement bears emphasis: both individual preferences and the overall priority system can be regarded analytically as a product or summation of the results of sets of two-element choices, or as an extrapolation from the results of such choices. That is, given a choice among three or more outcomes, justification can proceed by selecting any two options or outcomes as a point of departure; if reasons are found for preferring one of the options, the other can be discarded. The "winning" option is then matched against another element in the set, and the "loser" is again discarded. Such one-to-one choices are continued until only one option, or a number considered to be equally acceptable (which may include *all* of the set) remains. In practice, judgments of preference need only deal with the relative desirability of two outcomes or options, although each outcome may, of course, be quite complex and extensive. Once all of the choices have been made, a preference-ordering in the form "Outcome A is preferable to outcomes B, C, D, E...N" can be stated and defended. The preference-ordering, which is specific and particular, must be generalized, creating a priority, before it can be applied, even to the case where it originated. The priority can then be used to deal with any member of the same class of choices that appears in the future.

7

Preferences and Priorities: Justification

The justification of preferences or priorities, narrowly construed, is a daunting intellectual enterprise, subject to a formidable set of impediments and constraints and supported at present by only a very limited amount of cumulated knowledge and reasoning capacity. The overall field, and its "discipline," is rudimentary and inchoate; there is no recognizable body of "informed opinion" to serve as arbiter when differences in judgment appear; there is little agreement on either the fundamental purposes of normative inquiry or the canons of evidence and argument to be applied to the field; and few of the choices actually encountered in everyday life, either by individuals or by collectivities, have been worked out in a satisfactory manner. Moreover, there is a deceptive similarity between the justification of preferences and the justification of empirical theories and forecasts that tends to foster either unwarranted expectations about the kinds of arguments that should be produced to support normative judgments and about the best strategy for producing them, or despairing retreats into traditional moralism. Nevertheless, there is always some normative apparatus in place, and that can provide (if only because it *must* provide) the necessary point of departure for future improvement.

The chapter begins with a brief restatement of the fundamental assumptions on which the approach to the justification of preferences depends. That leads to a discussion of the factors that enter into an assessment of the adequacy of the conceptual apparatus—of the set of normative variables that is used to state the content of the outcomes. Those preliminaries are followed by a detailed examination of the process of justification, beginning with simple choices involving a single human life and a single normative variable and concluding with complex choices involving a number of different persons and several normative variables. Two major points are made with respect to the overall process of justification: (1) the "primacy of the negative"—the need to focus first on the elimination of unacceptable outcomes rather than seeking to maximize benefits or "strike a balance" of costs and benefits; (2) the procedures that are needed to avoid the kind of circularity that is implicit in any inductive approach to justification. The process is illustrated in its simpler mode by an example taken from agriculture, and in its more complex forms by contemporary medical practice. The chapter ends with a brief summary of some of the special problems that are easily resolved or avoided by adopting the recommended approach to justification.

Justification: Nature and Limits

As a preliminary to the discussion, two points bear underscoring. First, the goal is not an "adequate" justification, for there is no way to produce criteria of adequacy that could be applied in all cases. Instead, the aim is to show how the "best possible" justification for a real preference can be created, and examine its salient characteristics to the extent they can be specified. The quality of a normative argument is a function of the specific variables used to structure the options and the relevant body of normative knowledge embedded in the "discipline"; justification must refer to real past experience and real present cases. The content of the justification will vary with the overall purposes set for normative inquiry, and with a range of assumptions about the characteristic functioning of the natural universe and a variety of human capacities and limitations, particularly those that relate to intellectual performance. There is, in brief, no simple criterion of adequacy that can be applied to justifications.

Second, as an unavoidable corollary, justification cannot occur until at least the basic rudiments of a normative "discipline," a minimum body of knowledge and competence, is available. There is no alternative to building upon an existing normative apparatus. The key to improvement is argument, a systematic working out of underlying assumptions on which judgment depends, including those relating to past experience, focusing particularly upon the effects of accepting and living with given criteria of justification. The court of last resort is the consensus view of the current body of informed and competent persons, but there is no guarantee that a consensus can be reached. The basic apparatus needed as a point of departure is available everywhere, but there are today almost as many "disciplines" as there are individuals, and quality varies enormously. Usually, the normative apparatus in place is badly organized and for the most part unarticulated. The necessary first step, therefore, is to identify the main elements in current practice, whether the actor is an individual or a collectivity. Even simple stock-taking, however, is much complicated by the absence of an organized field of inquiry sharing agreed purposes and canons of argument.

The procedure to be followed in justification is fairly straightforward. It begins always with a real-world case, with a serious effort to justify or defend a particular judgment of preference. Whether the choice is made by applying an established priority or creating a new one, subsequent argument—which may involve only one individual "arguing" with the self or a number of persons engaged in open discussion— proceeds by "pushing-back" the reasoning and evidence step-by-step, seeking to locate data flaws or differences in assumptions. That procedure will lead either to agreement or to an impasse centered on known differences in assumptions or evidence which become points of departure for further inquiry and argument.

Put somewhat differently, improvements in the quality of argument and justification, including improvements in arguments that refer to the quality of the argument itself, are contingent on the development of an adequate "discipline" and a body of informed opinion able to use it critically, self-consciously, and with competence and integrity. That in turn requires systematic efforts to resolve real cases and to apply the conclusions reached—use them to direct real-world actions and in the process to create further evidence that can be used in justification. Imaginary instantiation has no standing in serious argument; illustrations, however illuminating they may be are not equivalent to evidence. *The "best possible" justification is achieved when the existing body of informed and competent opinion has exhausted its capacity to argue.* Judgment may at that point remain inconclusive. That may not sound like too formidable a criterion, but if it is all that lies within human capacity, then it must be accepted and employed.

In the circumstances, the absence of a body of informed opinion is perhaps the most serious impediment to development of a field of study able to deal in an effective manner with real-world choices or actions. It follows that the primary task at present is to create such a field of inquiry and begin systematic development of an appropriate "discipline." The first step, necessarily, is to set in motion a sustained effort to agree upon a set of fundamental purposes and assumptions for normative inquiry and then begin applying them systematically to real cases.

The fundamentals on which normative arguments depend, the rock bottom layer of assumptions in the intellectual apparatus, serve mainly as limiting and focusing devices: they are used to target inquiries, to check the validity of judgments and conclusions, and to determine questions of relevance. Priorities cannot be deduced from such premises. To illustrate, two of the fundamentals assumed here—that normative knowledge must be useful for directing human actions on defensible grounds, and that normative decisions must be based on the consequences of action for human individuals—can be used to rule out acceptance of normative variables that refer to non-human dimensions of the environment such as social states, but they do not determine the actual substance or meaning of those variables.

The Basic Perspective. In the remainder of the chapter, the kinds of justifications that are required, and can be provided, for a range of preferences of varying complexity, are discussed and illustrated. Both the discussion and the illustrations flow from a specific perspective, a set of assumptions relating to the purposes of inquiry and to human potential for achieving them that has already been spelled out in some detail. The basic elements, however, are worth restating, if only to underscore the contingent nature of the argument that follows.

It is assumed, first, that the overall purpose of normative inquiry is to develop the intellectual apparatus needed to direct human actions on grounds that can be defended within the limits of human capacity. If that purpose is accepted, and the following analysis is correct, the criteria of adequate performance adduced for the enterprise should be useful in both the conduct of such inquiries and the assessment of the conclusions reached. It is assumed further that the overall purpose of the normative enterprise (to maintain or improve the condition of life of a specific population) can be achieved by success in pursuing three second-order purposes: prediction of future events from present (or past) observations, projection of the consequences of deliberate action or change, and selection of the preferred outcome from among the range of options available to an actor.

The approach to fulfilling those purposes is controlled by four further assumptions; they make up the foundation of the normative apparatus, the "rules of the game" within which the required justification for normative knowledge claims will be sought. First, the primary unit of significance in human preferences, the "thing" or "object" that is pre-ferred, is an individual human life, treated holistically. Second, in the limited sense of life *qua* life, one human life is of equal significance to any other; if nothing is known of the lives affected by action beyond their "humanness," there can be no defensible grounds for preferring one to another. Third, the justification for preferences must be grounded in human experience with the outcomes; an "inductive" foundation is required, meaning in practice that the assumptions on which justifi-cation depends must be consonant with established knowledge and experience, and generalizations are contingent upon particulars. Fourth, priorities must be ordered transitively at all points where they intersect, otherwise the minimum requirements for calculability are not satisfied. Other assumptions needed for justifying specific preferences will be underscored as the discussion proceeds. The aim, to repeat, is to facilitate future development of the necessary normative apparatus by establishing its basic parameters and not to create a substantive structure.

From that perspective, the only tenable strategy for fostering the kind of critical competence on which normative improvement depends (beyond minor tactical suggestions, such as beginning with the action to be taken and asking who will be affected in what way as a consequence rather than beginning with a fixed set of normative variables and asking which of them will change values as a result of the action) is a sustained, self-conscious, and systematic effort to improve present practice. In the foreseeable future, cultural and other differences in conceptualization and priorities, long available in history and now increasingly visible in a world grown more interdependent and interacting, should provide a stimulus to efforts to rationalize differences as well as a rich source of new concepts and new reasons for preference. Given a human purpose of the kind accepted here to serve as an anchor for the enterprise, and assuming a commitment to grounding normative argument in past human experience, systematic efforts to deal with specific cases using the available normative variables but seeking ways of improving them can generate an overall conception of the significant dimensions of individual life, and of the relative desirability of different configurations of those dimensions, that informed opinion can endorse and deliberate action can reify in the appropriate context; universally applicable priorities are out of the question given the character of present-day social organization.

As with the improvement of hammers or medicine, systematic argument, conducted with competence and integrity and closely tied to practice, offers a means for stabilizing the underlying set of assumptions on which the normative apparatus depends and thus improving the justifications that are provided for preferences. Improvements in the conception of what human life *could* be, which are usually contingent upon increased knowledge or extended awareness, can lead to further improvements in normative performance, which then open the way for still further extensions and improvements in the conception of what human life can be, and so on. The overall apparatus can evolve in precisely the same manner that hammers and hammering is improved in use: improving the life along one dimension extends the potential of the improved life, and that opens the way to further improvements in the life, and more importantly, to a more sophisticated and potentially richer conception of "the quality of life," thus providing a way to improve the overall construct used to judge that improvements have occurred in the quality of particular lives.

The principal impediments to progress along these lines, already noted above, flow from the great diversity about fundamentals that appears in current normative inquiry, fundamentals ranging from the nature of the enterprise to the criteria of evidence, argument, and justification to be applied to normative affairs. Curiously enough, there is perhaps less disagreement about the substance of the normative apparatus, about the variables to be used and the priorities to be applied, than about the epistemological and methodological criteria used to assess or argue the decision to employ them. Unfortunately, the disagreements occur at a critical point in the normative structure so far as justification of preferences is concerned. Agreement on the kind of argument that should be accepted for a particular preference, and the reasons why such arguments deserve acceptance, is bound to be frustrated (or misplaced) until there is agreement on epistemological/methodological fundamentals. The function of argument, in normative matters as in science, is not merely to locate points of difference and find ways of resolving them to the satisfaction of those involved, but to assess the validity of points of agreement as well. Agreement on conclusions alone is meaningless; there must be agreement on the reasoning and evidence used to reach them as well, whether the conclusion refers to a theory, a concept, or a preference.

CONCEPTUAL ADEQUACY

Justification or criticism of preferences, or actions based upon them, is usefully broken into two separate stages: the adequacy of the conceptual apparatus used to project the available outcomes is examined first; the justification for a priority or preference-ordering, whose acceptability is contingent upon the adequacy of the normative concepts, can then be assessed. The ordering is analytic only; in real cases, the two aspects of preference are inextricably meshed. The discussion presumes that empirical questions relating to the accuracy and reliability of the theoretical apparatus used to project the available outcomes have already been settled competently and satisfactorily.

How to determine the adequacy of the selection of normative variables used to structure the outcomes available for choice? That question provides a good opportunity to demonstrate the function of the "discipline," and in particular of the generalized overview of human potential that it includes, in the justification process. It would be pointless merely to return to the real-world situation in which the choice occurs and begin searching for other aspects of the projected life situations that affect its quality. Without a frame of reference to serve as a basis for judgment, that would be equivalent to seeking a medical diagnosis without any knowledge of medicine.

In normative inquiry as in medicine, an overview constructed out of past experience with the conditions of human life found in real-world cases, and structured to show prior judgments of relative significance or preferability, is an essential ingredient in the analysis and/or diagnosis and criticism of performance. That overall structure may not appear in human consciousness as a fully ordered configuration of specific human situations, but it will include, among other things, a set of assumptions identifying the conditions of life that have been considered significant under a range of circumstances and a summary of the preference-orderings created from previous judgments about the relative preferability of specific configurations of those variables—an integrated priority system. Taken as a whole, that apparatus serves as a base from which the chooser or the critic can extrapolate to other aspects of life that should be considered when a particular preference is being justified—and as a base for assessing, tentatively, the relative preferability of the options available for choice.

The key to competent assessment of conceptual adequacy is the quality of the extrapolations made to particular situations. That in turn depends on the fecundity of the critic's imagination and the quality of the argument used to support what imagination has created. Both factors depend in large measure upon the richness and variety of the existing normative "discipline." As the Baroque artist or musician lived in an aural/visual/conceptual world that offered greater stimulus to creativity than the world of their more spartan predecessors, the normative inquirer living in a culture richly endowed with normative knowledge is, other things equal, better positioned to produce significant improvements in the established conceptual apparatus, as well as improvements in the arguments used to defend them as improvements.

The projections used in making choices may focus on information obtained through either a "microscope" or a "telescope"; both must be considered in defending a preference. Preferences are established in terms of particular configurations of specified selections of normative variables, and apply only to choices involving those configurations. The question of conceptual adequacy refers to the configuration, taken as a whole. The selection of variables employed will affect choice very significantly, for if different variables are used to project the content of a given set of options, the content of the "choice" will vary—which underscores once again the importance of developing a comprehensive set of normative concepts, of avoiding serious omissions.

The task of criticizing and improving the conceptual apparatus is complicated by a singularly unfortunate ambiguity in current practice. Conceptual differences are a major source of normative disagreements, but they are also an indicator of the way in which responsibility is allocated in situations where human capacities overlap. A classic illustration is found in the nexus linking individual and collectivity. A society may employ a selection of variables for making decisions that omits various aspects of a choice that are of great significance to the individuals concerned. What is perhaps less obvious is that society may be able to maintain its position even if it takes into account all of the relevant data, whether they come from a "microscope" or a "telescope." Indeed, it must already have done so if the judgment is to be defensible, for every option must be considered in terms of *any* normative variable that can be applied to it. Collectivities, and individuals, may with justification choose to ignore dimensions of the outcomes available to them that are very important to those who are affected.

To illustrate, a society may view with unconcern decisions in which the state of health of a particular individual differs in each outcome, although the individual involved, as well as members of the family, may attach a great deal of significance to the projected differences. Similarly, parents may regard with indifference choices that are of great importance to their children. Such variations of assessments are due to the differences in the level of responsibility accepted by, or assigned to, the actors involved. Responsibility helps to determine the set of concepts used to structure outcomes, and in contemporary industrial society at least, responsibility is determined ultimately by the national state. That is, individual decisions about the scope of individual responsibility take place within limits that are determined socially in a system of sovereign national states. The reasons for that seeming anomaly, or at least peculiarity, are explored in chapter 8.

JUSTIFYING PREFERENCES: THE BASIC PATTERNS

Because of the transitivity requirement, every choice can be expressed as a sequence of dyadic or two-element choices: the outcomes available for choice are assessed in pairs. Two aspects of each outcome are taken into account in the justification of a preference for one element in such a dyad: (1), the size of the population whose lives are affected by the action (are different in the two outcomes); (2), the relative normative significance of the changes induced in each life—the relative desirability of the projected future lives in each outcome. The complexity of the justification offered for a preference will be a function of both the number of individuals or classes of individuals and the number and type of normative variables whose values are altered by action for each individual or class. In a very simple case, the value of one normative variable, used to state the condition of one human life, differs in two outcomes. More commonly, of course, individual actions affect a range of individuals or classes, and collective actions can have an impact on countless millions of persons. Qualitatively, the normative dimensions involved can range from the utterly trivial to matters of life and death.

One-Life, One-Variable Choices

In the simplest choice possible, there are two options, the same person appears in each option, and only one of the normative variables in the full configuration used to project the available alternative future conditions of life of that person takes a different value in each option. In practical terms, that may seem a near-impossibility. However, the use of benchmarks to indicate values of specific normative variables (or complete configurations) that are either grossly unacceptable or highly desirable can produce the same effect. That is, if the one normative variable takes an unacceptable or highly desirable value in one of the two options and not in the other, that serves to create a one-life, one-variable choice. When that occurs, the preferred outcome is readily determined.

The reason why such choices are easily resolved is found in the character of the normative variables. The argument needed to support the judgment that a particular variable is "normative" will also establish the human significance of changing its value in specific ways. It would be inconsistent to claim on the one hand that some aspect of human life had normative significance, but maintain on the other hand that it was uncertain whether a higher or lower value of that variable should be preferred. The evidence and reasoning used to argue for the human significance of a particular variable or concept will also determine its preferred values. A decision about significance must be based upon the effect of changing the value of a given variable in a particular way on an individual life. The effect on that life of different possible values for the variable will therefore have been assessed prior to deciding significance, for that is the evidence on which the decision rests. If the quality of the life remained the same regardless of the value taken by a variable, that variable could hardly be regarded as normatively significant. It follows that the normative effects of different values for the variable must be estimated *before* normative significance can be judged. The preferred end of the value continuum for that variable will therefore be known.

The role of the benchmarks, the cut-off values of the normative variables, can now be clarified: although the values of the normative variable may differ in the two outcomes being compared, it remains possible that the choice is a matter of indifference, and the normative apparatus must be able to locate or identify such situations. There are three possibilities: first, the normative variable may take a highly desirable value in both of the available options, in which case the choice is a matter of indifference unless some basis for further differentiation is found; second, if the normative variable takes grossly unacceptable values in both options, the choice is again a matter of indifference;

third, if the value taken by the normative variable is either highly desirable or grossly unacceptable in one of the outcomes and not the other (it could not be both), that is sufficient to decide the choice.

A common normative concept such as "health" illustrates the overall process nicely. If "health" is accepted as a normative variable, if it refers to a normatively significant dimension of individual life (as is surely the case), then a life marked by a positive or "normal" state of health *must* be preferred to that same life in a negative or "poor" health state. That conclusion follows automatically, as a side effect of the argument used to qualify health as a normative variable. And that argument in turn depends on various prior assumptions relating to human potential accepted by the person rendering judgment. Before the normative character of a variable can be judged, it must be argued convincingly that changing the value of the variable changes the quality of the life either positively or negatively. If it can be argued convincingly that increasing the value of the health variable has a positive normative impact on the life, it would not be possible to "improve" the health yet by doing so debilitate the quality of the life. The "positive" value of a normative variable need not be preferred in all cases, of course; an inverse relation (less is preferable) would hold for such variables as the amount of pain experienced, or the level of physical disability entailed, among others. But once the preferred end of the continuum identified by the concept has been established, the generalized form of the judgment, the priority to be applied to that choice when it recurs, will follow automatically. Moreover, efforts to apply the normative variable to real choices will in due course force development of appropriate benchmarks, for a decision about action must be produced and justified. Where those benchmarks are placed, which values of the "state of health" variable are considered highly desirable or grossly unacceptable, will be a function of medical, individual, social, and other factors. The results obtained by applying the benchmarks will provide evidence that can be used to adjust both the conceptual apparatus and the benchmarks over time.

The "state of health" variable also serves to illustrate the various instrumental requirements for justifying preferences, and to underscore the primary importance of abstract or intellectual considerations in the process. The question how the state of health that can be produced by an action will differ from the state of health to be expected if no action is taken calls for an empirical decision, the application of a theory. The normative judgments involved in treatment decisions—that health is a normative variable, that one end of the continuum used to measure the variable is preferable to the other, and that particular values of that variable are either trivial or significant—depend unavoidably upon the overall conception of human health and its potentialities that is accepted by the actor or critic making the claim. Without some such reference point, there would be no way to produce reasons for regarding one state of life as an improvement on, as preferable to, another. Similarly, an overall conception of human life and its potentialities, which is a purely intellectual construction comprised of a number of complex, not necessarily well-integrated, assumptions (which include references to affective reactions of various kinds), is an essential element in a "discipline" adequate for justifying preferences.

One-Life, Multi-Variable Choices

Most human actions, even those that impact only one human life, will produce changes in the values of more than one normative variable. For each normative variable, the preferred value will be known, as in the case of single-variable outcomes, a priority (in the form "prefer the outcome containing the higher/lower value of the variable") will already have been established, and a set of benchmarks may be available.

One-Life, Multi-Variable Choices: The Simple Case. Two basic types of one-life, multi-variable choices are possible in principle. In the simpler case, the values of each normative variable in each outcome are assessed in the same way (highly desirable, grossly undesirable, or indifferent); the result is an easily-solved composite of single-variable choices. For if: (a) only one person's life is affected, and (b) the value of more than one normative variable varies, but (c) the values of all of the normative variables have the same status in each of the options, then the decision to be made (preference or indifference) will be equivalent to a single-person, single-variable choice. If every normative variable takes a preferred value in the same outcome, the preference is obvious and even trivial.

It is worth reemphasizing that a decision to *act* does not follow automatically from a judgment of preference; all of the available outcomes may be trivial. Even if the consequences of exercising the actor's capacity are distributed among the outcomes so that one option contains the preferred values of all of the normative variables, and it is an easy matter to locate the preferred option, it may not be possible to justify actions directed to achieving it. There is no contradiction involved, as will be clear once the nature of the judgments required is elaborated slightly. The actor or critic seeking to make or criticize a real-world choice must make two basic judgments, and not just one. First, the relative preferability of outcomes that include both desirable and undesirable values for different variables must be decided; second, a further judgment is required whether the difference between the content of the preferred outcome and the content of the other alternatives amounts to a significant difference in the human life affected by the choice. A "choice among choices" is a necessary preliminary to justifying actions. Such judgments require the use of an ordered continuum of outcomes (each outcome comprising a complex state of an individual life) marked with benchmarks that show the states of individual life regarded as "unacceptable," and those considered highly desirable or preferable, other things equal. Hence, an adequate normative "discipline" must include both a set of priorities or preference-orderings and a set of benchmarks.

To illustrate the justification required for simple multi-variable choices, assume that the value of the "eyesight" variable for a single person can be altered by the actor, and treat "eyesight" as an Input variable that can take two polar values, "normal" and "blind." Changing the value of the Input variable from "normal" to "blind" will produce undesirable values for a number of other variables whose normative significance is widely and generally agreed. Indeed, the consequences are so well known, and the consensus is so strong, that the choice would ordinarily be made without bothering to work out the full content of the options. When that occurs, the condition labeled "blindness" is treated as a normative variable rather than as an Input variable—thus providing a nice illustration of the way in which current practice can confuse. The use of blindness as a normative variable is justified only to the extent that the preferred value for each of the normative variables that change when the value of the "eyesight" variable changes will ordinarily be found in the same outcome when the choice recurs, and that cannot be guaranteed—in some (perhaps few) cases, loss of sight could have a salutory effect on some aspects of the life.

As in virtually all serious decisions, an acceptable justification for preferring normal vision to blindness requires the use of several normative concepts. The differential impact of changes in the value of an Input variable on all important aspects of the life involved must be captured by the conceptual network. The prime normative effects of total vision loss may not vary greatly with individual differences, but changes in other Input variables are likely to produce varied effects, depending on the specific attributes of the persons affected, and the general procedure followed in justification should take that possibility into account.

In principle, all of the relevant conceptualizations of the effects of change are explored before a judgment is made about the relative preferability of the available options (before a preference-ordering is produced and generalized); in practice that is very unlikely to occur. In matters of action or choice, completeness is an ideal to be striven for and not a goal to be achieved. The element of selectivity that is built into every action or choice is controlled by such things as experience, habit, tradition, and the available time and resources; their content, and therefore their effects, can vary enormously among persons. That is yet another reason for insisting that the first task in contemporary normative inquiry is to establish the content of current practice as clearly and accurately as possible.

A choice between blindness and normal vision serves to illustrate the variety of normative concepts that can be used to identify the significant dimensions of individual life and the kinds of reasons for preference that can be created by using them. It is demonstrable, for example, that a total loss of vision effectively bars the individual, usually for all time, from active participation in a wide variety of activities, or from occupying specific life states, that are widely agreed to be an important part of human life. Blindness reduces the individual's level of self-sufficiency, adds to the human and monetary costs associated with large and important chunks of "normal" living such as marrying, raising children, finding employment, moving freely from one place to another, and so on almost *ad infinitum*.

Somewhat more generally, it can be argued that the quality of any human life is contingent on access to experience and that vision is the primary avenue to "experience" for species members. It follows that loss of vision seriously impairs access to a range of experiences and in that way reduces the overall quality of the life.

Finally, in the case of blindness it can be argued that one outcome is virtually contained in the other, that living in a state of "blindness" can be approximated by an individual with normal vision merely by closing the eyes, hence that any "advantages" available to persons without vision, such as improvements in tactile or aural sensitivity, could be obtained (if they were actually desired) while avoiding the long-term disadvantages and handicaps associated with blindness. A difference between outcomes that appears in any of these, or other, ways of conceptualizing them can be a reason for a preference. How they are assessed will depend, obviously, on a very complex configuration of factors—which will be reflected in the content of the options.

The impact of blindness on individual life can be expressed using a wide range of concepts, an indication of the extent to which life is affected by such a major change in attributes. The reasons why normal vision is preferable to blindness, other things equal, are extensive and compelling; reasons for taking the opposite position are hard to find. The significance of the difference in conditions of life created by acting on the preference is readily established. In structural terms, virtually all of the major normative variables altered by the action take a positive or preferred value in one outcome and negative values in the other; that outcome is therefore the preferred outcome within the available set. An exception may appear in those societies where blindness qualifies the person for public benefits, thus changing the content of the choice in a potentially significant way, but for illustrative purposes, that possibility can safely be ignored.

Evidence to support the judgment of preference can be obtained from a variety of sources. The testimony of those who are presently blind and those with normal vision can be compared; even better information can be supplied by those who have lived under both sets of conditions. The subsequent experience of anyone who has previously made the same choice is obviously germane. But the results obtained from reasoned analysis, based on systematic study of the relevant body of knowledge and experience and making use of an overall construction of human potential included in an adequate "discipline," will be the most persuasive element in the decision. When actions produce complex outcomes affecting a number of persons in a variety of different ways, a broad and general statement of human potential, of what a human life can be under a variety of different circumstances, is the crucial factor in the justification of preferences. It makes possible the required assessment of significance by taking into account such things as the scope of the effect on the individual's life, the duration of the effect, its reversibility, and so on. Given such an overall construction of human potential, a society of humans having no direct experience with blindness would still prefer normal eyesight and could produce a strong argument to support the preference, just as the overall organization of the states of human health encountered in the past that is acquired through medical training and experience allows a physician to argue for preferring one hypothetical state of health rather than another. Even in a society where ill health was unknown but imaginable, a preference for good health could still be justified by such reasoning. Normative judgments, like empirical judgments, are based fundamentally on intellectual or cognitive considerations.

The case for preferring blindness to normal vision is extremely weak. The prospect of a large governmental subsidy, which may sound attractive and is certainly preferable to a situation in which no subsidy is provided, would be unlikely to command support from many persons aware of the full set of consequences involved in a choice between subsidized blindness and normal vision without a subsidy. Nevertheless, a judgment favoring normal vision could be challenged, and the simplicity of the illustration serves to clarify in a useful way the argument that would follow such a challenge. Why should exclusion from a range of particular activities be considered undesirable? The respondent would have to argue that such activities affect specific aspects of human life: the normative significance of those aspects of life would then have to be argued. If the judgment of significance is challenged, the argument to follow will be forced to return to the potential embodied in a human life and ask what past experience has to say about the kind of conceptual apparatus best able to probe its quality (what set of concepts identify life's important major decisions) and try to connect the answers to the position being argued. If every assumption in the ensuing argument is disputed until no capacity to produce further reasons for or against a preference remains, the judgment is then moot for that set of protagonists, although either or both could then question the competence or integrity of the other (appeal to informed opinion for support). Given the nature of the enterprise, the importance of coming to agreement on a basic conception of the potential represented by a human life in a range of real-world situations could hardly be greater. The principal danger to be avoided is the circularity latent in the mode of argument, and the concurrent possibility of mistaking what presently *is* preferred, particularly within society as a whole, for what *should be* preferred.

One-Life, Multi-Variable Choices: The Complex Case. A more complex form of one-life, multi-variable choice occurs when only one life is impacted by an action but (a) the values of more than one variable are projected to change, and (b) each outcome contains some preferred and some unacceptable values of the variables. A choice must be made between two configurations of normative variables (life states), but each configuration now comprises normative variables whose values range from "unacceptable," to "preferred," or "regarded with indifference." In that situation, almost all of the major difficulties that are encountered in efforts to provide a justification for preferences and priorities are fairly easily identified.

Faced with choice between two or more outcomes—each containing a different set of conditions of existence for a single human life, with a different set of values for each of the normative variables—and asked to determine their relative preferability, the actor or critic can make one of four basic judgments. First, one outcome, one condition of individual life, can be judged more desirable than the other. In a two-option choice, that judgment decides the issue; in a multi-option choice, the less desirable option is dropped and the preferred outcome is then compared to another member of the available set. Second, both outcomes may be deemed grossly undesirable. In a two-element set, either a decision can then be made by a random procedure such as a coin toss or the normative apparatus can be elaborated and extended in ways that produce a justifiable and significant differentiation between the two outcomes; in a multi-variable set, the remaining options can be searched for an outcome that is judged less undesirable. Third, both outcomes may be judged equally desirable. Again, in any two-option set, a decision can then be reached by random processes or an effort can be made to extend the normative apparatus sufficiently to provide a basis for differentiation; in a multi-option decision, the remaining options can be searched for an outcome regarded as even more desirable. Fourth, both outcomes may be judged to be trivial. In a two-outcome choice, the decision can be ignored, left to habit or custom; in a multi-outcome choice, the remaining options are treated as an independent choice.

The effort to decide brings into play the full set of limitations and complications created by the inability to specify and measure the fundamental normative continuum "preferability of individual life." Technically, the selection of variables that make up the overall continuum cannot be identified with certainty; some factors that influence its measured value may not be known. Accurate comparisons along the overall continuum are therefore ruled out in principle. But all of the judgments required in complex choices depend on comparisons; indeed, measurement, broadly speaking, *is* a comparison of a special kind. If the continuum cannot be measured, and that limitation is taken literally and seriously, any approach to judgment or justification that requires a measurement, either explicitly or implicitly, must be eliminated—clearly an unacceptable situation. Further, the use of an approach that involves balancing one effect against another, or compensating for a change in the value of one normative variable by changing the value of another ("cost-benefit analysis" and "trade-offs," among others) is ruled out from the outset. Although no normative variable is so dominant in human life that it can be treated as an absolute (used to determine the outcome in every choice in which it appears), some aspects of life are for all practical purposes "non-negotiable," at least in the limited sense that no amount of education can offset the effects of inadequate nourishment on a growing child, even though inadequate nourishment may be preferable to death or unending torture. A different approach to comparison must therefore be found or developed as a basis for preference and justification.

If the problem of comparison (and justification) is approached *ex nihilo*, it will fail unavoidably. Until some set of preferences is accepted, taken as a point of departure, no justification is possible. If, however, a priority system is available, if the results produced by past applications have been assessed and the results generalized to form an integrated overall pattern, a choice can be justified. Each of the available outcomes may be located on the overall pattern, or a preference-ordering can be extrapolated from that pattern, thus resolving the choice. The apparatus required is precisely equivalent to the preference-ordering of states of health which is available in the field of medicine, and it is created in precisely the same manner. The initial grounds for preferring one outcome rather than another, which provide the basis for the accepted normative system, are found in past human experience. Preference may rest on direct affective reactions in the first instance, but such affectively based judgments will be modified cognitively in due course. The justification for retaining the priority system is based on a comparison of the results achieved by employing it with the results produced by employing any of the available alternatives or suggested improvements carried out in terms of the overall normative apparatus in use.

Normative systems, and the "disciplines" in which they are embedded, evolve over time out of experience; they depend inextricably and unavoidably on previous judgments. There can be no guarantee of improvement, or that improvement will be accepted as improvement should it occur. The best strategy available in those circumstances is to try to maximize competence in argument as fully as possible and make it widely available. Beyond such generalities, progress is contingent on that ineffable human attribute we call intellectual capacity, and particularly the skill and integrity with which the normative system in place is managed or developed. That system must serve as the starting point for justifying and correcting normative judgments. An illustration, taken from the field of agriculture, will suggest the ways in which it develops, and indicate the basic structures and processes involved.

Justification of Complex Choices: An Illustration

The problem of justification is not unique to normative inquiry. Any field of intellectual activity that requires qualitative assessments of options, or judgments of preference, from medicine to the purchase of securities, must find a way to deal with it. And in fact a common approach to the problem seems to have emerged in most such fields, although specifics vary from one to another. A clear illustration can be found in agriculture, or in animal husbandry, where the assumptions, structures, and processes used to judge livestock offer a good analogue to the apparatus that is needed to justify preferring some conditions of life rather than others. Asked to select one hog from a collection and justify the preference, an informed and competent judge of hogs will employ analytic tools that are structurally identical to those used by an informed and competent individual seeking to deal with a choice between different conditions of human life. Regarded substantively, the gap between the quality of a hog and the quality of a human life is enormous; analytically, the kinds of assumptions, structures, and processes that are employed for making and justifying qualitative judgments are virtually identical in both cases.

The essential prerequisite to competent and defensible hog-judging within a field of inquiry concerned with raising and evaluating hogs is an adequate conception of "hog potential," an overall construction of what a hog could be, or "should" be, generalized out of past experience, but taking into account, and extrapolating from, current knowledge. The conception of "hog potential" that is needed for maintaining and improving the breed is not, as might seem plausible, the equivalent of a multidimensional, full-color portrait of "Super Hog." Instead, a broad and flexible construct, derived from the overall purpose assigned to the hog (such as optimizing a farmer's economic return), is created out of past experience with hogs and used to make the assessment. If hogs serve different purposes for different farmers, as human lives differ with respect to purposes served, a range of constructions of "hog potential" will be needed, each developed by the same overall procedure but differing considerably in content. Those integrated overviews make possible the comparisons needed for assessment and justification. The comparisons are made indirectly, by locating particular cases on the overall composite pattern incorporated into the conception of "hog potential." That pattern can be improved over time out of experience in precisely the same manner as the concept "hammering."

Obviously, the overall purpose of a human life differs fundamentally from the purpose that is used for qualitative assessment of hogs. The purpose of the hog is determined by forces that are external to the hog, and depends on the hog's relationship to its human owners; the purpose of a human life is defined at least partly in terms of its own internal qualities. A hog may live to fulfill a farmer's purposes, but human life is lived at least partly for the sake of living a human life—no external "purpose" is required. Having said that, it remains the case that the purposes of both hogs and humans are determined and assigned by humans. Further, since the calculations are made using the same intellectual apparatus in both cases, it is not surprising to find that the structures and processes involved in making and justifying preferences (by reference to purpose or potential) are basically the same.

Within the discipline concerned with hog raising, a set of variables has been created that identify the hog's important dimensions, given the purposes sought (by the owners). An overall conception of a "full" life, of what human life can be, is equally necessary for inquirers concerned with human normative affairs, given the role that has been assigned to "maintaining and improving the human condition," and is also generally available. In both cases, a selection of "normative" variables is created out of past experience with the pursuit of the overall purpose and is then used to make judgments of preference that relate to the achievement of that purpose in future. Living with the results of accepting a given specification of purposes can in principle at least produce reasons for altering them. The values taken by individual variables, and combinations of variables, can also be ordered (by reference to past experience) to show relative preferability, again with reference to the agreed purpose. Finally, a set of benchmarks must be created that identify particular configurations of individual hogs that are considered either grossly unacceptable or highly desirable, again judged by reference to past experience and the accepted conception of what a hog's life can be, what purpose it can fulfill. Obviously, a fairly complex body of assumptions may be needed to deal with all of the hogs exposed to judgment. The necessary apparatus is readily available in such evaluative fields as agriculture; it can also be found in everyday human affairs, but tends to be less consistent or coherent, more open to argument and dispute, in that arena.

In an agricultural context, the justification provided for the apparatus employed in choosing or preferring, and for the results obtained by employing it in real cases, depends primarily upon (a) an overall conception of what a hog *can be* that is defensible on both experiential and theoretical grounds, and (b) a clear statement of the purpose to be served by decisions of preference made with respect to hogs. Taken together, they allow the user to integrate at least partially the available or accepted sets of priorities or preference-orderings, and to add benchmarks that indicate those outcomes that are unacceptable, or grossly undesirable, as well as those that are highly desirable or strongly preferred. The area between the unacceptable and the acceptable is populated by the sets of conditions that the evaluative apparatus is presently unable to differentiate. Similarly, there may be little capacity for discriminating among those situations regarded as "grossly unacceptable" or those considered "highly desirable." Further applications of the apparatus to particular choices provide an opportunity to examine those conditions again, and perhaps find evidence or reasoning that will differentiate their relative acceptability or preferability in a useful and defensible way—or at least reinforce the original judgment that indifference is appropriate.

In effect, the priority system tends to develop from the extremes, beginning with identification of grossly undesirable and highly desired conditions or states, whether of a human life or a hog. Over time, further differentiation can be introduced, both within the extremes and among the outcomes previously considered to be equally trivial, and the ordering can be altered appropriately. The process is unending: it is inconceivable, for both logical and psychological reasons, that humanity should arrive at a point where every possible state of life has been ordered to show relative desirability, where no human situation remains unexplored, or where all of the available outcomes form part of an aggregate regarded as equally desirable, equally undesirable, or equally trivial, by every person.

Justifying Preferences: The Primacy of the Negative

Given a normative "discipline" of the kind required, however crude and incomplete it may be, a relatively straightforward procedure will suffice for evading the measurement problem that so complicates the justification of preferences. The content of a choice between two or more projected life states for a human (as for a hog) can be represented by two or more configurations of variables, each taking specified values. Each of the projected configurations is examined in the light of an integrated priority system and its accompanying benchmarks—embedded somewhat loosely in an overall construction of human potential. The order in which the options are examined is not important, but in the case of human lives it is probably wise to begin with the projected outcome expected to follow from inaction, from not exercising capacity, to make certain that it is not overlooked.

The assessment of options will focus initially on two points: first, the set of variables and their values that indicate *unacceptable* outcomes, whether in hogs or in the conditions of human life, as they appear in the accepted set of benchmarks; second, the values for the same set of variables that are considered to be "highly desirable." Judgment, and justification, is influenced first by extreme negatives; choice proceeds by first rejecting the grossly unacceptable outcomes identified by the accepted benchmarks. If one outcome contains extreme negatives and the other does not, that decides the choice. If neither outcome contains an unacceptable condition of life, the actor or critic proceeds next to an examination of the highly desirable dimensions of the options; again, if one outcome contains highly desirable elements and the other does not, that can decide the matter. If neither procedure establishes a preference, a decision can be made randomly, or reasons can be sought for adding a new element or factor to the priorities, and perhaps to the benchmarks as well.

Clearly, the decision to rely first on an assessment of the negative aspects of each outcome is a matter of prime importance. Why emphasize that focus? Given the measurement problem, and the consequent inability to "weight" the outcomes, the actor or critic faced with a choice between two outcomes could, in principle at least, arrive at the preferred outcome by referring to either preferability, or unacceptability, or by considering both. But if the normative system is to be defensible, primary consideration should be given to the presence or absence of "unacceptable" conditions in the projected outcomes, as they are identified by the benchmarks. And the influence of such negatives is not compelling merely because there is much wider agreement on the undesirable characteristics of a human life, and on the reasons for their undesirability, than on the attributes that are evaluated positively, although that seems to be the case. The fact that agreement may be more likely if argument focuses first on ways of ruling out particular outcomes is hardly an adequate justification for accepting the procedure.

What forces primary attention to the unacceptable aspects of the outcomes available for choice is a line of reasoning that relates to the basic character of human life. Perhaps the most significant feature of human life is the inexorability of its temporal dimension. Life is on-going, and time is implacable; the process cannot be stayed and events cannot be erased or repeated. *Human life is not replaceable once spent.* Some aspects at least of human life are not "negotiable"; they cannot be offset or balanced against other gains—only preferred to even more serious losses. Because lost life is irreplaceable, the need to avoid se-rious reductions in the conditions of life, or the waste of life they represent, plays a primary role in the justification of preferences, and greatly influences the way in which justifications are phrased. In the case of the classic "philosopher's lifeboat," where a choice must be made between throwing one person to the sharks or risking the loss of everyone on board, the decision to save the bulk of the occupants is readily agreed. But it is preferable, on the reasoning put forward here, to argue that risking the lives of the whole company involves potentially greater harm than the harm done to the individual who is sacrificed, rather than argue for the option because it maximizes benefits. That need not rule out causing temporary harm (such as pain) to an indi-vidual in order to gain long-term benefits, or using substantial benefits to some as a justification for actions that produce moderate debilitation in the lives of others. Such considerations are automatically included in the outcomes by the practice of projecting the full implications of action as far into the future as existing theory allows. The objection is to a *procedure* of justification based on the benefits to be attained through action or choice; for that procedure does not, and cannot, min-imize the amount of "life quality" that is lost as a consequence of voluntary actions; yet that seems the only principle that can be de-fended over the long run given the assumptions from which the present argument proceeds.

In effect, defensibility in judgment requires that the Utilitarian pre-cept (seek the greatest benefits for the greatest number) be inverted. The guiding principle in defensible choice is to seek the least amount of harm or damage to the fewest number of lives: "minimizing misery" replaces "maximizing happiness." The philosopher's hypothetical case, in which all the world save one person is benefitted but that one person must be sacrificed, is only a hypothetical case and can be dealt with if and when it arises. In real-world choices, a strategy that will minimize loss of "life" is essential. As a side effect, that strategy is likely to stimulate the search for other modes of action that will augment benefits while limiting the harm done to those impacted by the action. The effect of the strategy must be weighed over time across a range of choices, for the implications of focusing on harm rather than benefits can vary widely, depending on the manner in which responsibility is allocated between individuals and collectivities—a special problem reserved for discussion in chapter 8.

If "damage minimization" is the basic strategy to be followed in making and justifying preferences, and only one outcome in a given pair contains an "unacceptable" condition of life, that outcome can be rejected summarily—assuming the benchmarks are properly set. If neither outcome, or both, contains an "unacceptable" element, then any "highly preferable" conditions located during the comparison can be used to determine the choice. If the examination is completed without producing grounds for a decision, if neither negative or positive reasons for rejecting or accepting one of the options is found, then the choice is a matter of indifference given the accepted normative apparatus, and can, in principle at least, be made randomly.

Note that decisions are *not* "left to the individual." The implication that an individual can somehow find an adequate basis for judgment in matters where informed opinion has nothing to say is merely silly. Of course, it is highly desirable, particularly in situations where the conditions being chosen are of great human import, to regard stalemates as an opportunity to elaborate and refine both the priorities and the set of benchmarks. That is, the critic can return to the overall conception of human "potential" on which the normative apparatus depends, seeking reasons for preferring one of the two outcomes, either by reference to the values taken by the other, less critical, variables included in the overall configuration that goes to make up the content of an option, or by bringing additional experience to bear.

The Parallel to Causal Justification. A very good analogue to the way in which preferences are justified is found in the procedures used to create classifications, or establish "causal" relations, in the physical sciences or elsewhere. In an "inductive" knowledge system, priorities relate to preferences in exactly the same way that causal assumptions relate to the sets of specific observations from which they are generalized. Analytically, the search for a "cause" always begins with a particular event. The goal, strictly speaking, is to locate the necessary and/or sufficient conditions for that event to occur. Put differently, the "cause" of a specific event must be found in the set of antecedent conditions that appear in a real-world case. The search for a cause is guided by, and the likelihood of success depends upon, the amount and kind of present information and past experience relevant to the event that is available. Such data can be supplemented, if time and resources permit, by deliberate actions meant to generate specific kinds of additional information. Further, if a number of "identical" events can be examined concurrently, that may facilitate the task of isolating the cause in the particular case. But the cause of a particular event is found only in the antecedent conditions to that event; otherwise an uncontrollable unknown or "spook" is inserted into the knowledge system.

Once a potential cause is selected or assumed, experience with other examples of the same event can be searched for evidence to support or contradict the assumption. Thus, if X is assumed to be the "cause" of event Y, then history is examined to see if event Y has occurred in the past in the absence of X, if event Y has occurred invariably when X has appeared, and so on. Given the conception of "causality" required for directing actions, at least some cases must be included where condition X has been created by deliberate human action. If the causal assumption holds for the particular case, and has been generalized and then tested against other members of the same class of cases (the two steps are usually combined), the evidence can then be regarded as sufficient to justify acceptance, always conditionally.

The cause of an event is to be found in a particular set of antecedent conditions; the justification for assuming the cause, on the other hand, is found in summarized and generalized past experience. Solving a particular case and generalizing the solution produces a pattern that can be used to deal with the class of cases exemplified in the particular. It may be difficult to identify that class, but the problem can usually be resolved in application, by trial and error learning over time. The generalized solution is tested against other particular cases, as they have appeared in the past or as they appear in the future, whether as the result of the normal flow of events or as the result of human actions. The results of these additional applications or tests serve to strengthen or weaken the justification for the assumptions on which the generalized solution depends.

Similarly, preference begins, analytically, with a particular choice; the solution to that choice can be generalized to deal with a class of cases. The justification for the preference, like the justification for a causal assumption, is found in past experience, suitably summarized or generalized—in the substantive content of the "discipline." The principal difference between establishing a causal relation and justifying a preference is found in the different possibilities for testing created by the meaning of the two terms, and the resulting "justification" problem with respect to normative inquiries. The proposed alternative to direct comparisons and "weighing" of outcomes functions in a way that resembles in most important respects the development of causal theories in empirical inquiry. In the case of theories, a selection of variables is identified which are assumed to be so strongly linked to one another that for all practical purposes, the value taken by one variable in the set is controlled by the values of the others, however they may be induced to change, and can be projected given an appropriate rule. In normative inquiry, the values taken by a set of normative variables

(incorporated into benchmarks), alone or in combination, are assumed (also on the basis of past experience) to have such a strong impact on the quality of human life that they can be used to rule out outcomes in which they appear. Illustrations of the general procedure can be found in various fields, but they are nowhere more clearly visible than in medicine, where such "benchmarks" as death, disfigurement, total disability, or extreme psychic shock have been widely used for many years to limit choices made in the course of treating patients.

The principal difficulty encountered in the effort to develop and apply the needed apparatus arises from a separation of capacity and responsibility that is brought about by the role of social organization in human affairs. Strictly speaking, benchmarks indicate human conditions that should be altered, sought after or ignored in the choice-making process, other things equal, by those who exercise the capacity to produce change. However, the implied doctrine (that capacity entails full responsibility) is difficult to maintain in a world that is characterized by large numbers of interacting individuals living within a variety of disparate social organizations under circumstances that may differ grossly from one person to the next. For the moment, that problem will be set aside for discussion in chapter 8.

Multi-Person Choices: The Conflation Process

To this point, the discussion has focused on the creation and justification of preferences and priorities in choices involving only one human life. Preferences, which are solutions to particular choices, are justified primarily by developing benchmarks that identify the extremes of unacceptability and acceptability among the life states from which choices are made. Adopting an overall strategy or principle of minimizing the waste of human life provides a practical working base for the field. If more than one person appears in the set of available options, very little change is needed in the structures and processes used to make and justify preferences, although the argument may be more difficult both to formulate and to follow. The reason why the introduction of additional persons into the set of outcomes from which choices are made does not greatly complicate the process of making and justifying preferences is found in the effects of the equality assumption—the assumption that in the limited sense of life *qua* life, one human life is the equal of any other. That assumption allows the chooser to conflate individual lives, to aggregate attributes as though they pertained to a single person, and thus avoid the need to balance one life against another.

To illustrate, assume a choice between outcomes in which two human lives appear, each differently affected by an action. A simple matrix will show the outcomes schematically and illustrate the kind of simplification that can be achieved by conflation of individual attributes:

Person	Option 1	Option 2
A	Condition X	Condition Y
B	Condition O	Condition P

As it appears in the figure, the choice poses an essentially unsolvable weighting problem for the actor or critic. Given the equality assumption, however, it can be transformed into the following matrix:

Person	Option 1	Option 2
A (or B)	(X + O)	(Y + P)

The choice can now be resolved in precisely the same way as any single-person, multi-variable choice. If the elements in each option consist of more than one normative variable, and each outcome contains some normative variables that take "undesirable" values and others whose values coincide with the "desirable" benchmarks, that equates precisely with the problem faced in any single-person, multi-variable choice. In effect, the equality assumption allows the critic (or analyst) to conflate or collapse a number of individuals into a single "life" and proceed as if dealing with a single-person choice. Thus a choice between (a) deafness for person A and normal health for person B, or (b) blindness for person A and a serious liver ailment for person B can be reduced, other things equal, to a choice between blindness and a serious liver ailment for one person or deafness for one person—not a very difficult choice if it actually appeared in a real case. In principle, any number of persons can be collapsed into a single set of attributes and treated as a single "person." The justification required may become more complex as the number of variables affected increases, but the overall procedure remains relatively straightforward.

The conflation procedure is particularly valuable for dealing with collective actions that impact large and diverse populations. For the equality assumption, coupled with a strategy of "minimizing misery," and the use of established benchmarks, makes possible a radical simplification of the substance of a choice. If other things are equal, an option in which only a few lives are found to be in a grossly unacceptable state is preferable to another option in which a much larger population live "unacceptable" lives; if no "misery" is involved, the number of persons living under highly desirable conditions can then be used as a basis for decision. The procedure remains rough and crude: misery can be minimized only up to a point, even if the impact of change on the less miserable could be ignored; such limits are reflected in the content of the outcomes. The procedure can serve as a starting point: it is easy to apply and the results produced are fully amenable to improvement over time out of experience.

Avoiding Circularity: Developing and Validating "Disciplines"

In the approach to the justification of preferences sketched above, the principal danger to be avoided is circularity, arising mainly out of the need to begin *in medias res*, with an existing normative apparatus. Circularity can be managed or controlled, however, without further complicating the analytic apparatus or its applications. The multi-element character of the overall intellectual structure used to justify preferences provides a built-in safety factor; in the normal process of justification, the inquirer will be forced to examine these elements in a variety of combinations that should bring circular reasoning to the surface quickly and reliably.

Justifying a preference necessarily involves the use of a number of intellectual tools; the "discipline" employed in justification is a complex of several different elements. At a minimum, it includes a set of normative concepts, an integrated collection of priorities or preference-orderings, an overall conception of a full or optimal human life, a set of benchmarks based on that overall construction, and a number of methodological premises, of which the more important are those that relate to the overall purposes of inquiry and to the canons of evidence and argument to be applied in the field. There is also included a body of relevant past experience, particular and generalized, which will provide, among other things, information relating to (a) the conditions in which people have lived, (b) people's subjective reactions to living with those conditions, (c) judgments based on those reactions, and so on. And finally, there must always be a real-world choice for which a preference is to be established. Each of these elements is to some degree independent of the others.

Every choice involves a complex set of interactions among those elements; such interactions provide a means for reducing the risk of falling into a vicious circle inadvertently. Each application of the overall apparatus to a real situation requires, in principle at least, the application of several elements in combination, and thus provides an opportunity to examine their consonance. Collectively, those applications, if self-consciously made, provide the nearest thing to a "test" of the apparatus that is available.

Perhaps the best way to illustrate the nature of the "test" is to trace the career of a choice from inception to decision (including justification), focusing on three basic elements: the overall conception of human potential, the relevant body of past experience, and the details of the particular case. Assume, for illustrative purposes, that the choice is being made by an informed and competent inquirer. Note particularly that: (a) the validity of the concept of human potential is wholly contingent upon its consonance with the content of past experience, and (b) past experience and the particular case are largely independent of one another and at least partly independent of the concept of human potential, although the conceptual apparatus used to define its content has been used to structure the content of both past experience and the options available in the particular case.

The content of the real-world choice is checked first against the integrated priority system/benchmarks, looking for grossly unacceptable conditions within each outcome. In the process, assuming a competent critic, the construction of human potential is in fact compared systematically to both past experience and the particular case, taken together. That provides an opportunity to check each of its elements against past experience. Further, it raises the possibility, in principle at least, of redefining the content of both past experience and the particular case and thus extending the scope of the inquiry to include the whole of the normative enterprise. How frequently such a reexamination can or should be carried out cannot be established in general terms; it depends very much on the state of the field. Clearly, not every choice can be regarded as an opportunity to reexamine the normative apparatus; on the other hand, a field that remains unexamined for extended periods of time courts disaster. Here the functioning of a community of "informed and competent" practitioners can be expected to resolve the problem informally. Such persons are by definition likely to be among the first to become aware of the kinds of real or incipient inadequacies or inconsistencies that usually trigger a careful reexamination of an established intellectual apparatus. The inadequacies can be expected to emerge most often out of efforts to deal with real cases.

In effect, particular choices provide an opportunity to reexamine the "discipline," for that construct serves as the central focus of justification (because significance and preferability are determined there), and therefore as the principal focus of efforts to improve the apparatus. Four of its features or dimensions are particularly important: adequacy of scope, internal consistency, validity with reference to experience, and methodological acceptability. Every real-world choice provides an opportunity for a systematic check of any or all of these points. Improvement depends mainly on the extent to which users are sensitized to the opportunity for validation provided by each application to a real-world case.

The aspect of the "discipline" that is particularly sensitive to such testing or comparison is the relation between the priority system, the set of benchmarks incorporated into it, and the overall construction of human potential. Inconsistencies are most likely to emerge during efforts to provide a justification for a preference, for all three elements are then applied to a relatively limited and well-defined body of information. In general, the validity of each of the elements in the "discipline," the extent to which each one can be justified out of experience, is checked by multi-factor comparisons involving a present case, past experience, and one or more of those elements. Thus the adequacy of concepts, priorities, and benchmarks is checked by applying them to a current problem, but their validity is a function of both past experience and the overall construction of human life and its potential incorporated into the "discipline." The overall construction of human potential can be tested, in broad terms, by reference to past experience, but its relevance or applicability in the particular case determines whether it has remained abreast of current developments in related knowledge. The benchmarks, for their part, are created out of past experience with disasters and successes—within a framework provided by the overall conception of human life that is incorporated into the "discipline"— and are reexamined in that context. Finally, the basic construction of human life and its potential, which plays the major role in determining significance, is checked for discrepancies within the context of the currently available body of relevant knowledge. Such "tests" may be far removed from the kind of testing available in the physical sciences, but they constitute at least some protection against slipping into circularity or acting upon a set of incorrigible premises.

The methodological assumptions contained in the "discipline," the canons of evidence and argument accepted for normative inquiries, are assessed by a pattern of systematic reasoning that begins from a construction of human capacity and a set of real-world limitations. They in turn can be checked against best knowledge in the respective fields of specialization. If differences in judgment arising out of real cases are followed by systematic efforts to discover the reasons why such differences appear, that procedure should surface conflicting methodological assumptions and provide a point of departure for trying to resolve them—on the understanding that resolution may turn out to lie beyond present capacity.

Finally, it should also be noted that the effort to validate the elements of a normative "discipline," whether it results in a more defensible apparatus, provides the necessary opportunity to improve the quality of "informed and competent" criticism within the field, particularly if it leads to open discussion of issues raised.

In practice, the overall structure is unlikely to be as neat and trim as analytic processes suggest; disconnected priorities, and even outright inconsistencies, are to be expected. But the principles of development and testing are reasonably clear, and the overall process can in time generate an integrated, transitively ordered, priority system encompassing all of the life states that have appeared in the past and able to deal with recurrences directly—and with wholly or partly new situations by extrapolation—while avoiding at least the worst forms of circularity. As the apparatus matures, that capacity should increase fairly dramatically.

MEDICAL PRACTICE AS AN ILLUSTRATION

A good example of a field of study that applies the approach to inquiry and justification of preferences developed above is contemporary medicine, especially as it deals with physical ailments. Assuming a commitment to generating knowledge useful for directing human actions in defensible ways, and a further concern for improving the human condition, far more can be learned from an examination of medical practice than from moral philosophy or ethics. Indeed, either medicine or agriculture provides a better model for emulation for the human sciences (or arts) than the physical sciences generally, and physics or chemistry in particular. For medicine, taken as a whole, is an empirically rooted, inductively generated, and normatively driven enterprise, committed to developing knowledge that can be used to direct actions to the reification of a normative structure. It combines inquiry, normative judgment, and policymaking in a way that exemplifies almost perfectly the perspective on knowledge adopted here. The conceptual, normative, and theoretical problems encountered in medicine parallel very closely those outlined earlier with respect to the direction of actions generally, and that greatly facilitates learning, and even outright borrowing, by those working in other fields.

To illustrate, the concept "state of health," which is central to both normative and empirical concerns in the field of medicine, has precisely the same analytic character as the concept "condition of life." Indeed, health is one of the major normative variables in the overall set needed to deal with choice problems generally. As a normative variable, "state of health" is also a configuration of factors and subject to the same problems of definition and measurement as the more general concept "preferability of a condition of human life." Neither "state of health" nor "condition of life" allows the creation of a standard unit of measurement; neither can be reduced to a single variable; neither can be used to produce the kinds of testable propositions found in empirical inquiries. In medicine, the concept "state of health" is widely employed for imposing a preference-ordering on different conditions of life in both single-person and multi-person situations; in normative inquiry generally, capacity is less well developed, but the structures and processes required are identical. Finally, the field of medicine is committed to the same overall purpose that directs normative inquiry generally—maintaining and improving the human condition. That characteristic is particularly valuable for the prospective borrower in social science; a field of study that is unconcerned with human actions, however well it may fulfill its own empirical/methodological requirements, is unlikely to be a good model for another field committed to dealing with them.

Within medicine, as in policymaking generally, normative judgments (preferences) cannot be avoided. Physicians regularly judge whether an individual is "healthier" in one state of health than another; medical treatment, which is an essential part of the profession's function, requires a judgment to the effect that one state of health is so "grossly unacceptable" (unacceptable at a level that justifies the cost and risk of treatment) that treatment is warranted. The latter judgment requires the use of benchmarks or cut-off points at which members of the profession should try to alter the "state of health" given the present state of knowledge and technology in the field—ignoring, for illustrative purposes, the condition of the patient's resources.

In effect, medical and "general" judgments of preference involve the same set of considerations. Such judgments only rarely generate serious controversy among practicing physicians. Not everyone will agree with every medical judgment, of course, but within the community of "well-informed and competent" persons, such as the physicians who specialize in the same branch of medicine, agreement on diagnosis and treatment can usually be reached in all but a few special cases. And if the question whether one state of health is preferable to another is seldom openly raised, and might not be taken very seriously, that is a measure of the strength of the established "discipline" in the field, for the question is raised, and resolved de facto, regularly and often in practice. In some cases, decisions are left for the patient to make, but it is uncertain whether the explanation of outcomes that must be supplied by the physician does not already prejudge the decision. In any event, normative judgments create serious problems for medical practitioners mainly in a few "grey areas" where empirical knowledge is weak and projections of the consequences to be expected from acting (or not acting) are uncertain, or cultural norms are particularly powerful and inhibiting.

The kinds of information and argument required for justifying preferences are most clearly seen in the medical community's way of judging the need for action, for putting a policy into force. Physicians not only deal frequently with the question "Is person X healthier today that he/she was a year ago?" (which requires only a preference-ordering of two health states) but also with the much more difficult question "Does X's physical condition justify the use of medication or other forms of medical treatment?" or "Is there an achievable alternative state of health that is preferable to the one presently displayed by the patient if all of the side-effects are taken into account?" Such questions go well beyond diagnosis (pattern-recognition) or the development of a mode of treatment (policymaking contingent upon a prior normative judgment) into the realm of the predominantly normative problem.

To answer those questions, the patient's "state of health" must be assessed. That raises first the question, "What data should be gathered?" which leads in due course to the further query, "Why these data rather than others?" Analytically, that is precisely equivalent to asking, "What selection of variables should be used to structure the outcomes to be used as a basis for judgments of preference?" If pressed, that query leads unavoidably to a normative judgment and supporting argument or justification. Taken seriously, it will trigger an endless regress unless purpose and past experience can be combined to produce pragmatically based criteria for making decisions. In medicine, such criteria are already available for a wide range of situations. They were developed out of an expanding body of past experience, increasingly systematized and ordered by reference to the physician's need to decide whether medical treatment is required as well as the kind of treatment that is called for. The normative apparatus that has been created within the field provides a solid basis for assessing past performance. Medicine can, under some circumstances, produce the information needed to decide whether a particular state of health is unacceptable and should be altered. Such medical benchmarks are created using the same procedures followed in any normative inquiry seeking to identify the "unacceptable" and "highly desirable" conditions of human life.

In order to perform its functions, medicine must have available a body of generalized knowledge, empirical and normative, ordered to reflect or summarize the judgments that have been made on the basis of that experience and sustained by subsequent practice—a medical "discipline." That structure is precisely equivalent to the kind of "discipline" needed to justify preferences, but is restricted, in principle at least, to the "state of health" dimension of the whole life. Descriptive accounts of an individual's "state of health," measured in terms that are themselves a product of past experience, can be located on an ordered or stratified pattern of great complexity and detail. That integrated pattern summarizes experience and judgments relating to the range of health states that have been encountered in past medical practice. If a given state of health does not appear in the overall ordering, it can be interjected or extrapolated, tentatively, and the proposed location defended.

Over time, and with repetition, such judgments can be stabilized by the use of benchmarks that are created concurrently with other relevant knowledge given the overall purpose that medicine pursues—"death," "disfigurement," or "incapacitation" are among the more common such reference points employed. The importance of focusing first on the "negative" aspects of the available outcomes is firmly established in medical practice. And some capacity to estimate the "distance" between a given state of health and the established benchmarks has been developed out of past experience. Medical training serves to transfer the overall apparatus from one generation of physicians to the next, together with some awareness of the possibilities for extending and improving it—and a sense of responsibility for doing so if the opportunity appears. (In medicine, as in other fields, that function tends increasingly to be left to specialists.) In short, medical knowledge, empirical and normative, is refined and extended in the same manner as Norton Long's hammering, or other more general forms of knowledge. A close parallel to the overall procedure is found in the way that knowledge of agricultural practices, or hunting and fishing techniques, is developed and transmitted within traditional societies.

The question how the medical equivalent of an integrated priority system, and a set of procedures for validating and improving its elements, evolved historically cannot be answered here. But the analytic requirements for producing such structures and criteria as they appear in the field of medicine are quite clear, and their implications for the direction of normative inquiry are worth attending. Four points are particularly important: first, the meaning of the concept "state of health" is "induced" out of experience and practice; second, the selection of concepts used to measure and assess "states of health" is developed concurrently from the same experience base; third, a set of cut-off points or benchmarks is created for making judgments about the need to act in particular situations; fourth, self-conscious application or use serves to test the normative apparatus over time. The process makes use of criteria of performance that are also generated out of an overall conception of human health potential derived from the same body of experience. Agreement on such matters does not emerge full blown within a field of inquiry or profession; the process is evolutionary, and to some degree uncertain. The old adage "Those what has gets more" seems to apply, however, for as the overall apparatus is elaborated and refined, the capacity to deal with particular classes of events improves; improvements in the capacity to deal with specific events tend in due course to translate into improvements in the overall structure; that in turn facilitates still further improvements...

At any point in time, the medical "discipline" summarizes the judgment of the medical community (informed and competent opinion) with respect to the meaning of "state of health," the configuration of variables that should be used to measure the concept, and the preference-ordering to be imposed on specific configurations of variables as they appear in real cases. The special problems encountered in collective decisions are found only rarely within medicine. Perhaps the closest parallel to them appears in the emergency room, when judgments must be made about the priority of treatment to be assigned to particular "states of health." The criteria needed to make such decisions, the medical "benchmarks" used to compare states of health in different persons, are created in precisely the same manner as those used by hog raisers or others seeking to make reasoned and defensible assessments of quality.

Although medicine provides a particularly good model of the kind of normative apparatus needed for justifying preferences, a very similar structure can be found in any field where judgments of preference must be made. The automobile mechanic must deal with the same *class* of judgments as the physician, although the significance of the mechanic's concerns will rank lower on an overall preference-ordering developed for general use. In all cases, the most important prerequisite is an established "discipline," however crude that can serve as a point of departure. Once a beginning is made, experience can flesh out and refine the apparatus, and reinforce the justifications on which it depends.

Three more points remain to be made about the field of medicine as an illustration of an approach to knowledge development and use that is suitable for normative inquiry. First, medicine demonstrates particularly well the importance of a commitment to directing real-world actions, and to the creation of the necessary body of empirical and normative knowledge. That commitment makes possible a type of evolutionary development and improvement based on experience that is closed to formalistic inquiries, or those that lack a pragmatic purpose. It also forces attention to the need for empirical and normative knowledge to evolve concurrently and from an experiential/pragmatic base. Given a commitment to treating patients, or altering the "state of health" of individuals (changing the value of a normative variable), one major function, and effect, of systematic inquiry is to refine and clarify basic concepts such as "state of health" and provide them with increasingly accurate and comprehensive indicators. In the process, a fuller statement of the various factors that influence the normative variable can be produced, and the overall capacity to both measure and alter the value of the normative variable can be increased. That in turn forces further efforts to refine and improve the priorities applied to different configurations of the variables in use, and to produce a justification for considering those changes to be "improvements." In so doing, the normative foundation on which the field of inquiry depends can be elaborated and strengthened. Medicine, in short, is both driven by a normative commitment and driven to the elaboration and improvement of a normative system that can guide physicians in the fulfillment of their normative purpose. It is unlikely that the quest for knowledge intended for directing significant human activity can proceed in a defensible way without producing and applying, implicitly or explicitly, a normative apparatus of this kind. It follows that systematic examination and criticism of these "working" systems is an important part of normative inquiry as a whole, a source of data as well as a potential testing ground for proposed contributions to the field.

The second major point to emerge from this brief look at the field of medicine is the singular importance of learning to identify the extreme cases (of producing benchmarks), particularly those that mark unacceptable life states. The reason is found in the need to go beyond a simple ordering of cases, whether medical or more general, to identify those situations where action is either essential or highly desirable. The process of developing and applying preferences will tend to generate an overall ordering of life situations (whether specifically medical or more general in nature) that is most fully articulated at the two extremes, at the points where conditions of life or states of health that are considered highly desirable, and those that are grossly unacceptable (where the need for action is strongest) have clustered. Understandably, the attention of those concerned with directing actions will tend to concentrate in the area where the need is greatest, on the "unacceptable" end of the spectrum, because of the non-retrievable character of human life once past. An evolving overall apparatus will therefore tend to develop from the extremes, and particularly from the unacceptable portion of the continuum, into the central penumbra or layer of indifference. Because of that characteristic, one useful way of comparing levels of both individual and social normative development is to examine the content of the areas of indifference in their normative structures, as well as the areas where action is considered essential. A more fully developed normative apparatus need not be characterized by a narrower area of indifference—indeed, that area may in fact increase in size as capacity improves—but the borders between indifference and concern should become much more sharply delineated over time as the apparatus becomes more complex and sophisticated.

The third point can be briefly made. Medicine, more than most other areas of inquiry, shows the enormous importance that attaches to the integrity of each individual inquirer or practitioner. Unless one can rely on the other perfectly, the enterprise cannot function effectively, and perhaps cannot succeed at all. Given the trends of the times, it is a point that bears all of the emphasis than can be imparted to it.

SUMMARY

The parallels between the "justification problem" in normative inquiry and the "induction problem" in empirical inquiry are both striking and instructive. Neither is amenable to formal resolution; each can be evaded. The evasion procedure is roughly the same in both cases. In empirical inquiry, in efforts to create the knowledge required to mold the environment to human purposes, success depends on the availability of a broadly agreed conception of how the world that is accessible to the senses functions, how its elements interact or are interrelated, and how such knowledge can be produced and tested. Pragmatic success in achieving human purposes in the environment can provide the needed quality criteria for assessing proposed additions to the knowledge supply, or proposed efforts to produce them. In normative inquiry, the overall strategy is the same. Inquiries must begin with an established "discipline" that includes an overall construction of human potential and seeks to deal with real-world problems, else they cannot be justified.

Over time, successful normative inquiry both creates and is contingent upon two major tools or constructs. The first is an overall conception of the range of conditions that human life can occupy, a set of potentialities that can serve as a point of departure for the various judgments required in the justification of preferences. It functions within normative inquiry in the same manner as the overview of the functioning of the perceived world that is implicit in the established body of scientific knowledge. The second basic tool is an integrated priority system, an ordered set of states or conditions of human life, arranged to show relative preferability. It will be marked by a set of cut-off points or benchmarks that distinguish grossly unacceptable states of life at one extreme and highly desirable states of life at the other. Both instruments tend to function by extrapolation and metaphor rather than formal logical inference, but that weakness, if it is a weakness, cannot be avoided.

Making and justifying preferences, like the development of empirical knowledge, emerges as a predominantly intellectual, though not a logical, process, evolving over time, as with medical practice or hammer-making. It must be grounded in, and closely linked to, both past experience and present needs. Affective reactions are an important datum in the justification of preferences because they reflect important aspects of the conditions of human life. They are also useful for reinforcing the intellectual process, and they may even supply a healthy counterweight to over-hasty change. They are not, however, part of the process by which judgments are justified. Other things equal, the justification of preferences will focus upon the negative aspects of the available outcomes, on the extent to which actions produce unacceptable conditions of life for some population, rather than on positive or desirable effects.

The development of a normative system depends very heavily on the availability of empirical knowledge, on the capacity to project the consequences of action into the future fairly accurately. That capacity is presently quite limited; at best, judgments are usually based on short-run projections of uncertain quality. That need cause no special problems in justification, which refers to and depends on the information that is available at the time when judgment is made. But it does have one very important implication for the field of inquiry as a whole: judgments of preference require periodic examination. The process is necessarily ongoing, and to some extent repetitive, but at least potentially expanding. Deliberate efforts to improve are essential, hence the field should have a propensity to query the validity of existing assumptions built into its norms of inquiry. In normative affairs, the guideline usually offered to budding statisticians is the course of wisdom: if you cannot predict accurately, *predict often*. If the effort to check the acceptability of the normative apparatus is made self-consciously, and if some measure of reality control can be maintained, development and improvement of a defensible normative system lies within the capacity of a sentient creature blessed (or cursed) with human attributes.

Arguments intended to justify preferences will be grounded in and limited by the accepted construction of the field, by the basic "discipline." The overall structure will be extremely complex, and internal consistency is likely to remain a serious problem into the indefinite future. The belief that justification of preferences can be simplified by reducing the complexity of the apparatus used to deal with normative questions, particularly by reducing the number of variables in the configurations used to state the condition of individual lives and thus facilitating aggregation, must be resisted. For aggregation serves to increase the heterogeneity of the class of persons identified by the configuration, and thus reduces the accuracy of the projected effects of action. The procedure, carried to excess, leads inexorably to the so-called index number problem; as the size of the class increases, the number of valid features that can be attributed to all members is reduced—eventually to zero.

Finally, note once again that the overall strategy to be followed in normative inquiry parallels the strategy used to improve hammers, and the intellectual requirements are the same. Given a purpose in the environment, efforts to deal with specific cases of choice in a responsible and systematic way, using whatever apparatus is in place but seeking to find reasons for retaining or altering it out of experience with use, can over time produce a conception of the significant dimensions of individual life, and how they should be ordered, that informed practice can endorse (or reject) with appropriate reasoning and argument. A combination of real-world applications and intellectual analysis or manipulation is in principle sufficient to allow creation of an intellectual apparatus useful for guiding the development of the normative system, and itself improvable out of efforts to guide that development. Potentially at least, each party to a normative argument could accept a different set of fundamental assumptions; competent argument, conducted with integrity and combined with adequate information, should surface points of difference and, in some cases at least, resolve them. The key to success seems to be the same potent combination of clearly stated purposes, intellectual integrity and competence, and attention to real-world constraints (most particularly those that arise out of established social and intellectual institutions) that characterize all successful intellectual enterprises.

SOME SPECIAL PROBLEMS

Normative inquiries tend to raise a host of major and minor problems, some historical and traditional, others analytic or methodological, that must be managed in any successful effort to justify preferences and have the justification accepted by informed and competent opinion. In most cases, they need only be touched upon briefly here, for the analytic apparatus handles them more-or-less automatically. Thus, the relative helplessness or vulnerability of an individual must be taken into account when outcomes are being assessed, in the same way that the extent to which those involved are "deserving" tends to influence the willingness of critics to accept particular outcomes. Both of these considerations are easily handled within the analytic framework. Relative helplessness is a function of capacity, which is reflected in the set of outcomes available to the person; deserving, or meriting, reward can be built into the long-run outcomes considered when preferences are being structured through the set of concepts employed as Buffer variables.

At a slightly different level, the analytic apparatus can manage without difficulty such matters as psychological aberrations in reported "experience" or "affective reactions." Although reported experience may be quite real to the individual, the information needed to discount, or confirm, such reports is produced more-or-less automatically by extending the set of attributes of the person doing the reporting—in much the same way that dentists can provide confirming evidence to support reports of pain experienced. The same procedure can be used to deal with the problem of rewarding the undeserving or punishing the guiltless. The approach allows easy separation of actions based on valid justifications from actions that amount to "doing the right thing for the wrong reason," a particularly important matter in the assessment of public actions (and indirectly public actors). The difference between the two kinds of actions cannot be determined from an examination of the priority that is accepted and applied, but if the priority is examined in conjunction with its justification, the difference is usually obvious. Insisting that the justification be included in statements of preference (plus any available objective data) provides an essential check on purely subjective reporting.

The so-called "intergenerational" problem in normative affairs, the tendency for preferences or priorities to lose their validity or justification as circumstances change, tends to diminish within the proposed approach—although it cannot be eliminated. For the apparatus, properly applied, functions in precisely the same manner as a "discipline" in physical science; adaptation to different circumstances is built into the analytic framework. Thus the question "What level of obligation to future generations is owed by the present" vanishes if human life is taken as the basic unit of significance in choice. All that is required of the present generation is attendance to the conditions of life of the existing human population; the sum of those living at any given point in time already includes three or four generations, and the future time span they represent is well in excess of theoretical capacity to predict or control most aspects of life. Some "future" problems will remain, certainly—particularly those that are derived logically from present trends and extrapolated to the distant future. It is certain, for example, that irreplacable resources such as the fossil fuels will one day be exhausted. The "problem" implied is in one sense insoluble. But that situation does not constitute evidence against *any* use in the present; that would only make it more likely that the future would be a disaster. All that can reasonably be demanded is intelligent management of such resources in the best interests of those presently living on the planet. What is more important, human intelligence presumably cannot manage anything beyond its own capacity to project the future in terms of the past. That is enough, because it must be enough. It would be pointless to criticize human capacity in terms of everything that imagination can conceive.

The approach to normative inquiry and judgment recommended here provides in addition a relatively simply way of eliminating the unfortunate influence of personal bias from normative judgments, and reducing its influence on normative affairs generally, without resorting to complex and tortuous—not to say farfetched—sets of assumptions. In psychological terms, elimination of subjective bias is very difficult and may be impossible. Analytically, a simple procedure will achieve the desired effect: the *identity* of the individuals involved in actions and their consequences is suppressed in the justification offered for a preference. Nothing of substance is lost in the process. The identity of the actor must be known, of course, before capacity can be specified and outcomes projected. The identity of those persons impacted by action must also be known before the full set of normative consequences can be projected; such things as family relations, membership in organizations, the set of institutional arrangements in force, and so on will influence the effects that a given actor can produce on a particular individual, often quite significantly. But if the *justification* adduced to support a preference for one outcome rather than another is restricted to the attributes and characteristics of the individuals involved, including the relations that hold among them but avoiding "proper name" identification—if a child is described as "someone's son" and not "my son" or "the son of Peter the Great"—there is no way for personal bias to intrude except through the virtually uncloseable loophole in any intellectual structure, the willingness of individuals to lie or cheat.

The reason for trying to eliminate personal bias from justification is found in the set of fundamental premises accepted for the overall normative enterprise. Using the *identity* of those involved as a basis for preference violates the assumption that one human life is the equal of any other in the sense specified. The amount of significance attached to any given life can vary with its attributes; that is how "deserving" is built into preferences. But references to the specific identity or the person violate the equality assumption. Once accepted, that principle requires that within any set of priorities, human lives must be interchangeable so long as their attributes remain the same. Otherwise, each preference or priority would be valid only for a specific person. Further, separating the identity and attributes of persons in the justification of a preference serves to separate ethics from psychology and thus helps to focus attention on what *should be* done rather than what is likely to be done. Finally, that practice serves to rule out the use of such observer-relative concepts as "utility," and thus eliminates pure selfishness or solipsism as an acceptable justification strategy—in principle only, of course, for such practices are easier to rule out in an analytic discussion than in real-world affairs.

A brief illustration of one type of problem that is particularly difficult to deal with psychologically will suggest the value of the analytic technique as well as the difficulties that can be expected in efforts to enforce it. Assume that a fireman enters a burning building, finds two young children there, and can save only one child. Which child to take? If all that is known is that each is a human child, there can be no basis for preference: the fireman cannot "choose," although a basis for decision can be produced, say, by tossing a coin. If, however, he knows that one child is terminally ill and will die in a few months while the other is normal and healthy, there is little difficulty about justifying a preference for one life rather than the other, and for acting on it—providing, of course, that only one child can be saved. If, however, the desperately ill child is the fireman's son or daughter, and that specific relation is known to the fireman, the tension between the decision he is likely to make, speaking psychologically, and the decision that should be made, speaking normatively, is all too clear.

A contrived situation of this kind cannot be taken too seriously, but it does parallel precisely the dilemma facing those who agree that humans ought not to smoke cigarettes yet insist on doing so themselves. The fireman could argue legitimately that failing to rescue his own child would cause some damage to the family as an institution, as well as to him personally (psychically) and to his particular family—hence, that avoiding such damage constituted an adequate justification for violating the equality principle. The argument would carry *some* weight, but seems unlikely to persuade neutral observers who agree with the assumptions on which the approach to justification taken here depends. Eliminating the identity of those involved in choice avoids only the psychological dimension of the problem. Accepting the equality assumption does not imply that there can be *no* departures from absolute equality—only that such departures must be justified. The preservation of the family, if it were truly at issue, would certainly count as an adequate justification for at least some kinds of differential treatment of individuals. How much would depend on the specific content of the options.

8

The Social Context

It remains to examine the normative implications of the social context in which virtually all human actions occur, using modern large-scale industrialized society as a prototype. From a normative perspective, three features of the social environment are particularly important: first, it consists of large numbers of *interacting* individuals—the interactions may be irregular, infrequent and sporadic, or frequent and sustained, but no person lives in total isolation from other members of the species; second, those individuals are *organized* into groups, which also interact regularly and systematically in much the same way as individuals; third, almost all of the earth's surface has been divided among a set of national states, each claiming *sovereign* authority over a specific territory. Wittingly or not, almost every individual lives at the center of a complex set of overlapping and interlocking relations with others, most of which are at least partly controlled or influenced by social organization; the whole apparatus is embedded in the present national state system. That structured set of interacting organizations has a profound effect on the kinds of normative systems that have been, and can be, developed, on the manner in which they are applied, and of course, on the results produced.

The normative significance of the social context is a function of the logic of human interactions; three of its implications are particularly important here. First, given individuals as they appear historically, extended interaction can in due course be expected to force development of a normative system that rises above pure selfishness; even if one individual should gain absolute dominance over all others, that expectation would hold for the rest. Second, extended interactions can at the same time produce types of social organizations that make it possible to accept and apply a set of normative assumptions adequate

for directing human actions on defensible grounds. Third, the interactions of organizations, which are driven by the same logic as the
interactions of individuals, lead inexorably to the creation of organizations to control them—and, ultimately, to the creation of sovereign,
but not necessarily absolute, social authority. Once in place, a sovereign
authority becomes a powerful instrument for extending, applying, and
altering the normative system in place within its jurisdiction. Like any
other tool, sovereign authority is intrinsically neutral: it can be used
to apply and support a normative system based on the assumption of
human equality, a system that seeks to optimize the condition of life
of all of those whom it affects; it can also implement a normative system
based on assumptions that actually negate or nullify efforts to order
human affairs on normatively defensible grounds.

In this chapter, the normative implications of the logic of those processes at work in the social environment are explored very briefly. The
analysis begins with isolated individuals, noting the kind of normative
apparatus that isolation implies. The effects of introducing interactions
among those individuals on normative (and organizational) requirements are considered next. The relation between social organization
and the development of defensible normative systems can then be examined systematically. That leads to a survey of the factors that force
creation of a sovereign authority able to organize the interactions of
organizations as well as individuals on a specific territory (a goal at
least partly achieved in the modern national state). A summary of those
factors of social organization that most influence their potential function in the normative enterprise concludes the chapter and sets the
stage for the development of a strategy for normative improvement that
is appropriate given the present international system. The approach
remains methodological or analytic rather than substantive or historical; space constraints force a broad and general treatment of the topic.
The principal concern is with modern industrialized societies such as
the United States, and the argument is formulated with those organizations in mind; whether it will apply equally well to the kinds of
national states found in the Third World or elsewhere is uncertain, and
perhaps doubtful.

Introductory: Normative Systems and Social Organization

It is a commonplace that human survival would be impossible in the
absence of social organization; the need for a defensible normative
apparatus is equally absolute, though perhaps less widely appreciated.
In fact, one depends on the other: a defensible normative system is
contingent upon the availability of a particular kind of social organization, and vice versa. Put differently, the kind of normative system

that is acceptable, the set of normative assumptions that can be defended out of experience, is determined at least partly by the social context—and thus depends to a very large extent on the character of the social organizations in which human life is lived. The crucial factor in normative development, aside from the resources that are available to members of a given society, is the set of implications that flow from the nature and frequency of human interactions, individual and collective, and from the sovereign organization created to manage them.

The Logic of Human Interactions. Even in a world where each person lived in total isolation, a normative system would be required to direct human actions. But the kind of system that could be justified out of experience would differ radically from the kind of normative system required and justifiable in a world of extensive human interactions; no normative system is equally applicable or defensible in all circumstances. Thus, if each person lived in isolation, the *homo mensura* assumption would still be made, but it would be pointless to assume that all human lives were equal; the phrase would have no meaning in experience. The normative system would be grounded instead on the principle of selfishness, for maintaining and protecting the self would be the only preference base worthy of credence under such circumstances. Relations with the nonhuman portions of the environment would be controlled by the "exploitative" principle—maximizing benefits to the self, restrained only by fear of retaliation or self-damage. In that limited sense, pure selfishness is properly considered the most primitive form of normative system that is available to the species.

Introducing human interactions into a world of isolated individuals would create stresses for those involved that could be expected to generate pressure for change. Extreme or pure selfishness is untenable in a world of interacting persons. However, accepting and applying something as dramatic as the equality assumption, even in the limited form accepted here, would require major changes in the behavior of the interacting population; those changes could not be justified (would be a very poor risk) unless there was a social organization in place committed to maintaining or enforcing the equality assumption. For accepting the assumption would expose the individual to the danger of being "exploited" by those currently possessing significant amounts of capacity to affect the lives of others, in precisely the same manner that the natural environment, both animate and inanimate, is exploited by those who live in isolation and premise their actions on pure selfishness. Absent organization, Hobbes picture of a humanity constantly engaged in a war of "all against all" seems quite plausible. The only lines of escape from such a situation would be through domination or cooperation; both depend on organization. Whether an adequate organization could be created by mutual agreement or consent, or whether it would have to be imposed by force does not matter so far as the logic of the situation is concerned. Human interactions, particularly if they were sustained, could be expected to generate efforts to stabilize the conditions of interaction, to lead to the development of both a normative system and some form of social organization able to enforce it. The two structures would be mutually contingent: the kind of normative system created would tend to influence the kind of social organization put in place; the kind of social organization created would have a profound influence on the kind of normative system that could be produced and maintained.

Human interactions generate social organization at least partly out of a need to stabilize the normative system in use; organization in turn makes possible a major transformation of the normative system. Within an organization, selfishness can be, and to some degree must be, replaced by the equality assumption, although it is important to emphasize that equality does not emerge automatically, and it need not be applied symmetrically, even in the limited sense that departures from equality have to be justified. The point is peculiarly important because the equality assumption is an essential component in every defensible normative system (for interacting persons). But assuming human equality, and acting upon it, whether inside or outside of society, involves risks to the self. If the assumption is to be based upon something more than a simple act of faith, justification must be found in the potential for enforcement that society provides. That is not to say that society requires or implies equality, for it does not. Societies can be constructed and operated on the basis of inequality as well. All that social organization can do is to make it possible in principle for some, or even all, of society's members to accept the equality assumption at a reasonable risk level; that in turn makes a defensible normative system feasible. It may be that over time every human population will be forced to accept the equality assumption as an alternative to living with the consequences of sporadic efforts to achieve and sustain dominance, but the historical evidence is unclear, and the logic of interaction would in any case remain unaltered.

The reasoning on which the argument depends is straightforward. Equality, in its root meaning, requires that each person be treated as a member of a common class. If all that is known about any group of individuals is that they belong to a common class, there is no basis for differentiation. The equality assumption requires those who accept it to treat each human life as equal unless a justification for differentiating them can be produced. Such justifications must be found in other characteristics of the individual—in past behavior that makes the individual "deserving," and so on. Social organization has the capacity to create a class of persons (members) that can be identified, and to enforce the use of class membership as a basis for decision and action in certain kinds of cases by altering the consequences that follow from a range of actions affecting its population. Enforcement of social norms will be imperfect, of course (problematic in particular cases), but almost any level of enforcement could be sufficient to justify acceptance of the organization's authority if all of the available alternatives are sufficiently repugnant. Once some minimal level of equal treatment is achieved, the social forces pressing for normative improvement can be expected to try to broaden the class of persons for whom equal treatment is enjoined and widen the areas of application; recent trends toward developing and implementing a broader and more meaningful concept of "human" rights illustrate the overall process very nicely.

Society and Equality. The foregoing sketch of the relation between society and normative system is based solely on analytic considerations, for human existence in utter isolation is a practical impossibility. The results of the analysis are particularly important for those situations in which large numbers of persons are organized within a pluralistic society. One family living alone and in isolation need only be concerned about equality among its own members; it can function selfishly with respect to the rest of the environment. In a world populated by many interacting families, such "external" selfishness is untenable, for precisely the same reasons that it cannot be maintained by interacting individuals over time. Further organization is again essential before selfishness can safely be abandoned. That is, if there are many social organizations, such as families, then in the absence of any overriding authority or sovereign, their situation is precisely equivalent to living in a system of individual interactions without organization; only the scale of potential conflict has been increased. Absent an all-encompassing organization (sovereign authority), the relations among organizations can be expected to remain based upon selfishness, whatever the set of principles applied internally, unless agreements based on self-denial can be created among them.

In effect, social organization functions to create an area in which the equality principle *can* be accepted by providing the kind of guaranteed reciprocity that makes the principle a reasonable risk for each individual, and thus makes it preferable, even by purely selfish criteria, to the alternatives. That guarantee, obviously, ends at the boundaries of the organization's jurisdiction or authority, and is no stronger than the organization's capacity to enforce. So long as interacting organizations remain without sovereign control, the threat of conflict, or "exploitation," is unavoidable. The threat is very strongly reinforced by the organizational "imperative," the need for every organization to discriminate between members and nonmembers, to differentiate between the internal and the external populations in significant ways, to give unequal "weight" to the effects of collective action on members and nonmembers, and in some cases to introduce differentiation based on class membership, even though class membership may be wholly irrelevant to the kind of effects that are produced by differentiating.

Selfish behavior by interacting collectivities produces consequences that differ only in scale from those generated by selfish behavior on the part of interacting individuals. Efforts to avoid such effects may try first to achieve voluntary agreement among organizations rather than seek to create a single all-encompassing organization, for obvious reasons. But the logic of the situation is clear, and it applies equally to the thirteen American colonies in the late eighteenth century, or the national states of contemporary Europe. It poses a clear dilemma for humanity: given frequent and potentially harmful interactions, success in efforts to improve normative performance depend absolutely on the availability of an adequate social organization; efforts to create or expand such an organization raise the spectre of tyranny and lead to efforts to control the use of its power and authority. Historically, attempts to escape from the horns of the dilemma have been at best only partially and temporarily successful, and the price of even such limited success has often been heavy—a point to be discussed further in the Conclusions.

Pluralism and Sovereignty. The pluralistic character of contemporary industrial society strongly reinforces the pressure to extend the authority of sovereign organization. The industrialized states comprise a large number of overlapping organizations; most individuals belong to several independent units—familial, political, economic, religious, and so on. The priorities accepted and applied by each organization can differ as night from day. If priorities are strongly held, that creates a situation which is the normative equivalent of a world made up of unorganized, interacting individuals. The problems generated by ethnic or religious differences in contemporary society, or by political extremism, are to be expected in such circumstances. The classic case of an individual caught in a network of incompatible personal and organizational commitments was the medieval citizen forced to take sides in a conflict between church and state. The same situation recurs in contemporary society, but usually on a smaller and therefore a more manageable scale. In any situation where a decision must be made, and a conflict among priorities cannot be avoided, "live and let live" is not a viable option if the priorities are held strongly enough. So long as organizations with overlapping memberships accept and apply different priorities, each collective choice becomes a potential locus of normatively driven conflict.

In the case of an individual actor, such conflicts can perhaps be regarded as opportunities to refine and improve the individual's normative system. But if large numbers of persons are affected by a collective decision, and the consequences are serious, society may literally be torn apart in the absence of an overriding or mediating force, and the lives of individuals made miserable in consequence. The only possible tool available for dealing with the problem is an organization with sufficient authority to nullify the effect of the differences, a criterion that can be met, in principle if not always in practice, by a sovereign organization. It seems reasonable to assume, given past history, that living under conditions of intense conflict would prove intolerable and that sovereign authority that led to stable living conditions would be preferable, other things equal.

It may seem paradoxical that an inductively based normative system may depend ultimately on the availability of a sovereign authority, an entity or actor capable in principle of making and enforcing final decisions. Indeed, it may seem inconsistent, for the physical sciences, which provide the basic emulation models for inductively grounded knowledge systems, reject the notion of a "sovereign" authority and depend instead on a consensus of informed judgments for validation of knowledge claims. And it has already been agreed that there is no acceptable alternative to validating normative systems by the same means. However, a sovereign authority, even in its imperfect reification, the modern national state, is capable *in principle* of resolving the dilemma posed by conflicting organizational priorities, and no other means is readily available. In practice, "sovereignty" amounts to no more than the claim that a particular actor or organization could, if it chose, intervene to settle any conflict within its jurisdiction without external interference. Absolute authority need not be claimed and cannot be achieved. The primary effect of the claim is to make it possible in principle for society to cope with the problems raised by the logic of human interactions. From that perspective, sovereignty authority can serve the same analytic purpose in the justification of preferences that a gravitational field performs in the development of a mechanics of motion. Of the presently available repositories for sovereignty, only the national state comes close to fulfilling the requirements on the needed scale. That gives the government of the national state a potentially dominant voice in the development and implementation of the normative system in force in any human society.

To summarize, there is always a number of alternative sets of priorities that can be applied to a given choice or action, whether individual or collective. Given a need to act but conflicting priorities, each strongly and dogmatically held, the only way of resolving the impasse other than resorting to combat is through an appeal to some external authority. The consequences to be expected from relying upon physical force may be so serious as to make bowing to any authority preferable—as the medieval Russians, having concluded that they were incapable of ruling themselves, once summoned the Swedes to rule over them. Under present-day knowledge conditions, if an acceptable intellectual resolution to a choice problem is impossible, and the inadequacy of the arguments for each of the competing positions cannot be demonstrated to those involved by reason of their lack of competence, the only peaceful basis for resolution is external authority. Absent such authority, the disputants are left to settle the issue among themselves, one way or another. If those involved choose to fight rather than agree or acquiesce, which is a decision that lies beyond the power of any organization, no solution is possible unless one side or the other can impose it by force of arms. But less extreme cases, which are far more common, can be resolved by the exercise of "sovereign" authority (if it is accepted by most of those involved). Circumstances may force acceptance, even from those who suffer some injury thereby.

The physical sciences have no need for such an instrument as sovereign authority so long as they remain separated from policymaking. (What would happen, or has happened, when science accepts responsibility for making decisions is another matter.) Humanity generally cannot do without one. At present, the national states each lay claim to sovereign authority, although the extent to which it can actually be exercised tends to be severely restricted. Indeed, it can be argued that the modern national state came into existence precisely because of the pressing need to settle the kind of problems being discussed. What is at issue is not a matter of forcing the national state to become a normative instrument: the national state *is* and has been a normative instrument. The need is for explicit recognition of the potential normative role of sovereign authority in the contemporary world—particularly in implementing the all-important equality assumption—and a sustained effort to employ and extend it as far as possible while keeping its exercise under normative control.

SOCIAL ORGANIZATION

Human interactions make defensible (or at least acceptable) normative systems essential; social organizations make them possible at least in principle. Unfortunately, the conceptual apparatus available for dealing with the impact of social organizations on normative performance is not, to my knowledge at least, very well developed. The brief discussion that follows should therefore be regarded as a preliminary, and tentative, effort to deal with a major gap in the available analytic apparatus.

Strictly speaking, a social organization is only a convenient fiction, an abstraction of a very curious sort. It functions mainly as a symbolic device that can be used to refer to sets of complex individual attributes which are difficult if not impossible to characterize adequately in detail. Taken too literally, everyday usage can be highly misleading, for it tends to personify organizations, and to regard them as "entities" with certain attributes, including possession of authority. The practice can be dangerous, but it is also very convenient, particularly for dealing with the role that organizations play in various aspects of human affairs. In the discussion that follows, a social organization will therefore be treated as a "thing," an entity vested with some measure of authority and possessing the capacity to produce change in the environment. That usage allows organizations to be regarded as "actors" in the environment, which is particularly helpful for identifying the effects that organizations may have on individual lives (their normative impact), and therefore for assessing their potential role in normative affairs. Treating organizations as actors need not create serious problems so long as it is clearly understood that organizations "act" only by and through living human individuals.

Introductory

An enormous variety of social organizations can be found in the contemporary world. They range from simple and transient dyadic relations arising out of direct personal interactions through families or clans linked by blood lines to associations such as those used to deal with economic or educational activities, to the large and complex political associations controlling designated geographic locations and labeled national states. These national states presently claim sovereign authority over particular territories, and their claims are normally accepted by everyone involved. They now encompass, for all practical purposes, everyone living on earth. How the population that is subject to an organization's authority is identified, whether subjection to authority is voluntary or involuntary, permanent or renouncable, based on personal attributes or on geographic location, and so on, can vary enormously. Such differences, however, are unlikely to alter the role that organizations can play in normative affairs or the manner in which they affect normative development or applications, and they will be ignored here.

Whatever their size, authority, history, traditions, or function, social organizations are only instruments, a kind of tool created by humans for the fulfillment of human purposes. They are not, though they have sometimes been conceived as, "superior" entities in which humans aspirations or purposes are fulfilled. Regarded as tools, organizations, like any other human creation, have no intrinsic significance. Further, as with any other tool, the justification for an organization's existence is found in the contribution that it makes to the human enterprise, normatively defined—here, to maintaining and improving the conditions of life of some human population. What is essential, in context, is to avoid accepting the actions of any organization uncritically simply to "maintain the integrity of the society" or because of traditional beliefs or practices, for that could open the door to the kind of absurdity entailed in killing every member in order to save the organization.

The justification required for organizational (collective) actions or choices must satisfy precisely the same requirements as the justification of individual preferences. Regardless of the size, capacity, and purpose of the organization, the justification for exercising its authority in a particular way will be based on a comparison of the conditions of life projected for the affected population in each of the available options, using the same criteria and procedures employed in dealing with individual decisions. In most cases, the differences between individual and collective actions relate to the size of the population affected or the scope of the projected impact. However, a major difference does emerge when the claim to sovereign authority is taken into account. That claim sets the national state apart from all other organizations, for it includes the power to set the boundaries of its own jurisdiction, to determine the scope if its own authority and responsibility. That claim alone suffices to give the national state enormous influence over the normative systems developed and applied upon its territories, if only because being able to limit the exercise of specific classes of actions denies that capacity to society's individual members.

Rights and Obligations. Most of the features of social organization that are important for normative analysis are captured by the use of two basic concepts, "rights" and "obligations." The relationship labeled "friendship" or even "casual acquaintance," will serve to demonstrate the essentials as well as a large association such as a corporation. The "organization," in such simple cases, is found in a set of internalized rules, which may be wholly tacit and vague, that control and limit future interactions. In effect, a rudimentary organization consists in a more-or-less clearly understood set of rights and obligations, which need not be symmetrical, accepted by two or more "members." The crux of the "organization," to the extent that an "it" may be said to exist, is the internalized rule structure, a structure whose content may be very poorly articulated. There will be observable behavioral effects of accepting such rules, but inference from behavior to substantive content is treacherous, and the results must be treated cautiously. Strictly speaking, behavioral evidence can only rule out the possibility that particular rules are being applied or obeyed; it cannot establish them in positive terms.

In a two-member friendship, the organization created may involve no more than a set of rules that establish the rights and obligations of each member *vis-a-vis* the other. Thus one person may have the "right" to accompany the other on certain occasions, such as walking to school. The obverse of such rights is a set of obligations, in some degree binding on and accepted by the other person, to permit the exercise of the rights—to listen to what is said, to allow the other person to come along, and so on. In a simple case of this kind, it is easy to see how such rights and obligations emerge, and how they relate to the scope of the organization's authority. Further, it shows the value of the conceptual apparatus very well: a major function of every social organization is the creation of rights and obligations for members (with respect to one another). Each organization must have, *inter alia*, a set of members, authority or jurisdiction (the capacity to create and enforce rules of interaction), and a procedure for exercising that authority. The elements may be formulated vaguely and informally or embedded rigidly in a basic document such as a constitution. Over time, if the organization persists, the content of the fundamentals may be altered, and the amount and rate of change within an organization may themselves change. But the basic functioning of the apparatus will remain the same, as will its implications for normative development.

The larger and more significant types of social organization differ from those generated out of limited personal interactions primarily in terms of the amount of authority or capacity that they claim and the way in which that authority is exercised. Most large organizations have a recognizable "government," meaning simply that the exercise of authority is specified in terms of a set of persons or offices able to take part in the process, and access to such positions is controlled by rule. The organization that is most important for normative inquiry, the national state, is a large-scale association whose jurisdiction is defined by reference to a specific territory, and whose authority applies (presumably) to everyone who occupies it, whether permanently or temporarily. Subjection to the authority of a national state is a function of geographic location alone, although membership in the society (citizenship) may be based on other considerations such as biological descent, or voluntary accession.

In effect, the claim to sovereignty once accepted, the national state can create an outer envelope of normative rules within which every individual and organization on its territory must function. Further, the amount of authority exercised by a national state, the aspects of life to which its authority extends, is self-determined. The sovereign claim once admitted, control over the allocation of authority for every conceivable sort of decision is in principle placed in the sovereign's hands. Decisions that allocate authority are not made by the national states alone, of course; parents trying to decide how much autonomy to allow a child in the family, or corporations trying to decide whether to ban smoking in the workplace, face the same type of question. But the sovereign political association claims to be able to decide all such matters authoritatively, if it chooses to do so, without interference from any other organization, and to bind all of the individuals and subordinate organizations within its jurisdiction to that decision. Of course, the right to make a decision in principle may be quite a different matter from having the capacity to enforce it. Nevertheless, the potential entailed by the principle is of overriding importance for the discussion here.

The Dynamics of Social Organization

There are any number of different ways of conceptualizing what occurs when an organization's authority or capacity is applied or employed, but the more important of them can be treated as special cases of the ability to create rights and obligations for those subject to their jurisdiction. Thus, collective actions serve to aggregate and/or allocate resources of various kinds (a function that is closely related to the implementation of the equality principle)—to create rights and obligations for donors (involuntary) and recipients alike. From another perspective, collective actions serve to "load" or alter the specific content of the options available to individual actors. However conceptualized, collective actions can be regarded analytically as the application of an accepted normative system (the system applied by those who exercise collective authority) or as a way of influencing individuals subject to an organization's authority to accept particular outcomes.

It is also useful to think of a social organization as an instrument able to perform a range of functions for the population lying within its jurisdiction. First, it can serve as an insuring agency, spreading the costs and benefits associated with the fulfillment of particular individual needs across all or part of the total population. Second, it can perform like a unit of capital in an economic system, multiplying overall productive capacity by aggregating individual efforts and organizing them for the fulfillment of specified purposes. Third, organizations can serve as a connecting link among those subject to their authority, a channel through which the actions of one individual can affect the conditions of life of another. Finally, organizations can coordinate individual actions, allocating responsibility for particular situations or conditions within its jurisdiction to particular individuals and groups, thus greatly increasing efficiency or reducing the total cost of altering the conditions of life of specified populations within the society in particular ways. In short, social organizations are an instrument with enormous potential to produce changes, both beneficial and harmful, in the lives of those subject to their jurisdiction.

The centrality of normative considerations in collective actions is clear; each collective act affects the conditions of life of some population either directly or indirectly. Society, like every individual, is a functioning embodiment of a normative system, reifying the system by its actions. Its main normative function is to determine and enforce the set of benchmarks applied to the lives of society's members. In practice, social organization can do no more than make it possible in principle to obtain agreement on particular normative assumptions; it cannot guarantee that they will be accepted. Indeed, under some circumstances it may inhibit or even prevent normative agreement. For that reason, it is just as important for a population to create a social organization that is able to develop and implement an adequate normative system as to produce the normative system itself.

Loading the Options. Given a commitment to construing society as a device for creating rights and obligations, the notion that collective actions serve to "load" the options available to an actor, or alter the content of the outcomes available for choice in particular ways, is especially felicitous. It allows an accurate statement of every conceivable type of collective action, from paying salaries to waging war. And it provides a clear connection to the normative system that is accepted and applied by the organization, particularly to the benchmarks (the grossly unacceptable and highly desirable outcomes identified in the priority system), which provide the essential base for most decisions. In a defensible system for directing collective actions, the conditions actually generated within the society in the absence of collective constraints imposed and enforced by sovereign authority become the evidence used to support or recommend particular ways to load options. Unacceptable outcomes can be loaded with penalties (to the limits of the organization's authority or capacity) in an effort to force selection of a different alternative. If the "carrot" is judged to be more efficacious than the "stick," penalties can be combined with rewards of various kinds added to one or more of the available alternatives. The critical factors, aside from the availability of an adequate supply of resources, are the size and character of the population whose conditions of life are taken into account in collective decisions.

The concept "loading" calls attention very usefully to the need to make collective decisions in terms that are significant for the affected population rather than for those who exercise authority. The validity of the judgment on which the loading depends, which is an empirical rather than a normative matter, can be tested over time and the loading altered to produce results more closely in line with normative aspirations. In these terms, the prime responsibility of those who control the exercise of collective authority at any level is to decide which of the outcomes or options subject to the collective authority, or lying within the collectivity's jurisdiction, should be loaded and what kind of loading is most likely to avoid grossly undesirable outcomes.

Use of the concept "loading" has the additional advantage of forcing attention to the consequences of action (and away from the characteristics of the actions taken) when collective decisions are being made or subjected to systematic criticism. It thus facilitates the task of locating and avoiding actions based on inadequate reasoning. Focusing on outcomes is particularly important in collective affairs because it is usually easier to specify a set of *actions* to be punished or rewarded than to identify the sets of consequences which should be avoided or sought (to penalize speeding rather than penalize endangering life and property by the way in which a motor vehicle is operated, for example), and organizations, or those who direct the use of their authority, understandably if mistakenly prefer to deal with actions rather than outcomes. From a normative perspective, that practice introduces an element of ambiguity into the use of individual or collective capacity that virtually eliminates any possibility of providing an adequate justification for choices. A justification, to be convincing, must refer to the content of the outcomes available to a given actor; if the consequences of action, the content of the options, remain unknown or very uncertain, no justification can be produced and defended.

The problems created by focusing on actions rather than outcomes can be partially circumvented (at cost) if an agency such as the courts is allowed to modify the effects of loading actions by taking circumstances into account—in practical terms, by taking into consideration the specific outcomes available for choice. Thus a court may forgive a speeding charge because the driver was rushing an accident victim to a local hospital. Such court decisions serve to transpose action-based judgments into consequence-based judgments, and thus to open the way for adequate justification. Interestingly enough, such modifications are usually performed in the name of "equity," which may be an indirect way of giving tacit recognition to the normative inadequacy of decisions grounded in something other than the consequences of action.

Social organizations need not load options directly, or limit their interests to matters controllable through direct actions. Introducing changes into the overall environment in which individuals function can also serve as an effective way of loading the content of the available outcomes and thus altering individual and collective choices. Construction of a highway or an airport, for example, will add a new element to the range of options available to at least some part of the local population, otherwise there could be no justification for the decision. The question who has been affected in what way by the use of such indirect channels for influencing actions may be very difficult to answer, or may provide grounds for criminal action, but the principle involved is clear and the conceptual apparatus allows a very precise statement of actions and expectations, thus opening the way for criticism and improvement of performance.

Finally, use of the concept "loading" greatly simplifies discussion of the relations between individuals and collectivities, and serves to underscore some of the problems arising from those relations in a most useful way. Thus the general question to be answered by any actor functioning in a social environment is, "How have the available options been loaded by the various organizations whose jurisdictions extend to these actions?" Merely to raise the question in that form calls attention to the possibility that different organizations may load the same set of options in quite different ways (sometimes creating insurmountable dilemmas for the actor). Moreover, the likelihood of enforcement, which will vary from issue to issue and therefore further complicates the task of justifying the choice, is highlighted very effectively if "loading" is recognized explicitly as a collective imposition or addition to the content of the outcomes.

The Limits on Organizational Authority

In real-world affairs, each individual is subject to some level of control by a number of different associations. At the sub-national level, organizational actions are constrained by the authority of the sovereign national state. And the national state, however powerful it may become, is in some degree limited by both internal and external factors. No individual or collectivity can exercise absolute dominion over any person or group. And ultimately, each individual has the inalienable *capacity* to refuse obedience, to rebel against authority. The price of disobedience may be high, but if the individual is prepared to choose death rather than obedience, the limits of authority over that person have been reached. And if the inalienable capacity to rebel is exercised in concert by a significant portion of the total population, social organizations cannot enforce their decisions. With respect to large-scale collectivities such as the national state, it may be very difficult and costly to generate the kind of organization required to make rebellion effective, but the principle involved, that rebellion is one limit on the power of the most powerful of national states, cannot be gainsaid.

Aside from the extreme case of refusal and rebellion, there are other limits on the capacity of every national state; some are internal to the society and others are found in the surrounding environment. The internal limits are mainly practical, but effective nonetheless. Thus the cost of the kind of active monitoring of individual affairs required for absolute or totalitarian rule, even if it were technologically feasible, would be prohibitive, for costs escalate dramatically as the desired level of control is increased. Even under "ideal" conditions, such as high-security prisons, the level of control that can actually be achieved tends to be relatively low with respect to all but a few aspects of individual behavior. Further, present capacity to introduce changes into the lives of large populations that will endure over time, even if the indoctrination process is extended over several decades, apparently remains limited. The dramatic resurgence of nationalism and ethnicism that appeared inside the Soviet Union and its post-World War II satellites during the late 1980s illustrates such limits rather well.

In a rather different way, the national state is restricted by the microscope-telescope phenomenon noted earlier. Most of the significant dimensions of individual life can be monitored to some degree from a distance, but the conduct of everyday affairs depends on sets of considerations much too detailed to be observed using the kind of "telescope" available to a modern bureaucracy. Lacking the necessary information, those who govern cannot produce the instruments that would be required for a form of rule genuinely deserving to be termed "absolute." Perhaps the closest thing to "absolute" rule in Western history was the medieval monastery, where the individual became a "self-monitoring" system that could be used to imposed adherence to specific limits on thought as well as action. Such control structures are extremely unlikely on any significant scale in the contemporary world, although they may be possible for small, isolated groups of a highly special character.

The external limits on the authority of the national states are mainly a function of the overall system of states presently in place. National states differ from one another with respect to size, strength, and independence from external influence almost as much as do sub-state organizations. All national states claim sovereign status with respect to their internal affairs; no state can claim sovereignty in its external relations. In most cases, the claim to internal sovereignty can be discounted to some degree. No modern state can order its internal affairs solely by reference to events within its own boundaries; no state can be totally independent of external influences. Like individuals functioning in an environment characterized by human interactions and interdependence, states can be purely selfish only sporadically and incompletely. At a minimum, fear of retaliation forces consideration of the effects of action on the population of other societies. And even a very powerful and largely independent society would be forced to maintain its power at a level sufficient to guarantee its independence, whatever coalitions might be formed against it—which would amount to an "externally-imposed" burden on the society. And should the national state system be replaced by, or transformed into, a single political authority, its decisions would remain subject to some level of influence, which could be formidable, from internal sources. Such considerations refer, of course, to the longer run, and levels of authoritarian control that fall considerably short of absolutism may nonetheless prove intolerable in the immediate present.

The Organizational Imperative

Social organization is potentially the most powerful tool available to humanity for developing, and extending the application of, a defensible normative system. It is also, potentially at least, the most powerful barrier to achieving that goal. The source of its potential is in both cases found in the nature of organizations. As instruments, social organizations exist for the benefit of their users or members, or for the benefit of some part of the total membership. Indeed, it can reasonably be argued that organizations exist only *within* their members, in precisely the same way that a species of living things has no meaning beyond its particular members, past and present. The "organizational imperative" flows from that fundamental characteristic: the relation between the organization and its members and the organization and nonmembers must differ in some way considered sufficiently important to warrant accepting (or at least not rejecting) the obligations that membership entails. The benefits need not be tangible, and assessment of their relative value may vary considerably as between members and nonmembers, but some difference there must be, otherwise membership in the organization would be meaningless.

Put another way, organization *requires* differential assessments of the importance of individual lives, based on membership status—organizations require or depend on discrimination. The amount and kind can range from the trivial to the ultra-significant. Of course, organizations may also differentiate among their members, perhaps even more than they differentiate member from nonmember, but that is not enforced by the logic of organization, while differential treatment of members and nonmembers is absolutely essential for organizational survival. Without some important (to members at least) difference in the set of rights and obligations that accrue to members and nonmembers, an organization would have no way of attracting members or, in the case of involuntary organizations, maintaining acceptance of its authority or jurisdiction. Other things equal, the greater the differential between members and nonmembers, and the greater the significance of the distinctions involved, the greater the power of the organization with respect to its membership—bearing in mind that the difference is assessed by the members and need not be apparent to others. To the extent that those differences are regarded as significant, members can reasonably be expected to seek increases rather than reductions in the discrimination that distinguishes them from nonmembers.

In some circumstances, the differential treatment of members and nonmembers can be justified. As noted earlier, a justification is based on systematic comparison of the conditions of life of those affected if the organization continues to function with their conditions of life under the available alternatives. Since some social organizations perform essential and perhaps irreplaceable functions in human affairs, functions that must be performed to ensure species survival, not to say prosperity, justification is certainly possible, although it is rarely a simple matter. The nuclear family provides a very good example of an organization that is highly discriminatory, often in ways that produce grossly undesirable effects on individual lives, both within and without the particular family, yet elimination or replacement of the family as an institution would involve such staggering, and essentially uncertain costs, that it is hard to take the choice very seriously. However, that does not mean that such organizations should be treated as a special kind of natural artifact, whose functioning is to be accepted regardless of costs. The defining attributes of the "nuclear family" are so vague that they can conceal enormous differences in performance, and in the effects of performance. Normatively speaking, the priorities applied by an organization are a function of its putative purposes, as with any other instrument. The acceptability of organizational performance, for the competent consumer at least, is a function of the full set of consequences that it produces, the sum of its actions, compared to the set of outcomes that are produced if it functions on different principles— or ceases to function altogether.

Analytically, organizations, or more precisely, those who exercise organizational authority, particularly in the sovereign national states, are pressed by their own survival needs to use their authority in precisely the same manner as an individual living alone and isolated, to base decisions solely on "selfish" considerations, disregarding the consequences of organizational actions for nonmembers—or even for members other than themselves. Three factors tend to constrain extreme forms of discrimination: first, the possibility of internal revolt; second, the danger of retaliation, at least in cases where the effects of retaliation are held to outweigh the benefits gained by ignoring them or the cost of insuring against them; and third, intervention by an organization of greater strength or superior authority, real or potential.

Revolt, particularly in modern society where physical power is enormously enhanced by technological advances, is usually resorted to only in extremis. And in practice, retaliation is unlikely to be an effective barrier to unacceptable differentiation. It may in fact encourage making such distinctions with respect to populations least able to retaliate (protect themselves) or by discriminating so extensively that retaliation would be tantamount to revolt. Intervention by another organization therefore offers the best hope for curbing the unwarranted, and undesirable, element of discrimination lying within organizational potential, providing, of course, that the external organization can be expected to intervene for defensible reasons in an appropriate manner.

That suggests, first, the potential importance to the national state (sovereign authority) of developing and maintaining a defensible normative system within its own boundaries, and, second, the reason why some populations must look to international organizations for improvements in their conditions of life. Within a national state, the normative system in place provides a channel for meliorating the worst effects of discriminatory behavior by any subordinate organizations while retaining their valued features. However, accepting the national state as ultimate guarantor of normative performance raises the age-old problem, "Who will police the policeman?" Can the national state be restrained except by a more powerful organization? The question rarely appears in serious discussion, which is perhaps a fitting tribute to the power of the indoctrination produced by living in organized society. And it is perhaps a fitting commentary on the curious nature of the species that the amount of pressure generated for the creation of an organization of organizations, a sovereign authority able to control interorganizational conflict, seems not to relate to the seriousness of the consequences of such conflict. Demands for a transnational authority able to limit the outbreak of wars among national states have usually been sporadic and transient, despite the real possibility that the next conflict might actually render the planet uninhabitable. On the other hand, demands for actions whose consequences are unlikely to be lasting and in some cases are clearly trivial, are frequent, loud, and vehement. It is possible, in principle at least, that those who rule the existing national states might find it in their best interests, selfishly regarded, to support a defensible normative system within each society. But in the absence of powerful pressures in that direction from substantial elements of the population, that possibility should probably be regarded as extremely remote or even nonexistent.

9

Conclusion

If (1) the ultimate purpose of the human enterprise is to maintain or improve the conditions of life of the human population within the limits of available capacity; and if (2) that purpose is to be fulfilled through human actions, directed by an appropriate, corrigible, intellectual apparatus, and performed in the kind of social context sketched very briefly in chapter 8, and if (3) suggested ways of directing human actions, and judging the results, have to be justified using the criteria and procedures set forth in chapter 7, then the most important task facing humanity at present is not to produce "better" or "more moral" individuals but to learn how to use the power and authority of the governments of the various national states in normatively defensible ways, to convert those governments into effective normative instruments. That is the primary conclusion to be drawn from the foregoing discussion and analysis. It may seem only a commonplace, but that does not diminish its significance or alter the rather pessimistic outlook on the future that it implies. To implement that commonplace would require massive changes in present attitudes, practices, and institutions. At best, such changes are likely to be very slow in coming; and if past experience portends the future at all well, they seem highly improbable, even in the long run. Nevertheless, the argument on which the conclusion depends, and the more important of its implications for the way in which society is organized and operated (for both the primary institutional arrangements in place, and for the belief systems that support them), is worth stating explicitly; it points the directions where improvements in normative performance must be sought, and suggests some of the major obstacles to be overcome before the effort could succeed.

The "normative performance" to be improved refers to the actual conditions of life of some part of the human population, and not to the character of the currently accepted normative system—the latter might be no more than window dressing. Normative systems do not have any intrinsic significance; they are only tools that can be used to further human purposes, to improve the conditions of life of human populations, or to judge that improvements (or regressions) have taken place. They are assessed qualitatively by reference to the consequences they produce in application, by comparing the conditions of life they create when acted upon, or would create if acted upon, with the conditions of life to be expected if any of the available or suggested alternatives were accepted and applied.

The need for urgency in the effort to convert national governments into normatively defensible enterprises is implicit in the conditions of life that actually appear in contemporary society, whether it is industrialized or part of the "less-developed" world. As humanity nears the close of the twentieth century, despite the enormous increases in wealth and knowledge that have occurred recently, a substantial part of the world's human population continues to live under conditions that are indefensible in terms of the most elemental criteria of adequacy. What is worse, those conditions deteriorate as readily, and perhaps as often, as they improve. In the industrialized societies, the equality principle is much violated, and decisions are too often based upon the consequences of action for small portions of the total population, ignoring the impact on the others. Worse, grossly indefensible differentials among populations have been institutionalized more-or-less systematically almost everywhere on earth.

The extent of the problem often escapes notice, for institutional arrangements quickly become part of current folklore and habit, accepted unheedingly even by those whom they harm. In the United States, for example, "equality of opportunity," meaning primarily the absence of socially imposed barriers to self-improvement, is firmly established as a criterion of adequate political/social performance. In a frontier environment, where natural resources were plentiful and widely accessible, the conditions of life were in fact determined almost entirely by individual effort. In such circumstances, each individual could be made almost totally responsible for his or her own condition of life, leaving the society with two major functions (maintaining internal order and guarding against external threats). But in an era of large-scale industrialization and urbanization, and a consequent increase in both interdependence and helplessness for most individuals, the results of acting on the same set of premises are in large measure unacceptable. And there is every reason to expect the situation to worsen significantly if present trends continue unchanged into the near future.

The primary reason for seeking improvement mainly, though not exclusively, through the governments of the national states is that such conditions cannot be altered in an adequate way by individual efforts alone. That is, calling attention to gross inequalities in the collective treatment of individual lives, and increasing both the capacity for action and the intellectual competence of the citizens of the society, or even strengthening the citizenry's commitment to act individually in ways that are defensible on normative grounds, would not produce the needed changes without support from social authority. Nor does it seem advisable to replace the function of public authority by private organizations, for they are not amenable in principle to the same level of accountability—they are more difficult to control. Further, before the least controversial premises in a defensible normative system can be accepted and applied by individuals, there must be some guarantee of reciprocity in enforcement, however qualified or conditional, else the risks involved are unacceptable. Such guarantees are possible on the required scale only within the jurisdiction of a single public social organization. In sum, if large-scale human problems are to be dealt with systematically and effectively, there is at present no good alternative to using the national state as the primary instrument or channel.

Social organizations alone cannot solve humanity's normative problems; neither can they be resolved by isolated private actions, individual or organized. The two must work in concert if there is to be significant improvement in future. John F. Kennedy's famous dictum: "Ask not what your country can do for you; ask instead what you can do for your country" is therefore badly misleading, and the amendment produced by George Bush, "ask what you can do for your fellow man," though an improvement, is also inadequate, for it continues the same fundamental emphasis. The commitment to assist one's fellow man must be extended to using *both* individual actions and public organization—a strong element of collective responsibility is essential.

Under such circumstances, a society that fails to produce a citizen body that is actively engaged in exploiting the potential for human betterment implicit in the national state (or its government) and to create political organizations that not only permit but further such exploitation, is in normative terms a failure, whatever may be achieved economically or militarily. And historically, if the surest recipe for social disaster has been to concentrate excessively on organizing to conduct hostilities against other societies, it has been closely followed by overconcern with expanding the production of goods and services while ignoring society's potential function as a normative instrument, as a tool for maintaining and improving the conditions of life of the members of the species—with due regard to its special role vis-a-vis its own citizens, given the existing national state system.

Under present conditions, then, eliminating the extremes of discrimination and bias in the distribution of life's most basic necessities is a matter of some urgency, and would constitute an enormous achievement. Such changes cannot occur on a substantial scale without positive action by the national states. Tragically, political systems have in the past been so incompetent, and so normatively perverse (and there are few historical exceptions to which one can point), that the instrument itself has been seriously discredited and may for that reason be unable to fulfill its potential. Given the pronounced tendency to limit the realm of the "possible" by reference to past performance rather than present potential, much of the value of political organization to its own members, and to humanity generally, may already have been lost for a considerable period of time, if not permanently. Thus, if actions are presently labeled "politically impossible," that is usually taken to mean that a particular action *cannot* be taken; the caveat "under existing institutional arrangements" is commonly ignored. It is dismaying, but hardly surprising to find that such data are rarely regarded as evidence of the need to alter and amend the existing political system.

In principle at least, any political apparatus could be tailored to allow optimal development of a defensible normative system once political structures and processes are regarded as conditional upon normative requirements and not the converse. And in decisionmaking, the governments of the national states could be bound by the same procedures and criteria as those required for justifying individual actions—as indeed they must be if their actions are to be defended. Like individuals, governments should be required to examine *all* of the available options, and not just those within present capacity, and to create capacity deliberately in order to achieve normatively desirable conditions in future. The ability to alter and extend capacity is, after all, the hallmark of the sovereign national state; the claim to be able to set the boundaries of its own jurisdiction, within the limits of available resources and knowledge, sets it apart from other human associations and makes it the ideal locus for producing normative improvements. What is necessary, but very difficult to achieve, is the essential normative commitment—acceptance of the principle that the normative dimension of human existence is what politics, and economics, is "all about," and not the reverse.

Put slightly differently, the sovereign state, like any other instrument, can be used either to further or to impede the achievement of specified goals, depending on the intentions and the capacity of its users, the institutional arrangements in place, and the state of the international environment. From a normative perspecctice, the goal to be sought is a national state that is controlled by the same criteria of acceptability as an individual functioning in a normatively defensible way. The principal impediment to progress in that direction is what amounts to a self-fulfilling ordinance or prophecy widely accepted as a commonplace in Western societies. It is generally assumed that increases in the power or capacity of national governments are to be avoided at nearly all costs, and hedged with restrictions where they prove necessary. Lord Acton's aphorism, "Power tends to corrupt; absolute power corrupts absolutely," states the core of the underlying set of beliefs both accurately and succinctly. Much of modern "democratic" practice, including the doctrine of limited government, is premised on that assumption. And in consequence, much of the potential benefit of living within a sovereign organization is foregone, knowingly or not, in order to avoid, or at least lessen, the dangers associated with the exercise of a sovereign authority.

The doctrine of minimal government may be necessary in an interacting system in which pursuit of selfish purposes is the rule; in a society that is committed to acting on defensible normative grounds, it is not only unnecessary but untenable. The decision to limit its own authority, which lies within the capacity of any sovereign state, should be argued in the same manner as any other decision—by comparing alternatives. A decision to forego potential benefits to substantial elements of the population out of the fear of tyranny may be justified in this way, for the full effects of choosing to live with minimal government are presently uncertain. But if that option leaves the individual free to function in ways that can be defended by reasoned argument, it also eliminates for that same individual the social environment that would justify the decision to act on such premises. Further, minimal government allows some members of society to exploit their fellow citizens, safe from either internal or external marauders and without fear of intercession by higher authority. In effect, the doctrine of limited government serves to recreate in a modern setting the conditions that made possible the emergence of powerful feudal lords in the middle ages; economic power may have replaced military power, but the overall effect on the weak and helpless remains about the same.

The foregoing line of reasoning serves to rule out acceptance of "interest group" democracy as a defensible approach to governing, even if a commitment to serving "the national interest" could be enforced. Collective judgments are justified by reference to the consequences of the decision for the *total* population affected, including both members of society, temporary and other nonmembers occupying part of the society's territory, and still others wholly outside the physical-legal boundaries of the organization. The impact of any choice on the various populations affected must be assessed objectively, and the assessment articulated and justified. Government's cannot simply react to self-expressed complaints or other forms of group pressures, for that would place (and does place) an unwarranted premium on the capacity to organize for complaining. And if the effects of collective action on those external to the society's jurisdiction may be partly discounted (counterbalanced by the other effects of maintaining the organization), they cannot be disregarded completely. The sovereign national state, like the individual interacting with others in the absence of social organization, must be concerned with the actions or reactions of external agents, whether individuals or organizations. In these terms, what is referred to as the "public interest" appears, in a normative context, hopelessly parochial. If the primary concern is the conditions of life of the population of the society, and each member counts equally, that concern is best furthered by insisting that each decision be made on defensible grounds. In some cases at least, such decisions will be influenced by consequences of action for a population that is as far removed from the "public" that makes up the society proper as from the "interests" of particular elements of the population.

Such arguments against minimal government may persuade, but acceptance is in practical terms very unlikely. In modern industrial society, minimal government is well-suited to the needs and purposes of the affluent and the powerful. It is, and has been, disastrous mainly for the less well-endowed. What is worse, that judgment would hold for the future even if the affluent and powerful were sensitive, compassionate, and dedicated to using their individual capacities to assist others—which they are not. The logic is well illustrated in the area of national security: assuming that each individual citizen was willing to defend the society to the death, the force and effectiveness of the sum of such individual efforts could not reach the potential available to the members of society through organization. Construing the national government as referee over individual efforts to improve their own conditions of life is an open invitation to badly skewed benefits and gross exploitation of some for the benefit of others. It is hardly surprising to find that the invitation has been accepted.

Of course, the danger of misusing sovereign authority is real, and the population of any society needs to protect itself against abuse as fully as possible. In the past, the problem has been dealt with mainly by seeking to restrict the use of authority, particularly by the imposition of complex procedural limitations on the exercise of political power. The United States Constitution, perhaps the best exemplar available for the genre, created a system of government that now combines enormous economic and military power with an almost total lack of responsibility for its exercise. And more specific efforts to limit government's capacity to restrict, say, freedom of speech and so on, if they have functioned well at times, have failed miserably during those periods of stress when they were desperately needed. Further illustrations could be cited almost endlessly from every kind of society. Historically as well as analytically, there are few grounds for placing much faith in either mechanical or procedural constraints on the exercise of collective authority. One major reason why they are unlikely to succeed is the form in which they appear: stated in absolute terms, procedural constraints produce quite different results depending on the circumstances to which they are applied; the effort to maintain and apply them raises questions that the procedure is unable to cope with.

The need to control the use of authority against potential abuse raises, in fairly acute form, what is perhaps the principal difficulty to be resolved in any meaningful effort to optimize the conditions of life of *all* of society's members at a respectable level, leaving aside the special problems posed by the multiplicity of national societies. The best available solution to the problem is easy to stipulate in principle but almost impossible to implement—governments must be made responsible, must be required to justify their actions. But governments cannot be made "responsible" without having a population to be responsible *to*, and that population must have the time and competence must be both willing and able to assess the validity of actions proposed, to deal with outcomes that will remain uncertain or problematic in some degree despite best efforts, while ignoring particular obligations that may be of great importance to them individually. That is not a political program likely to generate enthusiastic support and ready implementation.

The intellectual character of the dilemma is clear. A viable solution to the problem of controlling the use of authority will certainly require those who exercise the authority of the national states to *justify* their actions or decisions, in precisely the same manner that any other normative decision is justified. Evidence must be provided to support the empirical assumptions on which the decision is based; an argument, grounded in past experience, and making use of the established or accepted normative system, must be offered to support the normative decisions or judgments that are made. In brief, maintaining the integrity of a political system involves precisely the same considerations as maintaining any intellectual system, normative or not. Agreement is needed on the nature of the political (normative) enterprise, on the fundamental assumptions used to carry out that enterprise, and on the canons of reasoning and evidence to be applied to justifications or arguments. The apparatus must be applied with competence and integrity.

But justification, to repeat, necessarily involves at least two parties: a competent body of actors, functioning in appropriate institutional setting, and a competent and informed audience, available to hear and assess the justification. The question "Who will make up the audience that is to decide authoritatively on the quality of the justification?" is therefore crucial. Because the enterprise as a whole will begin in an ongoing political system, and the kind of informed and competent audience required for genuine improvement is not presently available, the best that can be hoped for is slow, uncertain, erratic improvement. Many crucial questions cannot be answered out of present knowledge alone; decisions can be expected to change with circumstances. The enemy, as in all normative or intellectual matters, is dogmatism (not collectivism), and particularly the kind of "uniconceptual" critiques popularized by the Marxists of the nineteenth and early twentieth centuries, and widely used by various ideological groups in the contemporary world. A tentative, pragmatic outlook that takes for granted the need for change, and seeks to adapt with foresight rather than to react to crisis after the fact is essential. Can a large general public be educated to this level of competence? Very preliminary and tentative experiments suggest that it is possible both practically and in principle, but implementation might take many generations. In a society where levels of cognitive competence are improving, and people are habituated to proceeding experimentally rather than dogmatically, there is room for optimism, but those criteria are far more easily articulated than satisfied.

Implications: Harnessing the National State to a Normative Function

Given a national state with a political system committed to justifying its actions on normative/empirical grounds, and a competent body of informed opinion to serve as a check on the use of political authority, there is much to be said for allowing it a dominant role in the improvement of the conditions of life of those within its jurisdiction. A good illustration of both possibilities and limitations is found in the maintenance of public order, or national defense—functions that have been transferred to the national government in almost every society. The transfer cannot be complete; each individual must retain responsibility for some aspects of the conditions of life of those with whom he or she is in close and constant association, for example. How responsibilities should be divided is a matter for experimenting and argument over time, and the decisions themselves can be expected to vary with circumstances—there is no single solution that will fit all of humanity.

The most obvious of the potential benefits of transferring primary responsibility for maintaining and improving the conditions of life of a given population to a sovereign national state is the resulting gain in capacity. Whether the population in question is a small group of settlers in need of homes or barns, or a large population seeking means of transportation between home and employment, the advantages gained by relying upon organization are clear: it is the primary device available for taking advantage of the benefits of scale. Given a collection of people and resources, what can be produced in a given time period is increased significantly by suitable organization, even after the costs of constructing and maintaining the organization have been deducted from the benefits. That simple principle, which provides the fundamental underpinning for modern capitalism, serves equally well as one element in the set of assumptions used to justify primary reliance upon sovereign authority for dealing with the conditions of life of human populations.

Beyond a sheer increase in capacity, social organization provides a mechanism that can be used to increase the efficiency of resource transfers within its boundaries, to the benefit of both donors and recipients. In the absence of an organization that has been provided with proper authorization, the wrong persons may provide assistance to the wrong persons, to the ultimate detriment of both. The reasoning is fairly straightforward. Once the equality principle is accepted, an individual seeking to function in a normatively defensible manner *must* provide assistance to another person given awareness and capacity if the outcome created by providing the assistance is preferable on normative grounds to the other available alternatives. But expending resources on those terms invites a normative version of what has been called, to some extent mistakenly, the "tragedy of the commons." In effect, the procedure can over time produce outcomes that are, in the aggregate at least, far less desirable than the outcomes produced if actions are coordinated or controlled by an overall authority.

To illustrate, consider the situation of a tourist of modest means visiting almost any large city in Central or South America. In the course of the visit, that person will encounter any number of inadequately fed, clothed, and housed individuals and families. Up to a point, the tourist will presumably have the capacity to improve the conditions of life of those persons without seriously damaging the self. But if actions are based on the premise that capacity must be exercised fully and unavoidably, and that responsibility extends to the limits of capacity without exception, the tourist will soon be virtually penniless, and the overall situation will have improved only slightly and temporarily. Furthermore, assistance may be provided to individuals who are relatively better off than others for whom nothing is done. In collective terms, individual actions may seriously reduce the benefits, both short- and long-term, that can be obtained from a given outlay of resources. Such misdirections of resources can be avoided, in principle at least, by coordinating the aggregation and allocation of resources through a social organization. To what extent organization for that purpose should be "public" or "private" is a matter for experiment and learning rather than dogma. It may be that control over such affairs should be placed in the hands of a sub-sovereign organization, either public or private, but that is a decision for the sovereign to make based on a comparison of the expected consequences of locating control over affairs at various points in the society.

Given the increase in capacity to be expected from relying on social organization to function as a normative agent, it follows that a sovereign government is ideally suited to determine the benchmarks to be enforced for society as a whole, for they are a function of capacity and need, taken in combination. The benchmarks, which stipulate the conditions of life regarded as unacceptable and highly desirable within the society and therefore serve as indicators of the need for collective action, are in effect a statement of the minimum benefits attached to citizenship (and perhaps residence). Establishing and justifying benchmarks provides a way of giving concrete meaning to the term "rights of citizens." Given the equality assumption, the levels of unacceptability should be kept at the highest point possible, with due regard for exceptional circumstances. Of course, the benchmarks must be applied or enforced in an appropriate manner, and the rate of progress from present circumstances toward desired future conditions should be optimized. An admirable benchmark (usually stated as a "goal") that is loudly proclaimed but unconscionably slow in materializing, is for all practical purposes a meaningless piece of window dressing. The provisions of the United States Housing Act of 1949 that called for a "decent home and suitable living environment" for every American family illustrate the case perfectly, for those in authority had no intention of implementing them.

To sharpen the discussion somewhat, the primary function of any sovereign authority that must provide adequate normative justification for its actions is to put in place, and enforce in a reasonable manner, the equality principle. That does not imply a simple redistribution of the resources and facilities that are presently in place within the society, for that approach to the task could lead to avoidable equality in misery. In some cases, where populations are large and very poor and resources, present and potential, are very badly constrained, equality in misery may not be avoidable. But the question whether that outcome is accepted is determined by the same procedures and criteria as any other choice or decision. In an industrialized society, the equality principle enjoins an ongoing concern with *what* is produced within the society as well as the way in which it is distributed. As resources become scarce and increasingly expensive in real terms, and costs increase, as seems almost certain to occur over time, that task is likely to occupy government to an ever-increasing degree. In normative terms, there is no way to exclude sovereign government from active participation in the productive and distributive processes. That does not mean that ownership and control of *all* resources and productive processes should automatically be placed in the hands of national governments. Recent experience in China and the Soviet bloc suggests the high price to be paid for accepting such dogmas. But excluding government from productive and distributive systems, even to the degree presently practiced in the United States and some other Western nations, is as much a matter of dogma as its antithesis. Both total collective control and pure selfish competitiveness can be ruled out on the basis of both reasoning and experience. The proper balance must be learned experimentally, and cautiously, and may well change with time. Killing the goose that lays the golden eggs would only make things worse; tokenism is equally unacceptable when human misery is real and avoidable. The basic principle involved, that such decisions require sound normative judgments by sovereign authority, seems clear. Otherwise, significant future potentialities may be foregone and the members of society, both individually and collectively, will be the losers.

To summarize, bringing national governments into active partnership in the human enterprise seems an essential prerequisite to improving the normative system in place. The reason is not that governments are somehow a repository of superior intellectual ability; rather, it is a consequence of government's unique capacity to influence, and to apply or enforce, the normative system in certain fundamental ways—in effect, to reify the equality assumption. First, only a social organization can create the conditions that allow the individual to abandon extreme selfishness and accept the equality assumption. It can both restrict the opportunities for acting in a purely selfish manner and eliminate institutional features that reinforce or even require selfishness. The aim is not to eliminate selfishness, or achieve selflessness; even if that were possible, it would not be desirable in all cases. But it is highly desirable, and probably necessary, to limit its influence in areas where it conflicts most sharply with the equality assumption. Even if it is reasonable to assume that pure selfishness is built into the human individual at birth, that changes nothing, for it is also clear that selfishness can be limited by conditioning over time. If unselfishness is learned behavior, then efforts to enforce it can be justified for particular situations in the same manner as any other decision. The society's capacity to influence the degree of selfishness that characterizes human interactions (by loading options in an appropriate way) therefore remains a crucial factor in determining its potential role in normative improvement.

Some of the more obvious drawbacks to using the governments of the national states as the primary element in normative development, or of transferring responsibility for maintaining and improving some of the basic dimensions of human life to the national states, have already been touched upon briefly. The danger of tyranny or the misuse of authority, the need for social organization to discriminate between members and nonmembers, and the common practice of separating the society from its human population, regarded as individuals, and assigning primary importance to the collective, have already been noted. Along these same lines, transferring responsibility from individuals to collectivities cannot be more than partial, but it could lead to a total abdication of individual responsibility for using individual capacity to better the lives of others (a reversion to pure selfishness), or even to bettering the conditions of life of the self. Finally, most societies maintain institutional arrangements that literally make it impossible for either the society or its members to function in a normatively defensible manner in all cases. A political system that blurs and diffuses responsibility, for example, may very effectively rule out the kind of appraisal of the quality of the justifications offered for collective actions essential for controlling the use of collective authority. Each of these problems is, in one sense, only a technical problem arising out of the need to control the enormous power and authority that is vested in the modern national state, but in practical terms they may be difficult or even impossible to resolve in a dependable way.

Somewhat more generally and abstractly, those who exercise the authority of the national state must also deal with the special dilemma created by the imcompleteness of present-day sovereignty, with the reality of an international system in which no national state can function with total disregard for all other societies, yet no single authority can function effectively with respect to all of the system's members. That situation poses two kinds of threats to normative improvement. First, there are the practical problems that arise when the impact of future changes expected in the external environment must be assessed and dealt with: deciding what policies are most likely to optimize the future conditions of life of the population, for example. When dealing with such questions, the international context can be regarded as precisely equivalent to a situation in which individuals interact subject only to self-imposed restrictions. Under those conditions, the obvious danger of individual cheating is far less important than the effects of uncertainty. Obviously, external conditions can produce reasons for acting in particular ways that would override almost any internally generated imperative. That opens the way for serious errors of judgment, and more importantly, for deliberate misrepresentation of the risk represented by the external environment. The resulting actions could be both counterproductive and frightening, as recent disclosures of the chain of reasoning that guided the American government in the so-called "Cuban missile crisis" illustrate all too well.[1]

Finally, and most important of all, a reasonable long-run solution to the problem of developing an adequate normative apparatus requires an open mind, a receptive attitude on the part of the population, rulers and ruled alike. In particular, humanity should be regarded as an ongoing experiment in normative development, an experiment that is not predestined to succeed. It would then follow that members of a society have to play an active role in maintaining the integrity and viability of the policies that society approves and applies. In a system where actions have to be justified in normative as well as empirical terms, the quality of a government's operations is as much a function of the competence of its audience or critics as of its governors. Yet the truth is that in most large industrial societies, political apathy among the masses is commonplace and the kind of intellectual/normative competence needed to maintain the integrity of the intellectual apparatus is extremely rare among governed and governors alike. Most large industrialized societies rely upon hired mercenaries to operate their political as well as their military systems; they tend to be badly served in both arenas—deservedly, perhaps, for little effort has been made to learn how to select mercenaries. Even among those who govern, specialization of function is the rule, unfortunately if understandably. Not surprisingly, such political-social-economic systems tend to produce judgment without reasoning and criticism that lacks intellectual justification. Development of the kind of citizen body needed to operate an efficiently functioning national government is probably ruled out for the short-run, and could well be an overwhelming task even if ample time and resources are available. The catastrophic failure of mass education systems in the field of citizenship education is cause for serious concern—although as noted earlier, there are some reasons to suppose the problem is soluble in principle.

In the circumstances, should governments do what the population wishes done, as is assumed in much of modern democratic theory, or should it act in a way that is defensible in normative terms? The limited evidence I have been able to cumulate thus far suggests that following the voice of the people is likely to be a recipe for disaster. The kind of informed competence that is needed to judge sophisticated arguments about the consequences to be expected from complex and extended collective actions, as well as the relative desirability of outcomes whose probability is extremely hard to estimate, simply is not available—even within the academic community. In normative terms at least, those responsible for the development of the knowledge that society must have to conduct its affairs deserve chastising, if not the firing squad. The kind of citizen body needed to operate a modern nation state in a normatively defensible manner is nowhere available, nor does it seem likely to be produced in the near future; if anything, the best current prognosis is for little progress or even further deterioration. For critical competence depends upon acceptance, comprehension, and systematic application or use of fairly large sets of complex assumptions, reasonably well organized into an analytic framework that becomes the "coaching language" of the educational system, whose ultimate validity is primarily a matter of abstract reasoning and not affective reaction or social conditioning.

Furthermore, creating a competent government and installing it in a national state would not resolve the problem, even if that were possible; the population of a society must assess, and support, the government's actions for the right reasons, else the social enterprise loses its integrity, and with it the power to convince. The need for careful scrutiny of both a government's actions and the justifications offered to support them is unending, requiring a sustained commitment and appropriate institutions; momentary charitable impulses, and flashes of anger or concern, are inadequate for the task to be performed. In effect, the entire set of elements and processes in society, including education, the system of government, production and distribution of goods and services, relations with the external world, and so on, will have to be integrated into a coherent whole and subjected to ongoing and competent criticism, directed at both the parts and at the whole. Finally, some mechanism for translating valid criticism into meaningful changes in actions and institutions must be available for use.

None of these points of criticism is new, or even particularly radical. They sum to severe skepticism with respect to humanity's ability to create and maintain normatively competent social organizations. However, since the limits under which sovereign national states operate in the contemporary world are only vaguely and imperfectly understood, both the optimist and pessimist can find data in history to feed their respective prejudices. Some national states perform far more effectively and defensibly than others, in some areas at least, and that gives some hope for the future; the overall track record is dismal, and that dims the future outlook, particularly in light of present capacity to destroy the species. The low level of normative performance in most national states can be attributed to the inadequacy of the existing normative apparatus, and the relative absence of agreement on normative fundamentals. But the history of governmental performance suggests that: first, if the necessary knowledge were available, it would not be applied consistently and intelligently; and, second, if it were both available and honestly applied, the organizational/institutional arrangements now in place would interfere seriously with performance. Current efforts to maintain and improve the existing normative apparatus are dogged by an element of uncertainty and contingency that is impossible to eliminate without major changes in both intellectual capacity and existing institutional arrangements that seem very unlikely to occur in the short-run.

Optimists may argue, nevertheless, that the level of sovereignty already achieved by the national states opens the way, in principle at least, to development and improvement of a defensible normative apparatus within their boundaries, particularly in the larger industrialized societies. And recent efforts to promote generalized human rights (an obligation binding on each person to treat all other persons as members of a common class) can be regarded as a hopeful sign. Moreover, the first tentative steps toward creation of authorities that transcend national boundaries have already been taken, both for the world as a whole and for some of its regions, although they depend mainly on self-imposed, and therefore unenforceable, limits on the authority of the national states involved. Finally, and most important of all, it is demonstrably possible to create the needed intellectual competence on a large scale, even within the framework of existing educational institutions, with respect to the kind of "run of the mill" students that are found at present in the secondary schools, junior colleges, and state universities, in the United States and elsewhere. A major shift in educational emphasis would be required, but there is no reason to believe that a massive program, conducted with sound tools and directed with integrity, could not succeed.

On a more pessimistic view, man and woman's inhumanity to man and woman continues more or less unabated. And if the only way to bring it under control is through the human intellect, then, assuming that past performance is a trustworthy guide, it is very difficult to be sanguine with respect to the future. It took some centuries for the physical sciences to emerge from their intellectual morass, yet empirical conclusions had the great advantage of being demonstrable to anyone willing to watch and listen and were open to practical, and highly visible, applications. In context, it is disturbing to note the powerful vestiges of intellectual absolutism, of unwillingness to hear argument or evidence that conflicts with received beliefs, still present in the more "open" of today's societies—the apparent willingness to assert absolutes without argument or to dispute them on utterly irrelevant grounds.

If answering the kinds of questions raised by the present inquiry is a very difficult, and indeed, unending task, it remains important enough to warrant any amount of time and effort spent trying to succeed. And if there are few answers available, and none is permanent, the central question seems clear: How can the modern national state, particularly in its large-scale and heavily industrialized form, be organized, operated, and constrained or limited in order to optimize its normative potential? Is there one solution to fit all cases? Do all roads converge on some special "Rome" of the future or are there many different roads, each leading to its own long-range future for those who choose, for whatever reason, to follow it? Should attention focus on the structure and function of government? On the development of a better set of limits on the use of governmental authority and the creation of a system of courts or other institutions to enforce them? On the education of the population to higher levels of normative and political awareness and competence? Such questions are old and familiar intellectual companions to many of us, but traditional answers are as inappropriate as actual practice is inadequate. A better intellectual performance is required. It seems at present most likely to emerge under the general rubric of "defensible policymaking," and within the government of society itself, for the information that is needed to improve performance, whether it refers to real possibilities or real constraints, is available there and nowhere else. The challenge facing those who favor traditional "democratic" principles is to create a governmental system that is able to achieve the level of performance that such assumptions require, and a population that is able to make it function properly.

Notes

CHAPTER 1

1. Eugene J. Meehan, *Public Housing Policy: Myth Versus Reality*, (Rutgers University Center for Urban Studies, 1975); Eugene J. Meehan, *The Quality of Federal Policymaking; Programmed Disaster in Public Housing*, (University of Missouri Press, 1979); Eugene J. Meehan, "Looking the Gift Horse in the Mouth: Conventional Public Housing," *Urban Affairs Quarterly*, Vol. 10., No. 4., June 1975; Eugene J. Meehan, "The Rise and Fall of Public Housing," in D. Phares, ed., *A Decent Home and Environment*, (Ballinger, 1978).

2. Eugene J. Meehan, with Charles Reilly and Thomas Ramey, *In Partnership with People* (U.S. Government Printing Office, 1979); Eugene J. Meehan, with Charles Reilly, "Local-Level Development in Rural Latin America: The Inter-American Experience," in G. E. Jones and M. J. Rolls, eds., *Progress in Rural Extension and Community Development* (John Wiley, 1982); Eugene J. Meehan, "Urban Development: An Alternative Strategy," in D. Rosenthal, ed., *Urban Revitalization* (Sage Publications, 1980).

3. Eugene J. Meehan, *Economics and Policymaking: The Tragic Illusion* (Greenwood Press, 1982); Eugene J. Meehan, "A Critique of Economic Policymaking," in Redburn, F. Stevens, ed., *Revitalizing the U.S. Economy* (Praeger, 1986).

4. Eugene J. Meehan, *Education for Critical Thinking*, translated into Spanish at the University of Costa Rica and published by the University of Costa Rica Press, 1981; Eugene J. Meehan, *An Introduction to Critical Thinking*, 2 vols., translated at the University of Costa Rica and published by the University of Costa Rica Press, 1982; Eugene J. Meehan, "Improving Critical Judgment in Science," in R. Zeledon, ed., *Symposium on Creativity in Science Teaching* (National Council on Scientific and Technological Research, San Jose, Costa Rica); Eugene J. Meehan, "Reasoning in Social Science," presented at the First International Conference on Critical Thinking, Education, and the Rational Person, Sonoma State University, Rohnert Park, CA, Aug. 15–19, 1983.

5. For typical examples, see Richard B. Braithwaite, *Scientific Explanation: A Study of the Function of Theory, Probability, and Law in Science* (Harper, 1953); Carl G. Hempel, *Philosophy of Natural Science* (Prentice-Hall, 1966); Ernest Nagel, *The Structure of Science: Problems in the Logic of Scientific Explanation* (Harcourt, Brace, and World, 1961); Richard S. Rudner, *Philosophy of Social Science* (Prentice-Hall, 1966); or Israel Scheffler, *The Anatomy of Inquiry* (Alfred A. Knopf, 1963).

6. Eugene J. Meehan, *The Theory and Method of Political Analysis* (Dorsey Press, 1965).

7. Eugene J. Meehan, *Explanation in Social Science: A System Paradigm* (Dorsey Press, 1968).

8. Eugene J. Meehan, *Value Judgment and Social Science* (Dorsey Press, 1969).

9. Eugene J. Meehan, *The Foundations of Political Analysis: Empirical and Normative* (Dorsey Press, 1971).

10. See note 4 above.

11. See note 1 above.

12. See note 2 above.

13. Eugene J. Meehan, *Reasoned Argument in Social Science: Linking Research to Policy* (Greenwood Press, 1981).

14. Eugene J. Meehan, *The Thinking Game: A Guide to Effective Study* (Chatham House, 1988).

CHAPTER 2

1. The comparison of outcomes or consequences referred to here differs very significantly from the conception of "Consequentialism" as it is used in philosophic ethics. See, for example, Michael Slote, *Common-Sense Morality and Consequentialism* (Routledge and Kegan Paul, 1985); or Samuel Scheffler, *The Rejection of Consequentialism* (The Clarendon Press, 1982).

2. See Eugene J. Meehan, *Economics and Policymaking: The Tragic Illusion* (Greenwood Press, 1982, pp. 159–163).

3. See Lee Rainwater, *Behind Ghetto Walls: Black Family Life in a Ghetto Slum* (Aldine, 1970); or Eugene J. Meehan, *The Quality of Federal Policymaking: Programmed Failure in Public Housing* (University of Missouri Press, 1979).

CHAPTER 3

1. The rapidly-emerging field of tomography may change the situation quite dramatically in future. See, for example, Marcus E. Raichle, "Developing a Functional Anatomy of the Human Brain with Positron Emission Tomography," *Current Neurology*, 9:161–178, 1989.

CHAPTER 4

1. See Eugene J. Meehan, *Reasoned Argument in Social Science: Linking Research to Policy* (Greenwood Press, 1981).

2. See Nelson Goodman, *Fact, Fiction, and Forecast* (Harvard University Press, 1955, pp. 3–27).

3. See, for example, William Ascher, *Forecasting: An Appraisal for Policymakers and Planners* (Johns Hopkins Press, 1978).

4. Perhaps the most famous argument, or assertion, to the contrary is found in Milton Friedman's *Essays in Positive Economics* (University of Chicago Press, 1953).

CHAPTER 5

1. There are two reasons for the omission: first, the conceptual apparatus employed on conventional ethics is virtually useless as a basis for comparison; second, I wish to avoid the kind of "academic" arguments that could be expected to follow any effort to fit the apparatus set forth here into the context of contemporary ethical inquiry. The source of the problem is clearly visible in even the most casual survey of the relevant literature. For more or less typical examples see: Richard B. Brandt, *Ethical Theory: The Problems of Normative and Critical Ethics* (Prentice-Hall, 1959); Philippa Foot, *Theories of Ethics* (Oxford, 1967); William K. Frankena, *Ethics* (Prentice-Hall, 1963, Ch. 1); Roger N. Hancock, *Twentieth Century Ethics* (Columbia University Press, 1974); Alisdair MacIntyre, *After Virtue: A Study in Moral Theory* (University of Notre Dame Press, 1981); P. H. Nowell-Smith, *Ethics* (Penguin Books, 1951, Ch. 1); John Rawls, *A Theory of Justice* (Harvard, 1971); Wilfred Sellars and John Hospers, eds., *Readings in Ethical Theory*, 2d. ed. (Appleton-Century-Crofts, 1970); and "What is Ethics," in *Issues in Ethics*, Vol. 1, No. 1, October, 1987 (The Center for Applied Ethics, Santa Clara University). These sources describe the overall construction of the nature of the normative enterprise—the specific questions to be answered, the appropriate canons of evidence and argument, and so on.

2. The judgment is widely shared by critics of welfare economics. Kenneth Boulding, for example, writes:

It will no doubt be one of the great puzzles for future historians of thought as to how economists in the middle of the twentieth century managed to devise a whole discipline of welfare economics based on two absolutely preposterous assumptions. The first of these is the assumption of selfishness, that is, that the utility function of one person does not depend in any way on his perception of the welfare of another. The second even more preposterous assumption is that preferences, and the utility functions which express them, are simply given, are not learned, and cannot be changed. The first assumption makes nonsense of the attempt of welfare economics to define a social optimum; the second makes nonsense of social and economic dynamics.

See "The Network of Interdependence," mimeo, Paper presented to the Public Choice Society, Chicago, Ill., February, 1970.

CHAPTER 6

1. See note 4, Chapter 1.

2. Norton E. Long, "Foreword," in Eugene J. Meehan, *Value Judgment and Social Science* (Dorsey Press, 1959, p. vii).

CHAPTER 9

1. See Graham T. Allison, *Essence of Decision: Explaining the Cuban Missile Crisis* (Little, Brown, and Co., 1971).

Background Reading:
A Selected List

METHODOLOGY AND/OR REASONING

Ascher, William. *Forecasting: An Appraisal for Policy-Makers and Planners.* Johns Hopkins University Press, 1978.

Ashby, W. Ross. *An Introduction to Cybernetics.* Science Editions, 1963.

Bailey, Norman A. and Stuart M. Feder. *Operational Conflict Analysis.* Public Affairs Press, 1973.

Ball, Terrence, ed. *Idioms of Inquiry.* University of New York Press, 1987.

Beiner, Ronald. *Political Judgment.* University of Chicago Press, 1983.

Berlinski, David. *On Systems Analysis.* MIT Press, 1976.

Bernstein, Richard. *The Restructuring of Social and Political Theory.* Penn State University Press, 1978.

Bilsky, Manuel. *Patterns of Argument.* Holt, Rinehart, and Winston, 1963.

Blalock, Hubert M. Jr. *Social Statistics.* McGraw-Hill, 1960.

Blalock, Hubert M. Jr. *Theory Construction—from Verbal to Mathematical Formulations.* Prentice-Hall, 1969.

Blalock, Hubert M. Jr. and Ann B. Blalock. *Methodology in Social Science.* McGraw-Hill, 1968.

Braithwaite, Richard B. *Scientific Explanation: A Study of the Function of Theory, Probability, and Law in Science.* Harper, 1953.

Braybrooke, David, ed. *Philosophical Problems of the Social Sciences.* Macmillan, 1965.

Brewer, Gary D. and Peter deLeon. *The Foundations of Policy Analysis.* Dorsey Press, 1983.

Brodbeck, May. *Readings in the Philosophy of Social Sciences.* Macmillan, 1968.

Brown, Harold I. *Observation and Objectivity.* Oxford University Press, 1987.

Buchanan, James M. and Robert D. Tollison, eds. *Theory of Public Choice: Political Applications of Economics.* University of Michigan Press, 1972.

Burk, Arthur W. *Choice, Causes, Reasons.* University of Chicago Press, 1979.

Calabresi, Guido and Philip Bobbitt. *Tragic Choices.* W. W. Norton, 1978.

Carter, Lief H. *Reason in Law*. Little, Brown, and Co., 1979.

Cohen, I. B. *Revolution in Science*. Harvard University Press, 1985.

Connolly, William E. *Political Theory and Modernity*. Basil Blackwell, 1987.

Dahlberg, Kenneth A. *New Directions for Agriculture and Agricultural Research*. Rowman and Allanheid, 1986.

Dallmayr, Fred R. *Twilight of Subjectivity: Contributions to a Post-Individualist Theory*. University of Massachusetts Press, 1981.

Derrida, J. *Positions*. University of Chicago Press, 1981.

Direnzo, Gordon J. ed. *Concepts Theory and Explanation in the Behavioral Sciences*. Random House, 1966.

Dubin, Robert. *Theory Building*. Free Press, 1978.

Dunn, William. *Public Policy Analysis: An Introduction*. Prentice-Hall, 1981.

Eemeren, F. H. et al. *The Study of Argumentation*. Irvington, 1984.

Evans, J. S. *Thinking and Reasoning*. Routledge and Kegan Paul, 1983.

Falco, Maria. *Truth and Meaning*. University Press of America, 1983.

Fay, Brian. *Critical Social Science*. Cornell University Press, 1987.

Fay, Brian. *Social Theory and Political Practice*. Allen and Unwin, 1975.

Feigl, Herbert and May Brodbeck, eds. *Readings in the Philosophy of Science*. Appleton, Century, Crofts, 1953.

Feyerabend, P. *Against Method: Outline of an Anarchistic Theory of Knowledge*. New Left Books, 1975.

Fischer, F. *Politics, Values, and Public Policy: The Problem of Methodology*. Westview, 1980.

Fiske, Ronald W. and Richard A. Shweder, eds. *Metatheory in Social Science: Pluralisms and Subjectivities*. University of Chicago Press, 1985.

Flew, A. G. N. *Thinking About Social Thinking*. Basil Blackwell, 1985.

Foucault, Michel. *The Foucault Reader*. Pantheon, 1984.

Foucault, Michel. *The Order of Things*. Vintage, 1973.

Foucault, Michel. *Power/Knowledge*. Marshall, Medham, Soper, 1980.

Frankel, Charles, ed. *Controversies and Decisions: The Social Sciences and Public Policy*. Russell Sage Foundation, 1976.

Gadamer, H. G. *Truth and Method*. Crossroads, 1985.

Gale, George. *Theory of Science: An Introduction to the History, Logic, and Philosophy of Science*. McGraw-Hill, 1979.

Geach, P. T. *Reason and Argument*. University of California Press, 1976.

Geertz, Clifford. *Local Knowledge*. Basic Books, 1983.

Gibson, Quentin. *The Logic of Social Enquiry*. Routledge and Kegan Paul, 1960.

Goodin, Robert E. *Political Theory and Public Policy*. University of Chicago Press, 1982.

Goodman, Nelson. *Fact, Fiction, and Forecast*. Bobbs-Merrill, 1965.

Goodman, Nelson. *Of Mind and Other Matters*. Harvard University Press, 1984.

Graham, George J., Jr. *Methodological Foundations for Political Analysis*. Wiley, 1971.

Habermas, Jurgen. *The Philosophic Discourse of Modernity*. MIT Press, 1987.

Hempel, Carl G. *Aspects of Scientific Explanation*. Free Press, 1965.

Hindless, Barry. *Philosophy and Methodology in the Social Sciences*. Humanities Press, 1977.

Hogarth, Robin M. *Judgement and Choice: The Psychology of Decision.* Wiley, 1980.

Holton, Gerald and Robert S. Morison. *The Limits of Scientific Inquiry.* W. W. Norton, 1979.

Jarvis, I. C. *Thinking About Society.* Kluver, 1986.

Jencks, Charles. *What is Post-Modernism?* St. Martins Press, 1986.

Johnson-Laird, P. N. *Mental Models.* Harvard University Press, 1983.

Kahneman, D., Slovic, P. and Tversky, A. *Judgment Under Uncertainty; Heuristics and Biases.* Cambridge University Press, 1982.

Kaplan, Abraham. *The Conduct of Inquiry.* Chandler, 1964.

Kariel, Henry. *The Desperate Politics of Post-Modernism.* University of Massachusetts Press, 1988.

Kuhn, Thomas S. *The Structure of Scientific Revolution,* rev ed. University of Chicago Press, 1970.

Kyberg, Henry E., Jr. and Ernest Nagel, eds. *Induction: Some Current Issues.* Wesleyan University Press, 1963.

Lakatos, Imre and Alan Musgrave, eds. *Criticism and the Growth of Knowledge.* Cambridge University Press, 1970.

Leatherdale, W. H. *The Role of Analogy, Models, and Metaphors in Science.* North Holland, 1974.

Levi, Edward H. *An Introduction to Legal Reasoning.* University of Chicago Press, 1949.

Lindblohm, C. E. and D. K. Cohen. *Usable Knowledge: Social Science and Social Problem-Solving.* Yale University Press, 1979.

Louch, A. R. *Explanation and Human Action.* University of California Press, 1966.

Machlup, Fritz. *Methodology for Economics and Other Social Sciences.* Academic Press, 1978.

MacRae, Duncan Jr. *Policy Indicators.* University of North Carolina Press, 1987.

MacRae, Duncan Jr. *The Social Function of Social Science.* Yale University Press, 1976.

Margolis, Howard. *Patterns, Thinking, and Cognition: A Theory of Judgment.* University of Chicago Press, 1987.

Mayr, E. *The Growth of Biological Thought.* Harvard University Press, 1982.

Meehan, Eugene J. *Economics and Policymaking.* Greenwood Press, 1983.

Meehan, Eugene J. *Reasoned Argument in Social Science: Linking Research to Policy.* Greenwood Press, 1981.

Meehan, Eugene J. *The Thinking Game.* Chatham House, 1988.

Mills, Glen E. *Reason in Controversy.* Allyn and Bacon, 1968.

Minsky, Marvin and Seymour Papert. *Perceptrons: An Introduction to Computational Geometry.* MIT Press, 1979.

Mitchell, W. T. J. *Against Theory.* University of Chicago Press, 1985.

Mitchell, W. T. J., ed. *The Politics of Interpretation.* University of Chicago Press, 1983.

Mitroff, Ian A. and Ralph H. Kilmann. *Methodological Approaches to Social Science.* Jossey-Bass, 1978.

Mueller, Dennis C. *Public Choice.* Cambridge University Press, 1979.

Nagel, Ernest. *The Structure of Science: Problems in the Logic of Scientific Explanation*. Harcourt Brace, and World, 1961.

Nagel, Ernest and Richard B. Brandt, eds. *Meaning and Knowledge: Systematic Readings in Epistemology*. Harcourt, Brace, and World, 1965.

Nagel, Ernest and James R. Newman. *Godel's Proof*. New York University Press, 1958.

Nagel, Ernest et al. *Logic, Methodology, and Philosophy of Science*. Stanford University Press, 1962.

Nagel, Stuart S. *Policy Studies and the Social Sciences*. Lexington Books, 1975.

Natanson, Maurice, ed. *Philosophy of the Social Sciences*. Random House, 1963.

Newell, Allen and Herbert A. Simon. *Human Problem Solving*. Prentice-Hall, 1972.

Nisbett, Richard and Lee Ross. *Human Inference: Strategies and Shortcomings of Social Judgment*. Prentice-Hall, 1980.

Olson, Mancur. *The Logic of Collective Action*. Harvard University Press, 1965.

Paris, David C. and James F. Reynolds. *The Logic of Policy Inquiry*. Longman, 1983.

Polanyi, Michael. *Knowing and Being*. University of Chicago Press, 1969.

Polanyi, Michael. *Personal Knowledge*. University of Chicago Press, 1958.

Popper, Karl R. *Conjectures and Refutations: The Growth of Scientific Knowledge*. Harper and Row, 1968.

Popper, Karl R. *The Logic of Scientific Discovery*. Science Editions, 1961.

Popper, Karl R. *Objective Knowledge: An Evolutionary Approach*. Oxford University Press, 1972.

Putnam, Hilary. *Reason, Truth and History*. Cambridge University Press, 1981.

Quade, Edward. *Analysis for Public Decisions*. North Holland Press, 1982.

Quine, Willard Van Orman. *Word and Object*. MIT Press, 1960.

Quine, Willard Van Orman. *The Ways of Paradox and Other Essays*. Harvard University Press, 1976.

Rajchmann, J. and C. West, eds. *Post-Analytic Philosophy*. Columbia University Press, 1985.

Rein, Martin. *Social Sciences and Public Policy*. Penguin, 1976.

Rescher, Nicholas. *Empirical Inquiry*. Rowman and Littlefield, 1982.

Rescher, Nicholas. *Methodological Pragmatism*. New York University Press, 1971.

Revlin, Russell and Richard E. Mayer. *Human Reasoning*. V. H. Winston, 1978.

Ricci, David. *The Tragedy of Political Science*. Yale University Press, 1984.

Rieke, D. and Malcom O. Sillars. *Argumentation and the Decision-Making Process*. Wiley, 1975.

Riker, William H. and Peter C. Ordeshook. *An Introduction to Positive Political Theory*. Prentice-Hall, 1973.

Rock, I. *The Logic of Perception*. MIT Press, 1985.

Rorty, Richard. *Philosophy and the Mirror of Nature*. Princeton University Press, 1979.

Rosch, E. and C. B. Mervis, eds. *Cognition and Categorization*. Lawrence Erlbaum, 1978.

Roth, Paul A. *Meaning and Method in the Social Sciences*. Cornell University Press, 1987.

Rudner, Richard S. *A Philosophy of Social Science*. Prentice-Hall, 1966.

Runciman, W. G. *Social Science and Political Theory*. Cambridge University Press, 1963.

Ryan, Alan, ed. *Philosophy of Social Explanations*. Oxford University Press, 1973.

Salmon, Wesley. *Foundations of Scientific Inference*. University of Pittsburgh Press, 1966.

Scheffler, Israel. *The Anatomy of Inquiry*. Knopf, 1963.

Schelling, Thomas C. *Choice and Consequence*. Harvard University Press, 1983.

Simon, Herbert A. *Models of Man*. Wiley, 1957.

Simon, Herbert A. *Reason in Human Affairs*. MIT Press, 1983.

Skinner, Quentin, ed. *The Return of Grand Theory in the Human Sciences*. Cambridge University Press, 1985.

Smith, John E. *Purpose and Thought: The Meaning of Pragmatism*. Yale University Press, 1978.

Spence, Larry. *The Politics of Social Knowledge*. Penn State University Press, 1978.

Stinchcombe, Arthur L. *Constructing Social Theories*. Harcourt, Brace, and World, 1968.

Suppes, Patrick. *The Structure of Scientific Theories*. University of Illinois Press, 1977.

Toulmin, Stephen. *Foresight and Understanding*. Harper and Row, 1961.

Toulmin, Stephen. *Human Universtanding*, Vol. I. Princeton University Press, 1972.

Toulmin, Stephen. *The Philosophy of Science*. Harper and Row, 1960.

Toulmin, Stephen. *The Uses of Argument*. Cambridge University Press, 1964.

Vaillancourt, Pauline M. *When Marxists Do Research*. Westport, Conn.: Greenwood Press, 1986.

Weiss, Carol, ed. *Using Social Research in Public Policy-Making*. Lexington-Heath, 1977.

Weiss, Carol and Michael Bucuvalis. *Social Science Research and Decision-Making*. Columbia University Press, 1980.

ETHICS: ITS PURPOSES, MEANING, AND CHARACTER

Aiken, Henry D. *Reason and Conduct: New Bearings in Moral Philosophy*. Knopf, 1962.

Arrow, Kenneth J. *Social Choice and Individual Values*, 2d. ed. Yale University Press, 1963.

Barnsley, John H. *The Social Reality of Ethics: The Comparative Analysis of Moral Codes*. Routledge and Kegan Paul, 1972.

Barry, Brian. *A Liberal Theory of Justice*. Oxford University Press, 1973.

Beardsmore, R. W. *Moral Reasoning*. Routledge and Kegan Paul, 1969.

Brandt, Richard B. *Ethical Theory: The Problems of Normative and Critical Ethics*. Prentice-Hall, 1959.

Broad, C. D. *Five Types of Ethical Theory*. Littlefield, Adams, 1959.

Danielsson, Sven. *Preference and Obligations: Studies in the Logic of Ethics.* Filosofiska Foreningen Uppsala, Sweden, 1968.

Dewey, John. *Theory of the Moral Life.* Holt, Rinehart, and Winston, 1960.

Edel, Abraham. *Method in Ethical Theory.* Bobbs-Merrill, 1963.

Engelhardt, H. Tristram, Jr. and Daniel Callahan, eds. *Science, Ethics, and Medicine.* 3 vols. The Hastings Center, 1976, 1977, 1978.

Findlay, J. N. *Axiological Ethics.* Macmillan, 1970.

Fleishman, Joel and Bruce Payne. *Ethical Dilemmas and the Education of Policymakers.* Hastings Center, 1980.

Foot, Philippa. *Theories of Ethics.* Oxford University Press, 1967.

Frankena, William K. *Ethics.* Prentice-Hall, 1963.

Fried, Charles. *An Anatomy of Values.* Harvard University Press, 1970.

Gauthier, David P. *Practical Reasoning.* Clarendon Press, 1963.

Gouinlock, James, ed. *The Moral Writings of John Dewey.* Hafner Press, 1976.

Grassian, Victor. *Moral Reasoning: Ethical Theory and Some Contemporary Moral Problems.* Prentice-Hall, 1981.

Hancock, Roger N. *Twentieth Century Ethics.* Columbia University Press, 1974.

Hardin, Garrett. *Exploring New Ethics for Survival: The Voyage of the Spaceship Beagle.* Viking Press, 1968.

Harvard Educational Review, Reprint No. 13. "Stage Theories of Cognitive and Moral Development: Criticisms and Applications."

Kattsoff, Louis O. *Making Moral Decisions: An Existential Analysis.* Nijhoff, 1965.

Kemp, J. *Reason, Action, and Morality.* Humanities Press, 1964.

Kerner, George C. *The Revolution in Ethical Theory.* Oxford University Press, 1966.

Kohlberg, L. *Philosophy of Moral Development.* Harper and Row, 1981.

Lamont, W. D. *Law and the Moral Order.* Aberdeen University Press, 1981.

Lewis, C. I. *Values and Imperatives: Studies in Ethics.* ed. John Langa. Stanford University Press, 1969.

MacIntyre, Alisdair. *After Virtue: A Study in Moral Theory.* University of Notre Dame Press, 1981.

Moore, F. T. C. *The Psychological Basis of Morality.* Macmillan, 1978.

Moore, G. E. *Principia Ethica.* Cambridge University Press, 1903.

Najder, Zdzislaw. *Values and Evaluations.* Clarendon Press, 1975.

Newell, A. and H. Simon. *Human Problem Solving.* Prentice-Hall, 1972.

Polanyi, Michael. *Knowing and Being.* ed. Marjorie Grene. University of Chicago Press, 1969.

Raskin, Marcus G. *The Common Good: Its Politics, Policies, and Philosophy.* Routlege and Kegan Paul, 1986.

Rawls, John. *A Theory of Justice.* Belknap Press, 1971.

Rescher, Nicholas. *An Introduction to Value Theory.* Prentice-Hall, 1969.

Rescher, Nicholas, ed. *The Logic of Decision and Action.* University of Pittsburgh Press, 1967.

Richards, David A. J. *A Theory of Reasons for Action.* Clarendon Press, 1971.

Rokeach, Milton. *The Nature of Human Values.* Free Press, 1973.

Scheffler, Samuel. *The Rejection of Consequentialism.* Oxford University Press. 1982.

Sellars, Wilfrid and John Hospers, eds. *Readings in Ethical Theory*, 2d. ed. Appleton, Century, Crofts, 1970.

Singer, Marcus G. *Generalizations in Ethics*. Alfred A. Knopf, 1961.

Singer, Peter. *Practical Ethics*. Cambridge University Press, 1979.

Slote, M. *Common-Sense Morality and Consequentialism*. Routledge and Kegan Paul, 1985.

Smith, Adam. *The Theory of Moral Sentiments*. eds. D. D. Raphael and A. L. Macfie. Clarendon Press, 1976; first published in 1759.

Taylor, Paul W. *Normative Discourse*. Prentice-Hall, 1961.

Toulmin, Stephen. *The Place of Reason in Ethics*. Cambridge University Press, 1960.

von Wright, Georg Henrik. *The Logic of Preference*. Edinburgh University Press, 1963.

Wallace, G., and A. D. M. Walker, eds. *The Definition of Morality*. Methuen, 1970.

Wallsten, Thomas S., ed. *Cognitive Processes, Choice, and Decision Behavior*. Lawrence Erlbaum Associates, 1980.

Warnock, G. J. *The Object of Morality*. Methuen, 1971.

Warnock, Mary. *Ethics Since 1900*, 2d ed. Oxford University Press, 1966.

Wellman, Carl. *Morals and Ethics*. Scott, Foresman, 1975.

White, Morton. *What Is and What Ought to be Done: An Essay on Ethics and Epistemology*. Oxford University Press, 1981.

Winch, Peter. *Ethics and Action*. Routledge and Kegan Paul, 1972.

Index

About the Author

EUGENE J. MEEHAN is Curators' Professor of Political Science and Public Policy Administration, University of Missouri, St. Louis.